RAY STEVENSON

ONE CHORD WONDER

punk

THE WHOLE STORY

punk

THE WHOLE STORY

**LONDON, NEW YORK,
MUNICH, MELBOURNE, DELHI**

DORLING KINDERSLEY
Managing Editor **Debra Wolter**
Managing Art Editor **Karen Self**
Publisher **Jonathan Metcalf**
Art Director **Bryn Walls**
Production **Melanie Dowland**
DTP Designer **John Goldsmid**
Cover Design **Tim Lane**

MOJO
Editor-In-Chief **Mark Blake**
Art Editor **Lora Findlay**
Picture Editor **Dave Brolan**
Production Editor **Michael Johnson**
Deputy Editor **Pat Gilbert**
Designers **Carol Briggs, Isabel Cruz,
Kris Short, Peter Rogers**
Sub-Editor **Justin Hood**
MOJO Editor **Phil Alexander**
Publishing Director **Stuart Williams**
Creative Director **Dave Henderson**
Managing Director **Marcus Rich**

First published in Great Britain in 2006
by Dorling Kindersley Limited,
80 Strand, London WC2R 0RL
This edition published in 2008

A Penguin company

Colour reproduction by Rival Colour
Printed and bound in Singapore by
Star Standard

See the complete Dorling Kindersley
catalogue at **www.dk.com**

For more information about MOJO magazine
visit **www.mojo4music.com**

Mappin House, 4 Winsley Street,
London W1W 8HF

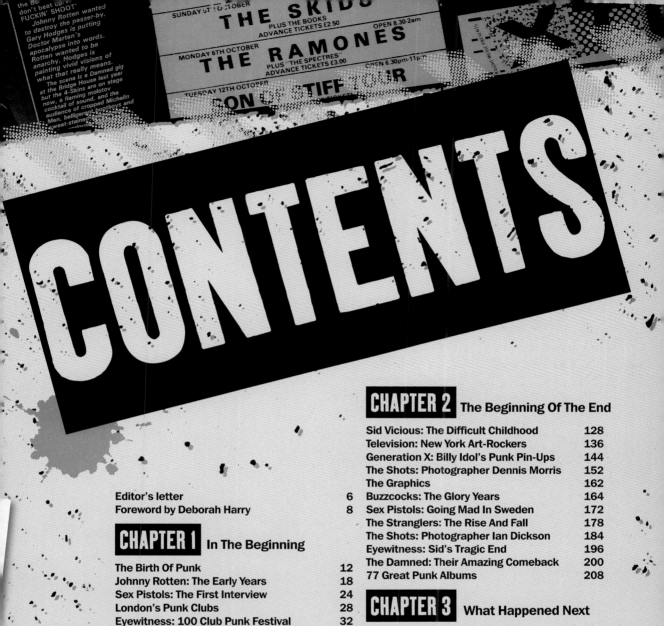

don't beat up.
FUCKIN' SHOOT.'
    Johnny Rotten wanted
to destroy the passer-by.
Gary Hodges is putting
Doctor Marten's
apocalypse into words.
Rotten wanted to be
anarchy, Hodges is
painting vivid visions of
what that really means.
    The scene is a Damned gig
at the Bridge House last year
but the 4-Skins are on stage
now, a flaming molotov
cocktail of sound, and the
audience of cropped Michelin
Men, belligerent bootboys and
sweat-stained...

SUNDAY 5TH OCTOBER
THE SKIDS
PLUS THE BOOKS
ADVANCE TICKETS £2.50
OPEN 8.30-2am

MONDAY 6TH OCTOBER
THE RAMONES
PLUS "THE SPECTRES"
ADVANCE TICKETS £3.00
OPEN 6.30pm-11pm

TUESDAY 12TH OCTOBER
SON OF STIFF TOUR

CONTENTS

PHOTO: RAY STEVENSON

Editor's Letter

SOMETHING CHANGED. It happened in Britain when the Sex Pistols appeared, swearing and uncontrollable, on a live TV show, and in America when the Ramones unleashed their soon to become trademark two-minute bursts of noise.

At a time when rock music claimed to challenge but had really grown complacent and way too safe, punk arrived to challenge everything. Its roots went way back beyond the Sex Pistols or The Ramones, but it was those bands and a cast of like-minded misfits that broke the movement: establishing the idea that – be it music, fashion or art – it all was up for grabs, it was all there to be messed with and re-energised by a new generation.

The writing contained here captures the excitement of punk's 30-year journey: its first flush of youth, its struggle to survive in a new age and its subsequent resurrection. Taken from the archives of MOJO, Q and punk's original champion, the UK weekly music paper SOUNDS, these stories ignore the hype and perceived wisdom to get to the truth, giving a voice to the bands, fans, writers and photographers who were there at the time, the people who saw it happen.

Whether it's exhuming the Sex Pistols' first ever interview, celebrating the poetic low-life New York glory of the Ramones, Patti Smith and Television, pioneering new territory with Siouxsie Sioux, Buzzcocks and The Damned, sounding a last post for The Clash's Joe Strummer or chronicling the moment Green Day outraged a nation, it's been an amazing ride.

Enjoy the trip.

Mark Blake
Editor-In-Chief

Foreword

By Deborah Harry

PUNK IN NEW York started in 1973. It was a very small scene, undiscovered and only really mentioned in the local press. It hadn't been developed, commercialised or exploited. Blondie didn't have any contact with the outside world of mainstream rock, record companies didn't pay any attention at all. It was just us and the other bands on the scene – Television, Patti Smith, Talking Heads, Ramones – pretty much making it up as we went along, experimenting, trying to find a new sound.

Our audience was our friends, other bands, kids from the Lower East Side. In New York, punk came out of a camp sensibility. Nobody had any money, so the look was all about creating a personal style. There was still a smattering of glitter, traditional leather, ripped-up shirts, elements of the mod style – because those clothes were easy to get in New York.

IN THE UK, the punk movement was much more political, and we could see it as soon as we got there. Everybody was very outwardly driven and politically minded and it was all in the music. It was really all about their economy, because their economy had turned to shit. A great percentage of people were on the dole, and there really was no future for these kids. People forget what a wreck the place was in the early 1970s.

I remember Blondie's first gig in England very well. The audiences were so demonstrative and tribal. They danced, they slammed, they jumped, they spat. It was hot, wild and exciting. American audiences were much more conservative. And the music was great – The Stranglers, The Clash, Siouxsie Sioux, The Slits, Poly Styrene. The Sex Pistols especially were wonderful. They actually reminded me of Beethoven, they were that grandiose. The whole execution of that band was based on criminality. They weren't worried about having

Picture this: Blondie in 1976, with (from left) Gary Valentine, Clem Burke, Jimmy Destri, Debbie Harry and Chris Stein.

Hot, wild and exciting. Punk was all about bursting out.

credibility or not; they existed entirely in their own realm, and their whole thing was to do with anarchy. They had the political rhetoric down, but they also wanted the money. And they got all that money just to get off the label. It really was The Great Rock'n'Roll Swindle.

I admired the way that some of the kids following the UK punk scene were part of it even though they weren't in bands. But they had a great tradition of creating their own looks. Punk came through in your music, how you dressed and where you hung out. It was very obvious, and I think it's had a lasting effect. Even though now anybody with style stands out like a sore thumb, punk is still around. It's all about bursting out; that first real expression of breaking away.

CHAPTER ONE

IN THE BEGINNING

By the mid-1970s, something was stirring. On both sides of the Atlantic, the disenfranchised and disillusioned were finding their own musical voice. Enter the Ramones, the Sex Pistols, The Clash and more. Punk's first youthful flush was about to begin...

NEWSDESK

Damned: first punx on wax

THE DAMNED beat the Sex Pistols to the punch when they release their debut single this week on Stiff Records (see review on page 36).

Title of the single is 'New Rose' written by lead guitarist Bryan James and it's backed by Lennon and McCartney's 'Help'.

As reported in last week's SOUNDS, the Sex Pistols were the first of t

The Damned will also be the first new wave band to play a major tour venue when they support Graham Parker and The Rumour, together w Sean Tyler, at Victoria Palace on October 26. The group are curren revamping their stage act and will be includ

Punk Rock Year Zero

The first rumblings of punk began long before 1976. Over three decades on, rock journalist Nick Kent recalls what it was like being there at the birth – and how he briefly became a member of the Sex Pistols.

DON'T TALK TO me about punk, punk. I was there at the barricades running around like a headless chicken telling everyone that punk rock was the imminent bright white future of youth music culture back when Joe Strummer was still a denim-clad folk singer called 'Woody', Malcolm McLaren a Teddy-boy revivalist haberdasher trying in vain to bankroll a film documentary on vintage UK rocker Billy Fury, and John Lydon a long-haired teenager who sold acid at Hawkwind concerts.

In the summer and early autumn of 1975, I spent three months in a rehearsal studio near White City helping Steve Jones, Glen Matlock and Paul Cook transform themselves from a '60s retro act intent on regurgitating Who and Small Faces songs into the most exciting young hard-rock band of the decade. Six months later, I was onstage at a Cardiff Women's Lib venue with Chris 'Rat Scabies' Millar, Ray 'Captain Sensible' Burns and Brian James performing the first ever live version of New Rose and other early Damned songs long before they'd even been recorded in demo form. It was all a thankless task, though, and culminated in me staring at a blood-stained knife being wielded two inches from my eyes by Jah Wobble as his thug accomplice Sid Vicious whipped my face and scalp repeatedly with a rusty bike chain.

For me, punk didn't begin in 1976; it started in 1971 when I first read US rock magazine Creem. The writer Dave Marsh claims he coined the phrase 'punk rock' in a review he wrote for the magazine in late '71 of a gig by ? & The Mysterians. But it was fellow Creem scribe Lester Bangs who really took the term and created a whole aesthetic for it.

For Bangs and his disciples, punk rock began in 1963 when Seattle quartet The Kingsmen hit Number 1 Stateside with the deliciously moronic Louie Louie, grew with the influx of three-chord one-hit-wonders from the US mid-'60s that fellow Creem correspondent Lenny Kaye paid fulsome tribute to with his influential 1972 double-album compilation Nuggets, and reached a crashing apex with the less successful Michigan-based MC5 and Iggy & The Stooges.

Both bands emigrated to London at the beginning of 1972 just as I was commencing my career as a rock journo, but they were too ahead of their time and failed to attract any solid following. One of the best concerts I ever witnessed was the MC5 playing a club near Piccadilly Circus called Bumpers to an audience of myself, Viv Prince – the former Pretty Things drummer

– a Hell's Angel companion of Prince's and a large Alsatian dog. And when The Stooges played their one-and-only UK showcase at the King's Cross Scala cinema that summer, they attracted less than 100 paying customers. Still, for me at least, that show was the pivotal event, a moment of epiphany that injected the very essence of punk into the post-hippy cluelessness of British youth culture.

For punk purists, The Stooges were the first and the best because their music was as deep, dark and brutally honest as the classic blues masters. All the bands that followed – from The Ramones to The Damned – revered and ransacked The Stooges' albums in the same way The Rolling Stones and The Yardbirds had looked up to their Howlin' Wolf and Muddy Waters records.

The New York Dolls also had a blues connection in singer David Johansen, a big-lipped, girlish-looking individual who'd once followed his idol Janis Joplin around the US on tour and who sang in a lascivious baritone growl like Big Joe Turner in a woman's corset and heels. The Dolls were quintessential glam rockers – three members had even imported flamboyant fashion clothing from Europe and sold it around Manhattan – but their musical shortcomings and the trouble-prone presence of Johnny Thunders, a guitarist notorious for blowing out the most PA systems in New York club history, also guaranteed the quintet a rowdy punk-rock kudos.

THE NEW YORK Dolls moved to London in late autumn 1972 in search of a record deal, just as The Stooges, MC5 and Lou Reed were packing their bags back to the States. But once again England proved cold and inhospitable.

I witnessed the Dolls for the first time supporting The Faces at London's Wembley Empire Pool. They looked exquisite but sounded so sloppy that the audience began jeering them and throwing toilet rolls before they'd completed their first song. Less than 24 hours later, their drummer Billy Murcia would die from an overdose

Steve Jones sold me a Fender he'd stolen. He had a real talent for shoplifting guitars.

Malcolm McLaren and Vivienne Westwood, king and queen of punk, June 1977.

(Inset) Original Pistols Paul Cook, Wally Nightingale and Steve Jones.

(Previous page) Iggy Pop, proto-punk and mooted Pistols vocalist, 1973.

of tranquillisers and alcohol at a London flat and the group would return to Manhattan.

In early 1973, I paid my first visit to the States and during the three months I was there reconnected with the punk rock pathfinders I'd first encountered in '72 in London. In Detroit, I found members of the by-now-broken-up MC5 struggling with substance abuse problems and uncertain of what lay ahead. In Los Angeles, I spent time with The Stooges, who'd just released their third album, Raw Power, and saw how Iggy Pop's recurring heroin addiction continued to destroy any chances the group had of mainstream success. In New York, I saw the New York Dolls recording a demo of their song Jet Boy and noticed how both guitar players were hopelessly out of tune.

The Dolls would soon follow The Stooges into the toilet, but they at least managed to release a strong, sassy-sounding debut album that came out in the summer of 1973, prompting a second tour of England and also Europe. I caught them in Paris in late '73 and had my first conversation with Malcolm McLaren, a nervous-looking little red-haired bloke who ran the clothes shop Let It Rock on London's King's Road. A blinkered advocate of vintage '50s and early '60s rock, McLaren

had given up on then-contemporary rock altogether until the New York Dolls traipsed into his store one afternoon and reignited his curiosity. He liked the music but mostly he liked their rebellious spirit and potential as models for his risqué clothing designs. I liked him because underneath his shyness he was raging with zany theories. I remember him trying to convince me that Johnny Kidd And The Pirates were more influential than Bob Dylan on the ultimate scheme of contemporary music.

McLaren invited me to his shop for a further exchange of cultural viewpoints and I went in January '74, bringing along my girlfriend, Chrissie Hynde. Chrissie liked the place so much she ended up working there. We got along with Malcolm and his girlfriend – a feisty little Northern woman with peroxide hair called Vivienne Westwood – and spent many evenings together. During our lengthy chat sessions we would lament the absence of a truly world-beating young London rock band and talk passionately about how the music needed to be dangerous again in order to survive as a potential art form.

EARLY IN 1974 I was introduced to Glen Matlock, a Faces-worshipping youth who worked at Let It Rock, which quickly changed its name to SEX and then to Seditionaries. In the early summer of that year, McLaren and I were standing in the upper foyer of the Kilburn State cinema for a concert featuring Ronnie Wood, Keith Richards and Rod Stewart to promote Wood's first solo album, when Matlock suddenly materialised with his mates Steve Jones, Paul Cook and Wally Nightingale. They didn't have tickets, so they'd climbed through the roof of the venue. Right then they had my respect, which grew when they related their exploits as cat burglars in piecing together the PA and instruments they'd ripped off to commence their own group, then tentatively called Swankers.

Steve Jones was the leader because he was the toughest and had personally done most of the ripping-off. He was just the vocalist at this point; Wally Nightingale was their guitar player. I never caught them rehearsing during 1974 – nor did I witness their disastrous sole live performance – but I frequently found myself around them. Jones even sold me a beautiful Fender Telecaster Deluxe he'd stolen. He had a real talent for shoplifting guitars – over 20, he'd boast. By the beginning of 1975, though, McLaren and I had both bade farewell to our thieving chums and reinstalled ourselves in America: me in LA, partly to see if The Stooges could be resuscitated, and him in New York to bail out his lost boys, the New York Dolls.

Trying to stimulate The Stooges back into action was a fruitless quest. Iggy lapsed between being charmingly straight and coherent to becoming a stoned menace,

Bare cheek from Chrissie Hynde (centre), Vivienne Westwood (second right) and Jordan (right) at SEX, King's Road, London, 1976.

and his name was poison around Hollywood. He felt there was a curse on The Stooges' name and had started fixing his hopes instead on working as a solo act under the aegis of David Bowie.

McLaren became the Dolls' personal Florence Nightingale: another thankless task. He got alcoholic bassist Arthur Kane his much-needed medical insurance, and attempted to detox Johnny Thunders and new drummer Jerry Nolan from their heroin addictions – all to no avail. He then compelled Vivienne Westwood to design red patent leather stage outfits for the band and coerced them into pretending they were communists, which only alienated the last remnants of the group's crumbling Manhattan fan base. By the summer he was back in London, frothing at the mouth about his recent humiliations with the Dolls. David Johansen was a prima donna and Thunders was a hopeless junkie, he said. Their golden days had come and gone. By contrast, the young cat burglars who still congregated around the shop were the voice of the future – untainted by drug abuse and young enough to be psychologically moulded.

Shortly after that, McLaren and his group – he'd named them QT Jones & His Sex Pistols – invited me to attend a rehearsal. Wally Nightingale's dad was a night watchman at the recently defunct BBC Studio complex near Shepherd's Bush, and it was in one of the abandoned building's large rooms that they had set up all their stolen equipment. They played a set that was both quaint and bloody extraordinary. The repertoire mostly consisted of spunky renditions of The Small Faces' Understanding, The Who's Call Me Lightning and other mid-'60s Brit-pop staples including The Foundations' Build Me Up Buttercup. But it came alive dramatically when the group, which now featured Steve Jones playing second guitar as well as singing in a manner that mimicked the lung-bursting bravado of early Steve Marriott, played the two songs they'd written so far: Scarface and Did You No Wrong. Actually they were the same song – same riff, same groove, same everything. Only the lyrics were different.

JONES SHOWED ME a scrap of paper on which his stepfather had written the words to Scarface, a song about a gangster. Almost every word was heinously misspelled; one line read, "'E dun 'im in." That didn't matter because it provided them with the chance to reprise Did You No Wrong, which was a little miracle. Written in part by Nightingale, who contributed the descending riff that he partly stole from Ron Wood's intro to The Faces' Pool Hall Richard, the song is the only one that would survive the Johnny Rotten era.

Indeed, the version they ended up recording two years later is virtually identical to the song I heard that afternoon, barring Lydon's howling replacing Jones's

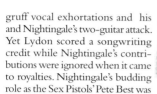

gruff vocal exhortations and his and Nightingale's two-guitar attack. Yet Lydon scored a songwriting credit while Nightingale's contributions were ignored when it came to royalties. Nightingale's budding role as the Sex Pistols' Pete Best was brought home to me that day when McLaren coldly told him that he didn't fit into the group and that he should basically fuck off and never darken their door again. This was a bold move as Nightingale held the keys to their rehearsal premises – but it didn't prevent both Cook and Jones, who'd grown up with him, turning against him too. McLaren told everyone I was the new guitarist. It was news to me too. Suddenly I was a Sex Pistol.

At first it was all rather exciting. I never sang a note with the group; I played guitar instead, filling out the sound made by Jones' limited strumming. People pretend the Sex Pistols could barely play their instruments but this wasn't true. By the time I joined they were already far more accomplished musicians than, say, the New York Dolls, and Matlock and Cook were shaping up as one of the most exciting rock rhythm sections ever to come out of Britain.

THE MAIN PROBLEM was their repertoire, which was too '60s-fixated. They couldn't see beyond copying the songs of their favourite acts, The Small Faces and The Who. I got them to drop Everlasting Love and Build Me Up Buttercup. McLaren chose two songs from his jukebox – Dave Berry's Don't Give Me No Lip, Child and Billy Fury's Do You Really Love Me Too, aka Fool's Errand – and we duly worked out new arrangements. I constantly played Jones and Matlock my Stooges albums – it was me who suggested doing No Fun, though we never played it together – and a tape of the first Modern Lovers album.

Hearing Roadrunner and Pablo Picasso for the first time inspired Matlock, and these sessions did much to transform the group's musical agenda from '60s nostalgia to the cutting edge of the

'70s. McLaren than decided they really needed a lead singer and started looking around. I phoned up Iggy Pop in LA to lure him over to London to front the Pistols only to discover that he'd just been committed to a mental institution. McLaren spoke to Sylvain Sylvain and Johnny Thunders in New York, offering them both the Sex Pistols' frontman spot – but they preferred to stay in Manhattan and score drugs.

After that we became desperate and spent many evenings travelling around the outskirts of London – Bernie Rhodes, Malcolm's designated gofer, was our driver – visiting youth clubs, social functions, even bar mitzvahs, in search of a teenager who could front the band.

McLaren's rap was always the same: "We're the Sex Pistols – the greatest group ever to have come out of London, the greatest city in the world – and we're looking for a singer. Have you got the bollocks to fit the bill?" Invariably the youths he was addressing would look at us as though we'd been beamed down from another planet and gruffly reject the offer. McLaren then decided to cruise the London gay bars for a suitable candidate. He found one youth and brought him down to a rehearsal, but the poor lad literally pissed his pants with fear when he stood next to the microphone stand and came perilously close to electrocuting himself.

Incidents like these started making me suspicious of McLaren's capabilities and also irritated Steve Jones, who still secretly saw himself as the band's vocalist. Jones and I then wrote a song called Ease Your Mind and recorded it at a friend's demo studio. When McLaren discovered we'd done this without him being consulted, he got Matlock to fire me. I didn't care. It had been an interesting three months but it couldn't have lasted much longer. I was four years older than the rest. Also, I was middle-class and had even briefly attended university. Poor Jones could barely read or write: he signed his name with a cross.

The Sex Pistols had to be introduced to the world as four authentic working-class social rejects, and if this meant no place for me, so be it. There was another reason: I'd become a heroin addict. Still, relations with McLaren and the band remained cordial – for a while, anyway. They were rehearsing in Denmark Street and I'd see them a lot. I remember walking down Charing Cross Road with McLaren when he told me excitedly that they'd found their singer, "this spastic-looking, red-haired kid who's always on acid… He's the best thing in the group… He came in the other day with this song he'd written called You're Only 29 – You've Got A Lot to Learn." That kid, of course, became Johnny Rotten, and the rest is his story.

I asked Iggy Pop to front the Pistols. But he'd just been committed to a mental institution.

It's always the
quiet ones:
the once-shy
Rotten erupts
onstage in
Holland, 1977.

ANGER IS AN ENERGY

John Lydon's childhood was scarred by poverty, illness and brutally strict schooling. Little wonder, then, that by the time he was picked to front the Sex Pistols the shy young waster was "an explosion waiting to happen".

THE BOY WHO would grow up to become Johnny Rotten was born with an attitude problem. Which is hardly surprising for someone who could never be sure where – or even exactly when – he was born. John Joseph Lydon's birth certificate apparently listed 31 January 1956 as the day he arrived in the world, though the document was subsequently lost, with no copy of it to be found in the Public Records Office. Lydon's father insists his son was born in London. "I'm not so sure," the singer later confided in his vivid autobiography, Rotten: No Irish, No Blacks, No Dogs.

John Lydon's account of his early life is so utterly grim it might have been lifted from the pages of a Dickens novel. His first-generation Irish immigrant parents, John and Eileen, initially led an itinerant life, living wherever the former could find work as a crane driver. Once they'd settled in the ironically named Benwell Mansions near Holloway Road, north London, Lydon had to share two rooms – a bedroom and kitchen – with his parents and two younger brothers, Bobby and Jimmy. Occupying the front room was a tramp who stank out the house. Completing this ugly picture, once a month Lydon's mother would plant her son in a tin bath and disinfect him using a brush and a bottle of Dettol. The young John would help his mother out in times of crisis, grabbing a bucket whenever – good Catholics that they were – Mrs Lydon was having one of her regular miscarriages.

However closely they were forced to live, Lydon now claims his parents were strangers to him. "I had no idea who they were," he told MOJO in 2005. "That's a terrible thing, innit? They were just basic Irish folks living in England. And that was bad. I ain't no romantic looking back at that time, there was fuck all for them."

The singer who would declare "anger is an energy" seemed to be driven by rage and hate, even in his early youth. He hated his father's job, particularly on the occasions that John Snr took him into the crane cab, feeling that although he was the envy of his friends, he was "way above all that". He hated his mother's Crimplene clothes and the smell of her hairspray. He hated the drunken family gatherings where his brother Jimmy would be encouraged to perform an Irish jig ("I'd be sitting in the corner going, 'This is awful'"). He hated the lengthy Irish holidays the Lydons enjoyed every summer, remembering, "I could never be wilful on a farm… the only things you can antagonise are the cows." Nevertheless, for all his rage and bluster, Lydon was a timid child. "For years, he was so shy it was unbelievable," claims his father. "He would never mix."

LYDON'S SHYNESS WAS probably not helped by the fact that Irish immigrants were looked on as third-class citizens in 1960s London. Even as an infant, making his way to the Roman Catholic Eden Grove primary school, he suffered abuse from English Protestant adults ("Dirty Irish bastards! That kind of shit"). Once there, the brutally strict nuns would rap his knuckles with a ruler if he got his sums wrong. Life was unrelentingly bleak, and about to get much worse.

One morning when John Lydon was seven, his mother couldn't wake him for school, finding him limp and lifeless. He was rushed to Whittington Hospital in Highgate, where he was diagnosed with meningitis. The illness, Lydon believes, was caused by him drinking water contaminated with rats' urine. "It frightened me, naturally," Eileen Lydon said after. "I had it when I was 11 and I knew what it was."

The young John Lydon was hallucinating, having visions of fire-breathing green dragons, and slipping in and out of consciousness. Eventually he fell into a coma lasting six months. When he awoke, much of his memory had been erased. Returning to school after a year away, damaged and disorientated, he soon realised how far behind his classmates he now lagged.

"I had serious learning problems and it took years to get back to normal," he told this writer in 2002. "I was known as Dummy Boy 'cos I didn't know nothing. I couldn't even speak, I'd forgot words. When your body's that inoperative, it affects everything. It's a great possibility that I have brain damage, but I'm damaged so much as to not know that."

John Lydon Snr recalls his wife patiently re-teaching their son how to read outside school hours. "He couldn't spell c-a-t," he says. "So his mum sat down with him every night. I didn't have the patience – I'll be honest about that. I suppose he had to learn everything twice. He learned the hard way how to get on. The kids would tease him – 'Dummy! Dummy! Dummy!'"

This horrific period in John Lydon's early life appears to have informed everything that he would later become, both mentally and physically. In his head, he was now boiling with anger, while the aftermath of the disease left him with a permanent hunch – caused by the injections to drain fluid from his spine – and impaired eyesight that gave him a manic stare. He also had a weak chest that filled with phlegm that needed to be frequently spat out. In other words, all the character traits that would become known as the hallmarks of Johnny Rotten.

Long before the dawning of punk rock, John Lydon learned to use his stare as a weapon. When his family moved to a council flat in Pooles Park near Finsbury Park train station in the late '60s, Lydon was enrolled in William Of York comprehensive school near Pentonville Prison. He remembers it as being "a shit hole". The future singer was showing an interest in literature, though he would often argue with his English teachers about their interpretations of books. Clearly bright, his passion for art was discouraged because painting and drawing were viewed as pursuits only for the academically challenged.

Displaying the antagonistic characteristics that would earn him infamy, he told his religious education teachers that he wanted to be a Muslim. When he couldn't wind up his superiors any further, he'd resort to the stare. "It was all about manipulating their anger," he wrote in Rotten, "annoying them

> ## "He was the vilest geezer I'd ever met… Everyone hated him. Everyone hated me too."
> SID VICIOUS ON JOHN LYDON AT COLLEGE

by staring without blinking through an entire lesson."

Outside of school, Lydon had similar delinquent tendencies. At night, he and his mates would break into factories on a nearby industrial estate and cause havoc. He discovered alcohol at a surprisingly tender age, and by 11 he was downing pint after pint in Finsbury Park pubs where the landlords turned a blind eye.

The young bad boy was not without a sense of responsibility, however. To

John Lydon with college 'friend' turned band-mate Simon Ritchie, aka Sid Vicious, 1977.

(Left) The pre-Rotten Lydon practises his trademark stare, 1974.

Dreaming. "A jean shirt, no jackets and hobnail boots painted bright green. Hair way down my shoulders."

As his teens progressed, Lydon found solace in music and was often to be found upstairs in the family flat, listening to his records. As his father remembered, "He'd sit up there almost 24 hours a day." Eschewing the prog and glam rock staples of the early '70s, he favoured Van Der Graaf Generator over Yes, Hawkwind over David Bowie, Captain Beefheart over Marc Bolan.

HE ALSO BECAME a huge fan of reggae, which he heard drifting out of windows in the increasingly Afro-Caribbean-populated Finsbury Park. He tentatively began buying reggae albums from a shop by the train station, waiting until the black customers had left before coyly taking a record up to the counter. "I don't go out of my way to listen to 'black' music," he explained to MOJO. "I grew up in Finsbury Park – the melting pot of the universe. I see no clear distinction between a reggae record or anything else."

One revelatory experience that would shape his later career as a Sex Pistol was witnessing Iggy Pop And The Stooges perform at the Scala in King's Cross when he was 16. "James Williamson was playing the most of out-of-tune guitar," he told Jon Savage. "Iggy wasn't liked. In fact, he was ignored. He'd run around and bash himself with the microphone. I liked it."

Nevertheless, these formative experiences appear to have had little effect on Lydon's own musical abilities. Schoolmate John Gray recalled how one progressive music teacher at William Of York brought a copy of The Who's Tommy into school for his class to sing along to and how Lydon mercilessly took the piss: "He went up and down like a yodelling cat being strangled. That was the first time I'd ever heard John sing. The teacher shouted, 'Stop, stop, stop! I've heard enough.'"

Soon after, he was kicked out of William Of York for his disruptive behaviour.

From there, Lydon sleepwalked through a succession of menial jobs – killing rats on a building site, laying concrete for a sewage farm – and enrolled at Hackney Technical College to complete his O-levels. There he met a fashion-conscious Bowie obsessive, Simon John Ritchie. Lydon thought he was "a wanker". The future Sid Vicious – nicknamed by Lydon after his hamster and the Lou Reed Transformer song – recalled his new friend as being "the vilest geezer I'd ever met… all misshapen, hunchbacked. Everyone hated him. Everyone hated me, too. We hated each other, but no one else would talk to us." Vicious's mother, Anne Beverley, remembers the future Sex Pistols singer. "He was shy. If I just looked at him, he went beetroot red. Couldn't say a word. I'd never met someone that shy before."

help out his permanently skint family, he took a job as a taxi controller in a local office at the age of 10. "I had fantastic fun," he recalled in his autobiography. "It was an easy enough job to tell the drivers where to go, since I knew the area. I got bored with it only because the manager was such a miserable old Irish git. He was one of those old Teddy boy sorts."

Though he would later decide never to trust a hippy, as Lydon hit his teens he grew his hair long, further stoking the ire of his teachers. "I was the freak of the neighbourhood," he told author Jon Savage when recounting his youth in the punk history England's

After Hackney, Lydon and Ritchie moved on to Kingsway College near Kings Cross, though they rarely went to classes. Along the way, they met John Wardle, later to become PiL bassist Jah Wobble, who remembers Lydon's almost overnight change into a proto-punk: "He came along with dyed, shaved hair… saying he'd found a new way of life."

Having decided to rebel against the long-haired fashions of the day, Lydon had hacked off his locks and dyed the remainder green. John Gray remembers his friend experimenting with Crazy Color, the blue dye blending with John's blond hair to produce a sickly, cabbage-like shade. Lydon remembers it differently, claiming it was a clothes dye. Either way, the result was the same: Lydon's father kicked him out of the house.

"Nothing stops me doing anything," he defiantly told me. "When I first dyed my hair green, that weren't no joyride."

BY 1975, THE 19-year-old John Lydon was sharing an unlikely squat that Ritchie had found in the leafy, moneyed north London suburb of Hampstead. Also living in the flat was a squad of hippies, whom Lydon learned to loathe, from the smell of their joss sticks to the silk scarves they draped over milk crates to make their environment look habitable.

Lydon and Ritchie were a pair of complete wasters during this period, permanently drunk or wired on speed. Nevertheless, for a time they were gainfully employed as cleaners by the longhairs who ran Cranks health food restaurant in Tottenham Court Road. Left to their own devices by night, they would help themselves to the leftovers in the kitchen.

Ritchie supplemented his income selling amphetamine, though Lydon was later strangely reticent when I asked him if it was true that – as Lemmy from Motörhead claimed – he regularly used to sell wraps of speed outside The Rainbow in Finsbury Park at this time.

"Lenny [sic] has been saying so," he sneered. "Well, poor Lenny. I mean, how would he remember? But get with the programme, y'know. When you're fucking poor, you've gotta make a bob or two. There aren't many opportunities. Free enterprise means something quite different to a working-class lad, and that's how it is."

Around this time, his overwhelming hate seemed to turn in on itself: Lydon began self-harming, burning his arms with lit cigarettes. "I don't know what prompted it," he mused in his autobiography. "Insecurity. There's scars all up and down my arm. I think it was a badge of self-pity more than anything."

Part of this self-loathing possibly stemmed from his lack of success with members of the opposite sex. At school, he would forlornly follow around a girl called

Sylvia Hartland, to no avail, setting the tone for what was to follow. He later claimed he "hadn't worked out" his attitude towards sex until he was 21 and already a Pistol. "I had loves early in my youth," he told Q in 1992, "but they were unrequited, I'm afraid. I just had to be a voyeur. I was so insecure, absolutely totally petrified by sex and that kind of commitment."

Still, there were brighter moments amid the gloom. Despite their acute lack of musical skills, he and Ritchie used to go busking in Tube stations, playing violin and

He stoops to conquer: Johnny at the Queensway Hall, Dunstable, October 1976.

(Above, right) Awkward outsider becomes punkette magnet, 430 King's Road, London, 1977.

guitar respectively, making a howling racket built around Alice Cooper's I Love The Dead (which, typically, Lydon reworked as I Don't Love The Dead) and crooner Tony Bennett's I Left My Heart In San Francisco (or, as it became, I Left My Heart In Some Crummy Disco).

All the while, the pair continued to develop their own idiosyncratic fashion sense, guided by Lydon, who gave Ritchie one of the original punk crops by hacking at his friend's hair until it was a mess of spikes. He also began slashing cheap suits with a razor blade and piecing them back together with safety pins. John Lydon Snr, for one, was appalled by his son's stylistic experiments: "If he had a pullover sweater, he'd cut one sleeve off."

LYDON'S WAYWARD INTEREST in sartorial trends perhaps inevitably led him to the centre of London's fashion world at the time, the King's Road. He later stated that he and his mates would parade up and down the street in their disassembled suits and skewed hairdos "just to annoy people", all too aware that they stuck out among the soul boys with their pleated trousers. John Wardle remembers, however, that there was an ulterior motive. Ritchie had discovered where his other hero, Roxy Music singer Bryan Ferry, lived on the road and he and Lydon had plans to knock on his door wielding a bottle of Martini and force their way in.

It never happened. And instead, fatefully, Lydon chanced upon the SEX boutique, then run by ambitious designer Vivienne Westwood and her partner, one Malcolm McLaren. "SEX were doing something different," Lydon told Jon Savage. "I loved the rubber T-shirt. I thought it was the most repulsive thing I'd ever seen."

"For years he was so shy it was unbelievable. He would never mix."

JOHN LYDON SNR

Though he initially didn't encounter McLaren or sales assistant Glen Matlock in the shop, Lydon was spotted by a curious Bernie Rhodes, future manager of The Clash. At the time, Lydon was wearing a Pink Floyd T-shirt on which the twisted youth had written the words "I hate" over the band's name. Rhodes passed on the word to McLaren, who was intrigued and asked Lydon the next time he came into the shop if he sang, only to receive a curt, negative response. Nevertheless, Lydon's interest had been stirred and he agreed to meet McLaren and the rest of the fledgling Sex Pistols in the Roebuck Pub later that night.

According to Steve Jones, the band had already met a string of "idiots" in their search for a singer and so Lydon presented a highly unusual proposition, with his safety pins and mad-eyed stare. Nevertheless, the guitarist still decided that Lydon was a "prick". "Paul and Steve hated me on sight," the singer said, "which intrigued Malcolm because he is a bit of a sick fuck, and it went on from there."

Repairing to SEX for a makeshift audition, they asked Lydon to sing along to one of the records on the jukebox. "They tried to get me to sing Maggie May!" Lydon later scoffed. Instead he chose I'm Eighteen by Alice Cooper and – more through embarrassment than anything else – gooned and mugged and howled his way through the song, using a shower head as a mock microphone. Of course, he thought the assembled would be appalled. Instead, they offered him the gig.

"It never occurred to me to be in a band and to make music," he reasoned. "It was impossible. It should never have worked. You must understand that when I joined The Sex Pistols, I had no prospects whatsoever and this was my last chance to do something."

Considering how much Lydon contributed to the punk ethos and look, it's perhaps unsurprising that his hackles would rise whenever he was reminded how Malcolm McLaren or the other punk bands had tried to claim the credit.

"I've got news for you," he pointed out to me with bug-eyed passion in 2002. "I had to earn my wings to get some kind of punk thing going, and the rest came in like it was a hairdressers' convention. But they didn't go through those punishing early years."

Looking back, it seems almost inevitable that this furious individual, railing against his piss-poor background and lack of opportunities, would undergo a Jekyll and Hyde-like transformation – from John Lydon, hunchbacked Finsbury Park loser, to Johnny Rotten, punk icon and Public Enemy Number 1.

"Until then I was a bit of a church mouse," Lydon later wrote. "Fuming inside. An explosion waiting to happen."

PARADISE LOST

If you can't play pubs, you could always try a sleazy Soho strip club. Which is where, on 4 April 1976, the Sex Pistols chose to entertain John Ingham before their first-ever interview.

THE SMALL, SLEAZOID El Paradise club in Soho is not one of the more obvious places for English rock to finally get to grips with the '70s, but when you're trying to create the atmosphere of anarchy, rebellion and exclusiveness that's necessary as a breeding ground, what better place? Name a kid who will tell their parents they'll be home really late this Sunday because they're going to a strip club to see the Sex Pistols.

The front is the customary facade of garish, fluorescent-lit plastic and enticing tit pix, gold-flocked wallpaper and a life-size gilt-framed lovely beckoning you within. Conditioning expects one to go down a hall or some stairs, but the minute you turn the corner you're there. A small room, 20 to 30 feet long, a bar at one end, three and a half rows of broken-down cinema seats (the other half seems to have been bodily ripped out). It's a shock at first but, after it gets comfortable, the thought occurs that perhaps it's not sleazy enough. It needs more black paint peeling from the sweating walls, a stickier floor…

This gathering has accumulated entirely by word of mouth and by midnight the place is jumping.

Flared jeans are out. Leather helps. All-black is better. There are folks in their late twenties, chopped and channelled teenagers, people who frequent Sex, the King's Road avant leather, rubber and bondage clothing shop. These are people sick of nostalgia. People wanting forward motion. People wanting rock'n'roll that is relevant to 1976.

At the moment, those criteria are best embodied in the Sex Pistols. They fill the minuscule, mirror-backed stage, barely able to move in front of their amps. They are loud, they are fast, they are energetic. They are great. Coming on like a Lockheed Starfighter is more important to them than virtuosity. This quartet has no time

earlier reports reckoned their time-keeping was somewhat off, to the point of cultivating an ethic of them being so bad they were good, Glen Matlock (bass) and Paul Cook (drums) seem to have the beast on the rails, and in this stripped-down form the beast is where it's at. One also has to remember that the Sex Pistols have only existed professionally since Christmas and that Steve has only played guitar for five months.

With inaudible lyrics, the music is very similar from song to song, but a cranial

"i WANT PEOPLE TO SEE US AND THEN GO OUT AND START SOMETHiNG." JOHNNY ROTTEN

for a pretty song with a nice melody. Guitarist Steve Jones doesn't bother much with solos, preferring to just pick another chord and power on through. ("There's two reasons for that – I can't play solos, and I hate them anyway." As he said that, I'm Mandy, Fly Me came on the jukebox and we both agree the only good thing in it is the solo.)

But imitating the roar of the Industrial Age doesn't mean they're sloppy. Although

trigger says, "That song is great" (applaud), but "That one is just OK" (don't applaud). Everyone else seems to think similarly. Which annoys singer Johnny Rotten endlessly. "Clap, you fuckers. Because I'm wasting my time not hearing myself." He begins a slow handclap; about three people join in.

John likes to confront his audience, not to mention the rest of the band. It's this Stooges-like aura of unpredictability and

violence that gives the Sex Pistols that extra edge. Paul reckons the broken glass attitude will only disappear when they get as old as Pete Townshend and just do it for the money.

The Pistols' roots lie with Paul and Steve, who left school with a healthy desire to avoid work. The obvious alternative was rock, even though neither could play an instrument. Their musical models were the Stones and The Who and the early Small Faces, which doesn't say much for '70s rock, and was the reason for starting a band. From the last six years, Steve rates The Stooges. Paul admits to being fooled by Roxy Music for three albums. Later, he added Todd Rundgren. "Yeah, that's what acid does to you," retorted Steve, adding proudly, "There's no drugs in this group."

Glen joined and they staggered on for a year, learning a Who/Small Faces repertoire ("But that didn't get us anywhere"), buying their threads from Sex and bugging Malcolm, the owner, to manage them. Having already spent seven months in New York handling the New York Dolls, he wasn't too interested, but he helped them a bit and, well, London could do with a '70s rock band.

Malcolm decided Steve was hopeless as a singer, got him to learn guitar, and the search was on. Into Sex walks John, who couldn't sing but looked the part. They tried to audition in the conventional manner, but settled on standing him in front of the shop's jukebox, telling him to pretend he was onstage. John had never even considered joining a band.

WE'RE SITTING IN a tacky pub in Charing Cross Road. Until now, John has been sitting politely, looking a bit bored while I talk to the others. He's wearing the ripped-up red sweater he wears onstage, a safety pin dangles from a thin gold ring in his right earlobe. So how come you're doing it, John?

The intensity level immediately leaps about 300 per cent. "I hate shit. I hate hippies and what they stand for. I hate long hair. I hate pub bands. I want to change it so there are rock bands like us."

This is delivered at full tirade, with a sneer to match the voice. He clocks my tortoiseshell earring, the five weeks' laziness straggling across my cheeks and chin and the sneer and the direct-eye blitz never stops. I'm inadvertently thinking, "Gosh, I'm not a hippie now – that was a childhood error, and I never was one in the first place." The kid's got style. You know what end of the switchblade he would have been on in 1956. I'd love to be present when the middle-aged boogers who pass for rock critics on the nationals finally confront him. But John's just winding up.

"I'm against people who just complain about Top Of The Pops and don't do anything. I want people to go out and start something, to see us and start something, or else I'm just wasting my time." This last phrase is a favourite. He says it with just the right amount of studied boredom.

The Pistols found their first public by gate-crashing gigs, pulling up and posing as the support band. At the North East London Poly they succeeded in emptying the room, the same stylish feat being

Paul: "The trouble with pubs is that you have to please everybody. If we wanted to please everybody we'd end up sounding like The Beatles."

That left The Marquee, 100 Club and the Nashville. Eddie And The Hot Rods asked them to support at The Marquee. It was the first time they had ever used monitors, and hearing themselves caused a slight OD, John leaping into the audience and the others kicking the monitors about.

IN THE LIGHT of what the Pistols consider the Hot Rods' overreaction to the incident, the group insist they did little damage to anything that wasn't theirs. They've also written a song on the matter. I think the photos speak for the particular violence of the 100 Club gig, but the band and the Nashville seemed to enjoy each other.

Allan Jones of The Melody Maker described it: "Their dreadfully inept attempts to zero in on the kind of viciously blank intensity previously epitomised by The Stooges was rather endearing at first… The guitarist, another surrogate punk suffering from a surfeit of Sterling

"THE NEW YORK SCENE HAS NOTHING TO DO WITH US. IT'S A WASTE OF TIME." JOHNNY ROTTEN

Shep Gordon's reason for signing Alice Cooper. At St Albans, where they supposedly played one of their worst gigs, they were asked back again.

St Albans was also the first place to recognise the Doctors Of Madness. In London they rapidly depleted themselves of potential venues. For a start, they wouldn't play pubs.

Malcolm: "The trouble with pubs is that they're bigger than the bands. They're all full of people playing what a crowd wants rather than what they want because they can make a reasonable living from it. If you want to change things you can't play pubs. You don't have the freedom."

Morrison, played with a disregard for taste and intelligence." Taste. Intelligence. "Who's Sterling Morrison?" asked Steve.

When last heard of he was a university professor in Santa Fe. "Oh. That's alright then. What's 'surrogate' mean?"

They are going to play the Nashville again, but their problem, apart from finding it impossible to recruit a band they're compatible with musically, is that it's still not the right environment.

Malcolm decided early that France would understand much better and envisioned a couple of weeks or more in Paris. The French promoter saw the Marquee gig and, fired with visions of

PHOTO: RAY STEVENSON

The Pistols in London's Carnaby Street, 1976: (from left) Glen Matlock, Steve Jones, Johnny Rotten and Paul Cook.

Gene Vincent and Vince Taylor, has booked them across France and Switzerland for May. Meanwhile, El Paradise…

If things work out, Malcolm will obtain the old UFO premises. Tonight, the police arrive about 2am, what with the noise of the steel rolling door going up and down as people left.

Basically, what Malcolm wants is a rumbling, anarchic, noisy, energetic rock scene, the likes of which haven't been seen in this country since the mid 1960s. Any comparisons with the New York rock/club scene are quickly brushed aside.

"Maybe it's because they're all so close to the media, but they're all so scared by them," Malcolm confides. "I used to talk to [New York journalist] Lisa Robinson, and the New York Dolls' David Johansen would pull me into the toilet and say, 'Don't you know who you're talking to? Don't say those things!' My God, if you worry about what you say to her…

"The trouble with the Dolls was that their hype was so much bigger than they were. They really had an opportunity to change it all around, but instead of ignoring all the bullshit about signing up with a company and a big advance they got sucked in. Every time the Ramones have a picture of them published it lessens their mystique. There's no mystery about the New York scene.

"The thing to do is just ignore all that. No one came to sign up the Stones, no one wanted to know. But when they saw a lot of bands sounding like that with a huge following they had to sign them.

"The trouble with pubs is that they're free, and people come for that reason. If you're at a Sex Pistols gig, it's because you wanted to go, you had to spend money to get in. I opened the shop because I wanted people to make a statement if they wore my clothes. The Sex Pistols are another extension of that."

As for what the band think of the comparisons that are being made with the New York scene…

"It has absolutely nothing to do with us," sneers John. "It's a total waste of time. All anyone ever talks about is the image. No one's mentioned the music."

But there's a remote connection with the aesthetic and their seeming to try and get on with the future.

"I like that word 'remote'," he says real blankly. (Is he always like this? "No, he was rather polite tonight.")

Steve and Paul deliver the fatal blows: "They're not like us. They all have long hair."

So they sit, waiting for a scene to build up around them, for the appearance of bands they can play with. They look rather glum at the prospect, and when you consider it, we can at least go and see the Sex Pistols.

"Yeah," says Steve Jones with a sigh, "I wish I could see us."

LONDON CALLING

Summer 1976, and live punk is about to explode across the capital. Tap rooms, polytechnic bars and sweaty clubs will host its unwashed greats.

VIRT

MONDAY JULY

Siouxsie
Banshe
Slits
Ants
+ D.J. NIC LEE

Licensed Bars 3 am

The 100 Clu

The Vortex

The Roxy

OXFORD STREET

WARDOUR STREET

CHARING CROSS ROAD

THE MALL

1
3
2
4
5
6
7

The Hope & Anchor

The Marquee

Charing Cross Pier

ON THE GREEN
PRESENTS A MIDNIGHT SPECIAL
SUNDAY AUG 29TH
MIDNIGHT — DAWN
STAGE
SEX PISTOLS
CLASH
+ BUZZCOCKS
TICKETS £1

THE NASHVILLE
Corner Cromwell Road / North End Road
(Adj) West Kensington (Tube) 01-603 6071
PARTY WITH THE
SEX PISTOLS
29th April
Ted Carrol's Rock on disco

WORDS: JOHNNY BLACK. PHOTOS: RAY STEVENSON, REDFERNS, REX

1 The 100 Club
Oxford Street, W1

Immortalised by The Clash in Deny, the 100 Club was – and still is – a jazz club, but flourished as a punk venue through the late '70s. The Damned debuted here on 6 July 1976, supporting the Sex Pistols, but the 100's days of thunder came on 20/21 September 1976, with the Punk Festival that saw the Pistols, The Damned, The Clash, Buzzcocks and Subway Sect all playing under one roof.

2 The Marquee
90 Wardour Street, W1

The Marquee largely avoided punk acts after unruly crowd behaviour when the Sex Pistols supported Eddie And The Hot Rods on Valentine's Day, 1976.

3 The Vortex
201 Wardour Street, W1

The Vortex opened on 11 July 1977 with Siouxsie, Adam Ant, The Slits and Sham 69, whose Jimmy Pursey was singled out and fined £30 for breach of the peace. After playing two shows at The Vortex in November 1977, The Heartbreakers decided to call it a day.

4 St Martin's School Of Art
109 Charing Cross Road, WC2

Stuart Goddard, later Adam Ant, was in headliners Bazooka Joe when the Sex Pistols played their first gig as support on 6 November 1975. A horrified social secretary pulled the plug after five numbers, but Goddard was sufficiently impressed to quit his band on the spot.

5 The Roxy
41-43 Neal Street, WC2

This former gay club became London's first famous punk venue. Generation X (supported by Siouxsie And The Banshees) ushered in The Roxy's period

of notoriety on 21 December 1976, followed by Johnny Thunders And The Heartbreakers the following night. From 1 January 1977, the club went totally punk, putting on The Clash, the Buzzcocks, X-Ray Spex, Wire, The Adverts, Slaughter And The Dogs, The Unwanted, Eater and Johnny Moped (featuring unknown guitarist Chrissie Hynde and Captain Sensible on backing vocals). The club closed after 100 days with Siouxsie And The Banshees headlining on 23 April 1977, then moved to the nearby Rock Garden.

6 The ICA
The Mall, SW1

When Patti Smith saw The Clash here on 23 October 1976, she was sufficiently carried away by the forceful music (and, apparently, by Paul Simonon's bone structure) to end up dancing onstage. By describing their musical style as "country", Adam And The Ants blagged their debut gig here on 10 May 1977. When Adam donned a leather mask to sing Beat My Guest, the management had the band unceremoniously removed.

7 Charing Cross Pier
Victoria Embankment, WC2

The Sex Pistols' boat trip to 'celebrate' the Jubilee – on 7 June 1977 – featured the band playing live onboard the pleasure boat Queen Elizabeth for the entertainment of a large contingent of media liggers. The rumpus attracted the river police, who forced the boat to dock, after which 11 passengers – including Malcolm McLaren – were arrested. Film of the event was included in 1979's The Great Rock'N'Roll Swindle.

White riot: Clash fans rip it up at the Rainbow, 9 May 1977.

8 Battersea Park
Battersea Park Road, SW11

Following a GLC ban on their live gigs, The Stranglers managed to organise an event in Battersea Park on 16 September 1978, supported by Spizz Oil and The Skids. Police were seen jostling for position at the front when strippers joined the band onstage and no charges were ever brought. Some of the gig was captured on the Live (X Cert) album.

9 Victoria Park
Hackney, E5

After an Anti-Nazi League march from Trafalgar Square on 30 April 1978, The Clash, Steel Pulse, Tom Robinson Band and X-Ray Spex played to 80,000 fans from the main stage. The back of a truck sufficed for The Ruts.

10 Central School Of Art & Design
Southampton Row, WC1

"A lousy set-up," according to former student Joe Strummer, the Central was still the scene of many early punk gigs, including Generation X's debut on 10 December 1976.

11 Electric Ballroom
184 Camden High Street, NW1

Scene of "Sid Sods Off" on 22 August 1978, the final live extravaganza by Mr Vicious before heading off to New York, where he OD'd. In the audience that night were Elvis Costello, Steve Jones, The Slits, Captain Sensible, Blondie and Joan Jett.

12 The Greyhound
Park Lane, Croydon

Scene of The Jam's first London gig on 27 October 1974, supporting Stackridge and Thin Lizzy. Stackridge fans pelted them with turnips.

13 Hope & Anchor
207 Upper Street, N1

A venerated if grubby pub-rock venue, from which future Stiff Records mogul Dave Robinson ran a recording studio. The pub's musical policy is illustrated by the Hope & Anchor Front Row Festival album, which documents three weeks of gigs in November 1977, including 999 and The Stranglers. The Clash played fund-raising gigs for the venue in 1984.

14 Man In The Moon
392 King's Road, SW5

Adam And The Ants played some of their earliest supporting gigs here. When they finally headlined, in May 1977, the punters walked out after two numbers, but the set was seen by Jordan (who had previously sold Adam a Cambridge Rapist T-shirt in Malcolm McLaren's nearby SEX boutique). She was impressed enough to go on and manage them.

15 Nashville Rooms
171 North End Road, W14

Long-time favourite pub-rock venue, which, come 1976, embraced punk and put on gigs by the Sex Pistols, The Stranglers, John Cooper Clarke and others. When The Stranglers were having problems with bookings because of their reputation, they chose the Nashville as the venue for a 'secret' show under the name The Old Codgers.

16 The Rainbow
232 Seven Sisters Road, N4

With punk's popularity cemented, the Rainbow opened its doors to the new breed, but soon fell into conflict with the artists. Strangler Hugh Cornwell induced GLC hysteria on 30 January 1977 by wearing a T-shirt emblazoned with a parody ot the Ford logo that spelt out the word 'Fuck' and soon afterwards Siouxsie was arrested for "obstruction" after a Heartbreakers gig. The Clash asked to have the venue's seats removed for the final date of their White Riot tour on 9 May 1977, and when the management refused to comply, the band encouraged the audience to do the job themselves.

17 Screen On The Green
83 Upper Street, N1

At the 'Midnight Special' Malcolm McLaren set up here on 29 August 1976, the Sex Pistols were supported by The Clash and the Buzzcocks. Some record company A&R men were reportedly too wary to even enter the cinema, although several rock scribes did. The headliners mysteriously benefited from the best sound, leading one writer to describe The Clash as "the kind of garage band who should be speedily returned to the garage, preferably with the motor running".

100 Club Punk Festival

How The Clash, The Damned and the Sex Pistols gathered in a London trad-jazz nitespot to start a musical revolution.

1 September 1976

Ron Watts (manager, 100 Club) It was the end of that long, hot summer. I'd been booking the Pistols into the 100 Club for months and people were starting to come from Manchester, Plymouth, Newcastle... A&R men had been down from all the major record labels, but they all turned their noses up. It occurred to me that some sort of event, call it a festival, was needed to put punk on the map. I was informally managing The Damned at that point and I got Malcolm McLaren involved because he was in with a lot of other bands, notably the Pistols.

Caroline Coon (journalist and founder of the drug charity Release) When I heard about the festival I told Melody Maker I'd cover it. They didn't like it. But it was obviously going to establish whether there was something really happening or not. No one even knew if there were enough bands to constitute a real new movement. Remember, there were no punk records in the shops and the Pistols and The Clash hadn't even signed to labels.

Vic Godard (Subway Sect) Malcolm wanted as many groups as he could get for the festival. When he saw us, we'd never played in front of an audience and he thought we were so awful that there was no way we could do it. So he booked us for rehearsals at a place in Chelsea and paid for it. We only had five songs.

Pete Shelley (guitar, Buzzcocks) We'd done the Screen On The Green gig with the Pistols and then Malcolm called and asked if we'd do the festival as well.

Siouxsie Sioux There was a vacant space and Malcolm was saying, "We need another band." I said, "We've got a band." We hadn't. The next day we rehearsed with Sid Vicious on drums, Marco Pirroni and Steven [Severin]. We'd just seen The Cry Of The Banshee on TV and thought 'banshee' was a great word.

Marco Pirroni (guitar, Banshees) We'd had an abortive rehearsal at The Clash's place on Monday. We realised there was no point in trying to learn any songs.

Caroline Coon I talked with the kids in the queue. Not many had the bondage look yet, but they had ripped chinos, brothel creepers, faces scarred with blades. Their look mirrored the despair of the times.

Andy Blade (vocals, Eater) We didn't know at the time, but the queue outside was like a who's who of people who were going to go on to form bands later: Shane MacGowan, Siouxsie, Gaye Advert, TV Smith, Chrissie Hynde.

Ron Watts Malcolm and the Pistols were up to something. They kept getting into huddles and going out to the cafe. I think he was signing them to a contract.

"Sid Vicious took a dislike to Stinky Toys – just because they were French." THE 100 CLUB'S RON WATTS

20 September 1976

John Ingham (journalist, Sounds) That first afternoon when people were soundchecking, Ron Watts was saying there were going to be hundreds of people that night. People told him he was out of his mind, but he went out, came back and said there were about 500 outside. This was the first time I'd seen a punk I didn't know in the street.

Glen Matlock (bass, Sex Pistols) After Malcolm McLaren showed us the contract, I read through it and took up a point about percentages, but John [Lydon] was really daft about it. John didn't even bother to read the contract. He just said to me, "You read it then?" I said, "Yeah, I read it." He said, "Well, if there's anything wrong with it, it's your fault." And he signed it without even reading it.

Nascent new wavers at the 100 Club's punk festival, 20 September 1976.

Andy Blade Ron Watts asked us to play, but on the day he couldn't let us because we were all so young, like 14 and 15.

Ron Watts Even though I'd advertised the order they'd play in, there was jostling for position all day. There was a real rivalry between the Pistols and The Clash. Sid Vicious was the worst problem. He took a dislike to Stinky Toys, purely on the grounds that they were French. He had a knife out and I had to get it away from him.

Caroline Coon Siouxsie and Sid were hanging around all afternoon trying to decide if they had the nerve to go on. Siouxsie was very un-self-confident, asking people what she should sing.

Ron Watts Bernie Rhodes and Malcolm McLaren got into a huge row about Siouxsie wearing a swastika on her arm.

Bernie Rhodes (manager, The Clash) I felt she wasn't aware of what she was letting herself in for. If she used it, we too would be associated with the swastika. I felt she was mucking about with a loaded gun, and we didn't want to have anything to do with it.

Door and The Lord's Prayer, Steve trying to turn his bass on, and Sid with his relentless banging.

Captain Sensible (bass, The Damned) Siouxsie was utterly useless. They didn't deserve to be allowed anywhere near a stage. As far as I could make out, she was just this kid with loads of dosh from a well-to-do family. She was the only person I knew then who could afford to spend £200 a time on S&M outfits from Malcolm's shop.

Marco Pirroni We did a Velvet Underground thing for what seemed like hours. It was horrible. I remember me and Sid looking at each other and we were fed up, so we just stopped.

Ron Watts I hardly saw any of the music because there was antagonism the whole day between the London and the Manchester punks. I had to break up at least three fights. It was an elitist thing. The London punks could see that their personal little scene was being invaded and they were losing control. It was awful, because that wasn't what punk was about. The old bands had been elitist. The punks were supposed to be different.

discussion about the bombs in Northern Ireland. It was pure luck, but it sounded absolutely brilliant. Apocalyptic.

Roger Armstrong (co-owner, Chiswick Records) I vividly remember one typical McLaren-type stunt that night. He had arranged for all his friends to bring along cameras with flashguns. Then, when the Pistols came on, he got them all to run up to the stage and start shooting, so you had all these flashes going off, which made it look very impressive.

Steve Mick (Sniffin' Glue fanzine) The Pistols were fucking brilliant. They were really on form. There were kids on chairs, tables… No one in their right mind could say they couldn't play.

21 September 1976

Eddie (drums, The Vibrators) When we turned up there was no PA system. Luckily we'd played a gig up in Holloway Road the night before, so we agreed to let them use our PA system. It was meant for little pub gigs, so it was really useless, too small for the 100 Club.

Ron Watts Chris Spedding [renowned guitarist] had been down the club to see a few punk bands play and he'd really enjoyed it. He sided with them, and asked me if he could be on the bill. He wanted to be associated with it.

Eddie Spedding showed up in the afternoon and said, "Alright, so what's this gig I'm supposed to be playing?" It was like he had seen an advert announcing he was playing but no one had told him anything about it. We spent the rest of the afternoon and the evening in the dressing room learning the chords for his songs.

"Onstage, the idea was to annoy people so much that they'd chuck us off." SIOUXSIE SIOUX

Siouxsie Sioux I wouldn't apologise for it because it wasn't political at all. I saw it as just the gear that I wore.

Joe Strummer The swastika thing went back at least a year. Bernie and Malcolm had worked together designing clothes. Malcolm had come up with this swastika armband and Bernie hated it. So when Bernie saw Siouxsie wearing it, it brought the old fight to a head again.

Siouxsie Sioux When we went onstage, the idea was to annoy people so much that they'd chuck us off. It was taking the piss out of all the things we hated: Marco with his feedback, me wailing over the top of it singing Knockin' On Heaven's

Joe Strummer The Clash were in the middle of this ludicrous Stalinist vibe where we decided it was uncool to talk to the audience. Inevitably we broke a string, so suddenly there's no music. Luckily, I always used to have a transistor radio with me because there were those cool pirate radio stations. We didn't have spare guitars, so I just switched on the radio and held it up to the mic. At the mixing desk, Dave Goodman was hip enough to put a delay on it and it happened to be a

Captain Sensible The Buzzcocks turned up with all their equipment in Tesco bags. They had these Top 20 guitars which were the cheapest thing you could possibly buy. Most only had four strings and they couldn't even tune them.

The Damned's Dave Vanian, later booted offstage by bassist Captain Sensible.

Pete Shelley People like The Vibrators were already better established than us, so they got the use of a dressing room. We just had to dump our gear in a little alcove with seats that had been cordoned off. There was a lot of talk that afternoon about the possibility that The Damned might get signed to Stiff Records. Stinky Toys were good. Their singer screeched incessantly like Yoko Ono. The more excessive you could be, obviously the more you were on the right track.

Knox (guitar, The Vibrators) I had loaned the Stinky Toys guitarist my amp and speakers, and he played so loud that he blew out the speaker cones. So we went on and sounded crap.

Captain Sensible We really couldn't play very well at all, but we were better than any of the others. I spent most of my time standing at the front of the stage shrieking with laughter at the other bands, which didn't much amuse them.

We always tried to upstage each other, so at one point I kicked *[Damned singer]* Dave Vanian and he went hurtling right off the front of the stage. It wasn't as bad as it sounds, because the stage was only two feet high, but that meant it was easy for the crowd to climb up and mob you. Anyway, he went off the stage and crashed right into Siouxsie.

Pete Shelley A friend of ours eventually turned up, so we left him to look after our gear and went out to get a burger. As a result we missed the famous incident with the smashed glass.

Caroline Coon I was standing up on a chair that I'd dropped against the back wall of the club, so I could see what was going on. I saw things being thrown and there was a commotion and I realised something was happening. I actually saw the glass shatter against the pillar and my impression was that it wasn't Sid who threw it.

Eddie People started coming into the dressing room. There was one guy with his forehead gashed open and pouring blood. All we could do was wrap towels around his head. Then a girl came in with blood coming out of her eye. I thought, Christ, if this is what punk's about, you can shove it.

Caroline Coon The ambulance came first and people were taken away, then the police Gestapo'ed in, mob-handed, and Sid looked the likeliest suspect so they started frogmarching him out.

Ron Watts I'm certain it was Sid. He wasn't trying to hit the girl. He was just pissed off at The Damned, because he saw them as the main rivals to the Pistols, so he threw a pint tankard at the stage. Instead, it shattered on a pillar and glass went into this girl's eye. One of my barmen saw the whole thing. When the police tried to arrest Sid, there was immediately about 30 punks all saying it wasn't him.

The Cat's Whiskers

In the mid-'60s, Ray Stevenson fell in love with the music of Buffy Sainte-Marie and pretended to be a photographer in a ruse to meet her. Before long he was resident lensman at the Folk Club in Greek Street, Soho, gaining an entrée into the world of Bolan, Bowie and Roy Harper. In 1976, with his brother Nils working for the Sex Pistols, he was perfectly placed to chronicle the punk explosion.

Feline alright with the crew

Sue Catwoman, 1976

One of the Sex Pistols' early inner circle, 'Catwoman' famously appeared on the Today show in December of that year, when guitarist Steve Jones abused host Bill Grundy.

SEX gang

The Bromley Contigent, London, 1976

From the suburbs of south-east London arose the Sex Pistols' most fervent early fans. Some of the flamboyant bunch (including Billy Idol, not pictured here) would be inspired by punk to form their own bands. (From left, back row) Debbie Juvenile, Siouxsie Sioux, Steve Severin, Sharon Hayman, Simon Barker, Philip Salon, Berlin; (centre) Linda Ashby; (bottom) Sue Catwoman.

"Cheers!"

**Johnny Rotten,
Le Chalet Du Lac, Paris,
4 September 1976**

In-between weekend gigs at the Screen On The Green in Islington, north London, the Pistols and their entourage made their first trip abroad, flying to Paris to play two nights at a disco called Le Chalet Du Lac in the Bois de Vincennes region to the east of the city. There was no entry charge on the first night, and Siouxsie Sioux, wearing her peek-a-boo bra and swastika armband, was punched, while members of the band were threatened with knives. This picture of Rotten gooning was probably taken on the second night, for which an entry fee was imposed. There was little trouble – and very few attendees.

Vive le rock

**Sex Pistols, Paris,
3 September 1976**

Before the Chalet Du Lac gigs, journalist Caroline Coon suggested they rendezvous at Les Deux Magots, the legendary Left Bank cafe frequented by Sartre, Picasso, Hemingway and punk's favourite surrealist, André Breton.

Quiet riot

**Joe Strummer and Paul Simonon, Anarchy tour,
December 1976**

According to the photographer, this shot was taken in a lift. The two men sport similar clothes to those worn in the Kate Simon shoot that was used for The Clash's first album cover.

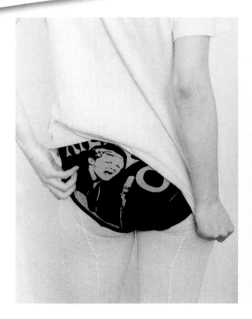

Great balls of fire!

Let It Rock knickers

Opening in 1971 as a supplier of
'50s memorabilia and Teddy-boy
drape coats and winklepickers, Let
It Rock was the first incarnation of
Vivienne Westwood and Malcolm
McLaren's shop at 430 King's
Road. After a gradual shift to
customised biker jackets and
'40s zoot suits, the shop changed
its name to Too Fast To Live Too
Young To Die in 1973. However,
the Let It Rock tag was retained
as the label for the couple's own
designs, such as these knickers
with an image of original rock'n'roll
bad boy Jerry Lee Lewis and the
legend: "The 'Killer' Rocks On!"

All you need is hate

Johnny Rotten, London, 1976

Rotten gives the Fabs the finger in
a Soho record shop. His disdain
for the 'classic canon' of crafted
pop-rock was always a point of
contention between Rotten and
Glen Matlock. The Pistols' melody-
loving bassist would quit the band
on 28 February 1978.

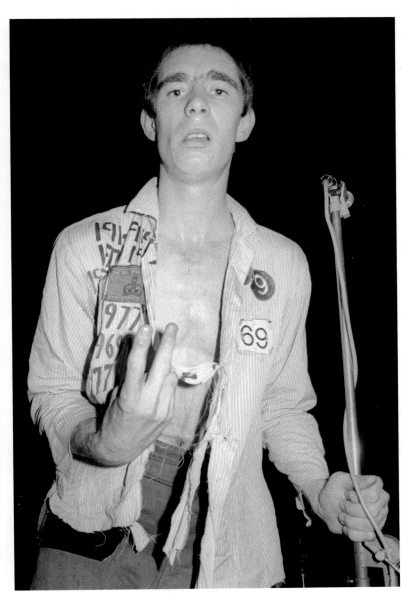

Love is the drug

Nancy Spungen, 1977

Heartbreakers groupie and later Sid's doomed lover and drug buddy, Nancy was reviled by the London punk fraternity. "When Nancy Spungen came into my shop it was as if Dr Strangelove had sent us this dreaded disease," said Malcolm McLaren.

Hanging around

Sex Pistols, Paris, 1976

The band performing at the Chalet Du Lac, 3 September. The Paris trip was the first time Rotten was seen in Westwood and McLaren's latest twist on punk couture, the bondage suit, with fetish elements such as buckles, straps, crotch zips and the all-new 'bum flap'.

V for victory

Jimmy Pursey, 1977

The Sham 69 singer giving it punk attitude onstage. Ray Stevenson noted: "Nobody ever lost money by underestimating public taste." Pursey would go on to become a punk hero when he joined The Clash onstage at the Anti-Nazi League rally in Victoria Park, east London in April 1978, much to the chagrin of Sham's right-wing fans.

44

First time The Boys, 1977

One of several groups to emerge from original punk hothouse the London SS, The Boys played their first gig at north London's Hope & Anchor in October 1976. So taken were they with Stevenson's press shot celebrating Chrysalis's signing of another scion of the London SS – Generation X – that they insisted on re-creating it, as seen here. Their own experience on signing to record label NEMS was less happy, though. The self-titled debut album was recorded in early May 1977 but its release was delayed by wrangles over the production, which the band considered too polished. When it did emerge three months later, availability problems saw it stall at Number 50. The death of Elvis Presley on 16 August meant that NEMS' distributor, RCA, was suddenly preoccupied with The King's back catalogue and halted pressing of The Boys' album.

Bodies

Pistols entourage, 1976

SEX shop habitués Debbie Wilson, Siouxsie and Philip Salon with Malcolm McLaren. A close friend of Boy George, Salon would become a well-known face on the burgeoning London club scene over the next couple of decades, both as partygoer and host of the capital's Mudd Club.

Cut off

Sex Pistols, London, 1976

"Working with the Sex Pistols was going to be my big break, I even left my cushy BBC job for them," says Stevenson. With his brother Nils taking the role of McLaren's co-manager, Ray acted as the band's unofficial photographer for two years. But he found himself unceremoniously dumped by Malcolm McLaren when he took pictures of clothes from rival King's Road punk store BOY for London listings magazine Time Out.

Under a vest

Jordan, King's Road, London, 1976

Born Pamela Rooke in 1955, Jordan worked at Malcolm's shop at 430 King's Road, becoming a living embodiment of the SEX aesthetic. She used to commute to work from the South Coast in full rock'n'roll/fetish/retro regalia. "Sometimes I'd get on a train and all I had on was a stocking and suspenders and a rubber top – that was it," she said. "I had a lot of trouble, but what did I expect?"

In love with rock'n'roll, but often at war with each other, the Ramones were a gang of suburban New York misfits who lit the punk-rock powder keg.

THE

WARRIORS

WORDS: BEN EDMONDS. PHOTO: KATE SIMON

49

PHOTO: ROBERTA BAYLEY

IT WAS 11 July 1975. A car carrying the Ramones crossed the Triborough Bridge, leaving New York City and speeding north towards Waterbury, Connecticut. Inside, the four members of the band were anxious. After months of playing their tiny downtown club circuit to an audience of friends, members of other bands, drunks and the occasional Brit journalist, they were about to share their recharged rock'n'roll vision with 'the real America' for the first time. Waterbury was only 90 minutes outside the city, but it felt like the beginning of a world tour.

When the quartet took the stage of the Palace Theatre to deliver a warm-up set for Johnny Winter, they were greeted with a wave of applause. What the Ramones didn't know was that the audience, uninformed of this last-minute addition to the bill, assumed it was Winter making his onstage entrance.

They tore into their set: short sharp pop nuggets of compressed energy. As was their habit, they spat out three songs before stopping for a breath. When they did, they heard it: a rolling wave of boos, followed by glasses, bottles, cigarette lighters and anything else the mob could get its hands on. Shaken, the Ramones don't remember if they even finished their 15-minute set. The message was clear: America was in no hurry to shake hands with its future.

TO UNDERSTAND the Ramones you have to go back to Forest Hills, a middle-class enclave in Queens, a 20-minute subway ride and a metaphoric million miles from Manhattan. Suburban jewels like Forest Hills were built at the turn of the century as the living embodiment of the American dream: where every man was a king and could afford his own castle. Never before had adolescents had the time and access to enough technology to make a noise loud enough to drown out the boredom.

"When you're 16, angry and bored, you have to be very creative to stir up some excitement," said Dee Dee Ramone years later. Life in Forest Hills, he admitted,

"Dee Dee was creative with the facts. That's probably what made him such a great songwriter." TOMMY RAMONE

consisted of listening to music, taking drugs (LSD, weed, smack, glue, anything) and dropping abandoned TV sets out of windows. This quest to beat the boredom would manifest itself throughout communities like Forest Hills, and coupled with a sense of rejection among displaced, alienated teens, would bring on the birth pains of American punk.

Tommy Erdelyi was displaced in the most literal sense. Born in Budapest in 1949, his family fled Hungary in 1957 after the Soviet takeover and he came to the US unable to speak a word of English. "I arrived to find rock'n'roll had broken wide open," he says. Learning his

English from the street and his radio, Tommy attended Forest Hills High. On his first day he met his future partner-in-crime, John Cummings.

Tommy: "At lunch we all sat at assigned tables and somebody took me over to Johnny's to meet him. Johnny stood out. He was exotic looking. He was tall, skinny, and he had a bowl haircut. He was smart, funny and charismatic, and he liked to have people gather around him."

Johnny's taste in music impressed Tommy, who at 14 had already formed a band named Tiger 5 with his neighbour Richard Adler. By 1966 Johnny had joined them both as the bassist in the Tangerine Puppets. Though named after a Donovan song, they followed the Anglo/garage template of the mid-'60s, a living jukebox that alternated Them and Yardbirds with Young Rascals.

"We weren't very original," Erdelyi confesses, "but we put on a wild show. John wore his bass high and played it like a machine gun. We were notorious in Forest Hills because we had played a school talent show where John had hit a girl with his bass and injured her."

John Cummings always used music as a weapon. This anger would serve the future Johnny Ramone well, but the Tangerine Puppets never developed original material that matched their attitude. After one single for a small label, the band split. Yet Johnny and Tommy soon met another local self-confessed "social deviant" who would play an integral part in their future.

Tommy: "We met Doug Colvin – Dee Dee – not long after he moved into the neighbourhood. He was an army brat who'd grown up in Germany. We got to talking, he said he played music and listed this incredible equipment he had, including a huge Vox amp. We were very impressed, but there was always some reason why we couldn't go check out his killer gear. That was our introduction to Dee Dee as a teller of tall tales. He was charming, eager to please and very creative with the facts. That's probably what made him such a great songwriter."

While Johnny, Tommy and Dee Dee viewed themselves as outsiders, they looked like solid citizens next to fellow Forest Hills High pupil Jeffrey Hyman. Tall, sickly thin and hunched over, Jeffrey was a strange young boy who liked Herman's Hermits, science fiction and making tape-recordings of thunderstorms.

Tommy: "He was always just there. Lurking. He was almost mute. He was a drummer. Not a very good one, but he had this gigantic baby-blue drumkit with double bass drums that looked bigger than Keith Moon's. The rest of us would have had some kind of lives if there wasn't a Ramones, but I'm not sure you could say that about him."

While Joey, Johnny, Tommy and Dee Dee had all met by 1969's "summer of hate" (as Dee Dee called it), it would be a while before they reconnected.

His high-school days over, Tommy drifted away from rock'n'roll, towards Manhattan and apprenticeships in film editing and studio engineering. A 1971 trip to England and exposure to T.Rex made music seem promising again, a promise confirmed when he saw the New York Dolls at the Mercer Arts Center on his return to the States. "The Dolls demonstrated that if you possessed the essence of rock'n'roll, it didn't matter how good you could or couldn't play," says Tommy. "It wasn't like I didn't already know this, but it hit me like a thunderbolt. I was reminded of how I felt about early rock'n'roll."

BACK IN QUEENS, John Cummings no longer owned a musical instrument. The angry young Stones fan who'd taken a bag of rocks to throw at The Beatles at Shea Stadium had graduated to harder stuff. "I know he was having emotional problems and got involved with unsavoury people and drugs, which led to criminal activities," says Tommy. "By the time I started calling him again he'd cleaned up, got a construction job, got married, and become sort of bourgeois. He was fiercely blue collar but very status-conscious."

Jeffrey Hyman, however, was "lurking" ever closer to music. Alan Vega, singer with pre-punk duo Suicide, recalls his first encounter: "Suicide was playing a rehearsal space showcase. The band that opened for us, Sniper, had a lead singer who was this tall skinny creature with black gloves and little glasses who looked like he was from another planet. I was totally struck by him. After the show he gave me his number and said, 'If you know any guys I could play with, would you please have them call me.' He said his name was Jeff Starship."

By March 1974 the pieces fell into place. Tommy pesters John Cummings about forming a band. John and Dee Dee succumb and buy guitars. They rehearse with drummer Jeffrey Hyman and a soon-departed bass player. Jeff is moved upfront when Dee Dee, now the bassist, is unable to sing and play at the same time. By July would-be manager Tommy sits down behind the drums, which he's never played before. Somehow, amid this group Dee Dee calls "a bunch of ill-mannered lowlifes", there is order and an incredible energy.

"I saw them do one of their first shows," continues Alan Vega. "It was like, '1-2-3-4 BRRAAAGAWGGH!' This roar. Then somebody would break a string and they'd all walk off. They'd come back on, '1-2-3-4' and the same thing would happen. We're standing there laughing our asses off. Yet the intensity of the music was astonishing. It was the best thing I'd seen since The Stooges. It changed my life. And to top it off, their singer was Jeff Starship! He was Joey Ramone!"

They'd become the Ramones at the second band meeting, with Dee Dee suggesting the name. A goof on McCartney's *nom d'hôtel*, Paul Ramon, it was both cartoon-like and menacing. The reference points within their image were knowing and deliberate. Dee Dee and Johnny adopted pudding-bowl haircuts, in homage to Brian Jones and Fred 'Sonic' Smith. The ripped jeans were Iggy circa '69. Unlike The Stooges, though, the Ramones' rips were pristine and strategically positioned.

Key to the Ramones identity, though, was the black leather jacket. "Johnny was a movie nut and loved The Wild One," explains their friend and designer Arturo Vega. "The jacket was the way he saw himself, this kind of bold, all-American rebel. 'What are you rebelling against?' 'Whaddya *got*?' That was John."

And the image matched their street-tough music perfectly. "They looked perfect, sounded perfect, stood perfect, the songs were perfect," says Danny Fields, recalling his first sighting at CBGB of the band he would later manage. "The show was over in 11-and-a-half minutes. I was swept away."

"We were like The Beatles on speed," deadpans Tommy. "Or, if you were a reader of Superman comics, we were a Bizarro-world version of The Beatles."

> ## "Joey said he heard voices or saw visions, and they weren't pleasant." TOMMY RAMONE

CBGB was not a punk scene, but part of New York's bohemian underground. So while the class of '75 – Blondie, Television, Talking Heads – shared the Ramones' do-it-yourself attitude, they were not acts that attempted to mirror their audience as the former Forest Hills hoodlums did. Behind the Ramones' caricatures lay a fierce intelligence that saw them establish their own sound, look and vision.

In September 1975 they entered a New York studio with ex-New York Dolls manager Marty Thau as producer. The results are scratchier versions of I Wanna

Sign of the times: Joey Ramone at home in New York's Bowery district, 1977.

PHOTO: KATE SIMON

Be Your Boyfriend and a clattering, harmony-heavy Judy Is A Punk. While Johnny's guitar is low in the mix, Joey's vocals emerge as the perfect amalgam of Brit-beat phrasing crossed with his New York drawl.

Thau's interest in the band galvanised other labels, notably Sire, whose A&R man Craig Leon had already recommended them to the label's president, Seymour Stein, believing the band could record "a revolutionary album". After a private audition for Stein, in January 1976 the Ramones signed their record deal at Vega's loft.

MUCH HAS BEEN made of the fact that the Ramones' debut album cost only $6,200 to produce. This reflected the fact that a gamble was being taken, but it was also because they were ready. They entered Plaza Sound Studios on 2 February 1976 intending to record their set in chronological order, and were done 17 days later.

"The studio was strange," recalls Tommy. "Plaza Sound was in Radio City Music Hall, a huge old place. We were all isolated. They put me in a booth at the other end – you had to go through four doors to get back to the control room, so communication was difficult. The studio staff would snigger but never to our faces – they were a little afraid of these strange guys in leather jackets."

Still, after acclimatising themselves, with Craig Leon producing and Tommy as his associate, the band began to relax. Tommy: "We were confident that the music was together, so we ended up having a lot of fun, stacking the tracks like it was an old Beatles album, and fooling around with ping-pong stereo effects."

The 14 tracks recorded showcased the band's distillation of influences from bubblegum pop to horror movies to real life. Lead track Blitzkrieg Bop opened with the band's "Hey! Ho! Let's Go!" rallying cry. Beat On The Brat saw Joey recalling the boredom and "rich ladies with bratty kids" of Forest Hills. Joey's lyrics on Judy Is A Punk regaled us with a true-life tale of two Ramones fans, Jackie and Judy. 53rd & 3rd depicted a pick-up spot for male prostitutes who'd turn tricks to buy heroin, a subject songwriter Dee Dee refused to discuss, fuelling speculation that it was autobiographical.

Today, it's easy to see the album as a world-changing debut. On its release on 23 April 1976, however, the LP was met with overwhelming hostility in America. Radio was unimpressed by the Nazi imagery of Today Your Love Tomorrow The World and the low-rent sentiments of Now I Wanna Sniff Some Glue. The Ramones' debut failed to challenge the soft rock supremacy of The Eagles' Greatest Hits or Frampton Comes Alive! at the top of the album charts, peaking at 111.

While fans identified with the band's last-gang-in-town image, their intra-band relationships were fractious. If Joey was the shy misfit, Dee Dee the self-destructive army brat and Tommy the worldly-wise outsider, the ever-volatile Johnny described himself as "a control freak". Driven by fear of failure, he ran the band violently. "Dee Dee was terrified of Johnny, because Johnny would punch him in the face," sighs Danny Fields. "They'd been childhood juvenile delinquents together, and this was how they resolved their issues. It would always be after the show, and about something like, 'You did a B-major when you should

The Ramones with ex-Voidoids drummer Marc Bell, aka Marky Ramone (right), who was with the band from 1978-83 and 1987-96.

(Right) Joey and (far right) Dee Dee, both in Plaza Sound Studios, January 1976.

> **"The studio staff were a little afraid of these strange guys in leather jackets."** TOMMY RAMONE

"I saw Johnny strike Joey once," winces Tommy. "Joey had left something at home of so little consequence I can't even remember what it was. But Johnny got so mad he slugged him. It was a punch on the arm, nothing like he and Dee Dee, but I was shocked. Who would want to hit Joey? It's like striking the infirm. It never happened again, at least while I was in the band."

While Tommy would quit the Ramones after Rocket To Russia, their third album, to be replaced by Marc Bell (aka Marky), by then the band understood Joey's quirks were deeper than mere eccentricity.

"There was no way not to be aware of it," Tommy says, "but we didn't know what it was. It wasn't yet diagnosed as obsessive-compulsive disorder. He had to keep touching things according to a certain order. Before crossing a street he'd step off the curb – on and off, on and off – until he arrived at a number that made sense in his head. When I asked him about it he would sometimes say that he heard voices or saw visions, and they weren't pleasant."

"Joey was treated with kid gloves," nods Danny Fields. "This was a band of brothers. Tour manager Monte Melnick and Arturo Vega took extra time with him. Those two were Ramones as much as the guys onstage."

THE CREATOR OF their iconic presidential eagle logo, Mexican-born artist Arturo Vega was at the first Ramones show at CBGB in August 1974 and became their lighting director and designer, staying with the band until their last performance in 1996. He met Dee Dee in 1973, and before long the bass player and Joey had moved in to Arturo's Bowery loft space. Arturo's relationship with Dee Dee had its own dangers, especially when it involved the latter's girlfriend, Connie Gripp. A stripper and fellow drug user, her presence did little to pacify the already wired Dee Dee. The couple finally split up after a fierce argument.

Arturo: "They were going at it, and Joey and I were hiding the knives in the kitchen and trying to stay out of the line of fire. She finally screamed, 'I'm sick of your shit. I'm leaving you!' This scene had gone down so many times, but she threw her things into a suitcase and slammed the door. We all ran to the window and she

have done a C-minor.' You'd hear glass shattering and bodies slamming into walls."

"We got known as the group who would punch each other out onstage, but it rarely actually occurred," counters Tommy. "Mostly John gave people dirty looks. It was effective because you knew what was behind it. John always prided himself on his control, but he had a very short temper."

No band member was immune from what Dee Dee called "Johnny Ramone's rules".

looked up and yelled, 'I hate you, you motherfucker!' Dee Dee answered, 'I'm glad to see you go.' Then he sat down and wrote that song right there."

While Glad To See You Go would eventually appear on the Ramones' second album, Leave Home, the episode demonstrates Dee Dee's ability to keep his songwriting circuitry intact while frying the rest of his system. This innate ability kept Dee Dee in the band. "Dee Dee's drug use drove Johnny crazy," Arturo explains. "But Johnny adopted the attitude that as long as it didn't interfere with the band's business, it was OK. Dee Dee would throw up at the side of the stage, but he'd never stop playing. We never cancelled a show because of Dee Dee. Never."

Dee Dee's charisma was also a major part of the Ramones' appeal.

"Dee Dee was such an asset," recalls Danny Fields. "All you had to do was point a faggot at him, and you would get a favour. I'm not going any further into that... but he was very sexy, and of course he played it up. The flirtiness, the feigned interest...

"I think Sid Vicious had a crush on Dee Dee, and I don't know for a fact, but I've got a pretty good idea what went on. I mean, after Nancy Spungen, wouldn't you rather have Dee Dee Ramone in your bed? Whose cock would you rather suck? Sid genuinely bonded with him. Of course, they were junkies. But Dee Dee had a lot to do with the Ramones being embraced by the English punk peerage. He was one of them, more so than anybody else in the band."

Dee Dee, however, did not see himself as an asset. In his autobiography, Poison Heart: Surviving The

The Ramones' galvanising UK debut at the Roundhouse, north London, 4 July 1976.

(Right) Johnny Rotten has a wee drink courtesy of Johnny Ramone.

PHOTO: JILL FURMONOVSKY

Ramones, he describes himself as "the most fucked up and weakest one in the band". While Dee Dee's self-loathing was rooted in his adolescence, it was symptomatic of the band's sense of worthlessness after the failure of their debut album. Their resignation crystallised in 1980 when, despite courting the mainstream with the Phil Spector-produced End Of The Century and appearing in the Rock'n'Roll High School movie, a breakthrough still eluded them.

"I think Sid Vicious had a crush on Dee Dee Ramone. Sid genuinely bonded with him." EX-RAMONES MANAGER DANNY FIELDS

Vindication came slowly. When, in 2002, the band were inducted into the Rock And Roll Hall Of Fame, they had been retired for six years and one of their number was dead – Joey from cancer in April 2001. Dee Dee would die of a heroin overdose in June the following year. Johnny followed them in September 2004 after a battle with prostate cancer, leaving Tommy as the only surviving founder.

IF THE RAMONES stood outside of mainstream America for their entire career, when they toured the UK in '76 they were given a heroes' welcome, playing a gig at London's Roundhouse where the audience was a Who's Who of the nascent punk scene.

Danny Fields:"John Lydon, Sid Vicious, Mick Jones, Paul Simonon and Chrissie Hynde were all there. The Ramones were astonished by this frenzy, because in New York we still couldn't get a gig in New Jersey."

Arturo Vega:"There were a lot of times people hated them. But at every show there were people who fell in love with the Ramones. If there was one person in Oklahoma, there would be two or three next time. They were pioneers and explorers."

Indeed, when the Ramones got back to a city for the second time, there'd suddenly be a new local band to open for them – the Real Kids and DMZ in Boston, X and the Dickies in Los Angeles, the Nuns in San Francisco. And as the band carved their niche across America, they created a new sense of industry around them based on their identifiable merchandising, which Arturo designed.

"Necessity is the mother of invention!" Vega laughs. "The first time we were going to the West Coast, the record company didn't want to pay for me to go. I had a silkscreen and proposed making some shirts to cover my expenses. The guys were sceptical, but I convinced them we should try it. There were times that money kept the band going."

By the time the Sex Pistols arrived in America to self-destruct at Winterland in January 1978, the Ramones had established their modus operandi. Musically they relied steadfastly on the musical template of the first album – something that proved to be a blessing and a curse. They'd also realised that they would have to compensate for their lack of radioplay with roadwork. And touring would lead to T-shirt sales, a crucial part of their survival.

Danny Fields: "The Ramones might have envied the Pistols' ability to self-destruct, but they figured out pretty early that they were probably going to have to spend the rest of their lives touring."

Indeed, if punk had been seized upon by some in the 'No Future' crowd as a way to flame out, the Ramones demonstrated that in America punk was not about fashion or merely a noisy suicide note. For four suburban misfits like Joey, Johnny, Dee Dee and Tommy it was a way for them to walk through this world, to go the full distance. It was a way to live.

I DIDN'T GET to know Joey Ramone until after the band retired. We began an occasional correspondence, usually accompanied by cassettes of the Ronnie Spector tracks he'd been working on. Despite all that was accruing to the Ramones' legacy, Joey couldn't mask his disappointment at the distance between his hopes for the Ramones in America and the actual tally sheets. One day, however, he indicated that he understood the Ramones' contribution was not that they stood apart, but that they helped to hold it together.

"We're really just one link in the chain," he said. "I always thought it was cool to see how it went from generation to generation, like those family tree things. To see our name mentioned with all those others is a thrill. But none of those names is as important as the chain. We did something new, but we were just trying to keep something alive, and we did. It goes on."

Over 30 years since they started, you can hear, see and feel the Ramones everywhere. The chain goes on.

THANKS TO HARVEY KUBERNIK, JAAN UHELSZKI, MONTE MELNICK (WHOSE BOOK, ON THE ROAD WITH THE RAMONES, IS RECOMMENDED), RACHEL FELDER, KABI JORGENSEN, CLEM BURKE, JEFF WHITE, JASON PADGITT AND LINDA RAMONE

read all about it

Punk magazine defined the mid-'70s underground rock scene in New York – and inspired Britain's Sniffin' Glue fanzine.

"**T**HE IDEA WAS to do a rock'n'roll comic book. I'd always read underground comic books and I was a big rock'n'roll fan, so it just seemed natural to put them together," explains John Holmstrom, editor, illustrator, writer and all-round dogsbody of Punk magazine, the 1976-1979 New York publication that ignited the punk fanzine craze.

A graduate of the New York School Of Visual Arts, Holmstrom teamed up with filmmaker Eddie McNeil and college student Ged Dunn in 1975. With no thought beyond simply getting out one issue, the trio had noted the blossoming CBGB club scene and knew their title was perfect for its times.

"Ged was always talking about decades defining themselves in the middle," recalls Holmstrom. "In the '50s it was rock'n'roll, and the '60s were defined by the period from '65 to '67. We knew the CBGB scene was hot, so I guess it was the right place, time and idea."

Punk's impact was instant. It was a success helped greatly by having Lou Reed on the first cover and by the unique visuals and articles in the magazine.

"We printed on New Year's Eve 1975, and then had to hand-fold and collate the issues a couple of days later," recalls Holmstrom. "So Eddie, who by now was going under his punk moniker, Legs McNeil, went out into the street with a couple of copies, and the first people he approached went, 'Wow, it's like a new Rolling Stone.'

Within a week The Village Voice called us The New Zeitgeist, which we had to look up in the dictionary, but it was exactly what we wanted to be."

Imported into the UK by Rough Trade, Punk became the direct inspiration for native titles such as Sniffin' Glue.

"Chris Stein from Blondie came back from Britain and told us how everyone was going mad for Punk," says Holmstrom. "Legs did a story about throwing up in a subway car, and Chris said kids were now deliberately throwing up on trains because they thought it must be punk."

Ironically, Punk wasn't particularly wedded to punk-rock music, but any attempts to move the

(Left) Punk magazine editor John Holmstrom.

"Legs wrote about throwing up in a subway car. Kids thought that was punk." JOHN HOLSTROM

magazine away from the CBGB scene seemed cursed. "Every time we tried to expand, a disaster happened," recalls Holmstrom. "Issue 9 had Kiss on the cover, and that would have put us over the top, but the printer disappeared with all our money and artwork."

With the New York scene's decline, Punk began to lose influence. While the final issue in 1979 sold well, the fortune the team dreamed the title would yield never materialised and Punk was forced to close.

Punk never fully died: a special edition accompanied the release of 1980 film DOA, a Best Of Punk book

Issue 8:
Sex Pistols

March 1977

"A guy called Steve Taylor did this cover," says Holmstrom. "Instead of drawing with a pen, he'd use an ink dropper or a broken quill and scribble with that and get ink everywhere. He didn't want a firm control over the ink."

Issue 4:
Iggy Pop

July 1976

"I wanted to make Iggy look like the Incredible Hulk, plus make it very commercial too, because I wanted it to look like a magazine everyone would buy. I believed comics and rock had similar heritage."

Issue 10:
Blondie

Summer 1977

"Bobby London did this cover. This was our benefit issue after Issue 9 disappeared. We had a show at CBGB with Patti Smith and Blondie."

Punk
T-shirt

"We figured we should have a Punk T-shirt. Unfortunately, it was black writing on a white shirt and everyone wanted white on black."

59

Sniffin' Glue Christmas Special

1976

"We were sat around wondering what to do," says Perry. "Then we thought, 'Oh, let's do a Christmas special for a laugh.' It was having a joke really. Magazines nowadays are designed to fuck – style over content. We were taking everything back to basics. What you saw was what you got. It was a DIY statement and an economic statement."

Sniffin' Glue Issue 5

December 1976

"I disliked the Sex Pistols and their fans when they were really cliquey and slagged off The Damned and The Hot Rods. They tried to dictate what was and wasn't punk, but with Sniffin' Glue we just wrote about what was exciting. We would never be dictated to. Because we thought the Hot Rods were punk, we said so. In the previous issue I'd argued the point with Joe Strummer."

Sniffin' Glue Issue 3½

September 1976

"Issue 3 came out just before the the 100 Club Punk Festival, so I wanted to get a post-festival issue out quick. I put it together the day after the festival and it was on the streets a week later. It's a good issue, it really reflects the time. Mainstream journalists told me it was important that they read Sniffin' Glue to find out what was going on. We were, in effect, the voice of punk."

Advert for Issue 6

October 1976

"This was a complete one-off because we'd had access to a colour photocopier. The article was in a Glasgow paper about the problems with glue-sniffing on council estates. We changed bits of it so that they refer to the magazine. I was invited on to Radio 4 a couple of years later for a serious discussion about glue-sniffing. They tried to blame it all on me!"

appeared in the '80s, and Holmstrom relaunched the magazine again in 2002. "The fanzines were great, but nobody put in as much effort as us. We figured if we put out a good magazine, eventually good things would come."

I T TOOK SNIFFIN' GLUE just a couple of months to become *the* British punk publication. The magazine hit the streets in the summer of 1976 with cover features on the Ramones and Blue Öyster Cult. The guidebook to the scene, its hand-typed, freehand-drawn, photocopied pages embodied punk rock's ethics in print. Sniffin' Glue was the brainchild of Deptford lad Mark Perry, or Mark P, to give him his punk nom de plume.

"I was a massive rock fan, and went to loads of gigs," he explains. "The first time I remember hearing about punk as such was the Ramones. So I was quite keen to see them when they came over in July 1976, and that was it – I was converted."

With the scene initially confined to a small word-of-mouth following, Perry recalls an almost religious fervour as people discovered the Sex Pistols: "They were starting to call themselves punks. Straight away, it seemed to be about the actual life you were living in 1976 rather

"Getting into the Sex Pistols was a lifestyle choice. That's how dramatic it was." MARK PERRY

than some old-fashioned American rock'n'roll ideal from the '50s. Getting into the Sex Pistols wasn't like, 'Oh, I quite like this new band.' It really was a lifestyle choice. If you got into the Pistols, you changed your life. That's how dramatic it was."

W ITH ONLY SMALL crowds attending these early gigs, and coverage in the national music papers limited, Perry felt there was room for a new kind of publication devoted to punk.

"I'd written a letter to a music paper in 1973 about Emerson, Lake And Palmer, and that was about the nearest to rock journalism I'd ever come. I had no ambitions to be a writer at all, but they often say that you only have to have one good idea and it will make you. Sniffin' Glue was my good idea and I was in the right place at the right time."

Perry produced the first issue in his bedroom and then had 20 issues photocopied. The record shops sold out immediately and soon demanded more.

"I was making the best use of what was available, and because that worked there was never any need to change it," he explains. "In a way we were making a statement – you don't need to be flash. Anyone can have a go. After a couple of months it was being called the most important punk fanzine. We were like the bands, playing a gig one minute and getting signed up two minutes later."

Sniffin' Glue relocated to a spare room at the Rough Trade record shop and then to Dryden Chambers off Oxford Street. "We had all-night parties there, bands used to rehearse, every wall was graffitied."

Perry soon came into contact with some important contributors – Harry T Murlowski, a photographer and business organiser; Steve Mick, who briefly edited the title; and old schoolfriend Danny Baker. "Danny was definitely the next most important person on Sniffin' Glue," says Perry. "The last few issues are defined by his approach, very powerful and hard-hitting."

However, with punk starting to fade out – Perry cited The Clash signing to major label CBS as its end – and Perry's band Alternative TV starting to take off, Sniffin' Glue closed in 1977. It had run for 14 issues.

"We'd become part of the new punk establishment," he says. "Remember, punk was meant to be anti-hero. I started to think of other ways to put over the message."

So was it tough closing Sniffin' Glue? "Not for me," explains Perry. "It was tough for the people I worked with. I think Danny Baker says it was like his meal ticket going. I didn't want Sniffin' Glue to lose its edge and, looking back, it was the right thing to do. In its time and place, Sniffin' Glue was the best rock magazine in the world bar none.

"I know that sounds really big-headed, but I do honestly believe that."

DESOLATION ROW

The Clash began life hungry and penniless in a dilapidated rehearsal studio, but soon they'd become the Sex Pistols' greatest rivals.

"**A**RE YOU IN or out? You've got 48 hours to decide." As offers go, it was one the singer couldn't refuse. He just didn't know it yet. When future Clash manager Bernie Rhodes approached Joe Strummer after a gig by Joe's band The 101'ers, the singer had little knowledge of what he might be getting into, other than the vague notion that Rhodes was putting together a band like the Sex Pistols. However, so smitten was Strummer with the Pistols, even something so nebulous piqued his interest.

Elsewhere in West London on that same day, 25 May 1976, Rhodes' new band members, guitarist Mick Jones and bassist Paul Simonon, were unaware that Rhodes was making any such approach on their behalf, let alone who he was making it to. Joe, Paul and Mick had only met twice: once in a dole queue when Strummer thought the others were about to attack him, and then at a chance meeting in Portobello Road when Jones informed Strummer that The 101'ers were shit.

No matter. The fast moving Rhodes was on the phone the next day, wiping 24 hours off Strummer's deadline. It can't have been easy. For all the pointers towards The 101'ers being a musical dead end, their debut single was about to be released. But a switch had been flicked in Strummer's head and although this nascent scene didn't even have a name yet, his gut told him the future was here.

Jones and Simonon had been members of the London SS, a short-lived band of Stooges and New York Dolls fans that at times included Tony James (later of Generation X), future Clash drummer Topper Headon, and guitarist Brian James and drummer Rat Scabies, who'd join up again in The Damned. The London SS had begun auditioning in autumn 1975, but never played a gig. After the group's demise, Jones, Simonon and a second guitarist, Keith Levene, had begun trawling the toilet gigs of London looking for a singer. Although they hated The 101'ers, something about Strummer's foaming delivery intrigued them.

WHILE HIS BAND dithered, the day after he shortened Strummer's deadline, Rhodes drove the singer over to meet the rest of the band. The pair he met in the living room were not what he was expecting: it was the two guys he thought were about to attack him in the dole queue, who'd told him his band were rubbish. A swift jam later and Strummer's mind was made up. He liked the cut of their jib, and went back to his squat to tell the other 101'ers they were history. It was

the first, but in no way last, cut-throat career move by The Clash, the kind of behaviour that would define them as both people and a band as they ruthlessly pursued their goal of rock'n'roll death or glory.

The 101'ers weren't the only ones left high and dry by Strummer's decision. Roger Armstrong, co-founder of Chiswick Records and the producer of The 101'ers' impending single, Keys To My Heart, found out about his star attraction's defection in an equally abrupt manner. "I was at the bar of a gig," recalls Armstrong. "Joe came up to me and said, 'Have I done the right thing?' I said I had no idea what he was talking about, so he says, 'I've left the band, I'm in a band with him now,' and pointed at the skinny kid standing behind him – Mick. What the fuck was I supposed to say? I had

"They were hell-bent on success – so focused."

EX-CLASH DRUMMER TERRY CHIMES

a record to put out and suddenly there's no band to promote it. I was delighted."

Armstrong bears no ill-feeling today, whether to Strummer, the other members of The Clash or the man probably most instrumental in poaching Strummer, Bernie Rhodes. "I really didn't feel any malice towards Bernie," Armstrong says. "Everything was moving so fast then, it was no surprise Joe left – there was obviously something going on with punk, if it even was punk then."

The sway that Rhodes held over his new charges should never be underestimated, although the suggestion that The Clash were mere avatars for his political philosophies is questioned by Caroline Coon, then a writer for Melody Maker and later Rhodes' replacement as band manager. "The politics always gets put

WORDS: ANDY FYFE

The Clash at
the Lacy Lady,
Ilford, Essex,
November
1976.

(Previous page)
Strummer,
Jones and
Simonon by the
Roundhouse,
Camden, north
London, 1976.

PHOTOS: (PREVIOUS PAGE): SHEILA ROCK, (THIS PAGE) JOHN INGHAM

down to Bernie," she says. "He and Malcolm McLaren were old hippies and so they brought a lot of leftist hippy politics to what they were doing. They encouraged the bands to be political and the bands were very receptive. Bernie wouldn't have been bothered with a band not interested in purveying some of his political ideas, and the band wouldn't have been interested in a manager who was only into haggling."

Rhodes moved the group into two rundown rooms in an old gin warehouse near Chalk Farm's Round-house that became known as Rehearsal Rehearsals, and made the band rehearse daily. It was still only June, a mere two months after Jones and Simonon had first forged their alliance, and Strummer had only just agreed to join. Everything was indeed moving quickly. The group made the space their own, Simonon even making it his home – as did roadie Roadent a few months later. That parts of it were near to falling down and it stank of decay was more of a problem to Roadent than Simonon. "Paul had very little sense of smell," says Roadent. "We had a faux leather sofa, three sheets, one blanket and a one-bar heater. There were huge rats, no hot water, and it was a bit damp, a bit rank."

Securing a drummer, though, would be a major headache. First on the stool was Pablo Labritain, an old school chum of Joe's and later a founding member of 999. Although he passed the audition, Labritain was uncertain. "I wrote to Joe on Monday and said, 'I don't want to let you down, I don't think I'm up to the task.' On Tuesday I had a moment and thought, 'Oh sod it.' I went to the foreman at the factory where I was working, said I was leaving, and moved into Joe's squat."

IT WAS A relentless period of change and discovery for everyone. Rhodes drilled the band in the importance of being important, and the only way to achieve that goal was to start anew, to mark a line in the dirt over which only the chosen few could step. According to Micky Foote, the 101'ers' soundman, it was Rhodes' way of exerting total influence.

"Bernie separated people," says Foote. "There was a process of pulling people away from where they were and from their friends, and he was fearful of people who would go against him. He'd ring up Rehearsals and say, 'Who's there? Oh yeah? Tell him to fuck off, I've told Mick not to bring him down there!'"

But Rhodes didn't see himself as merely a manager. According to Armstrong, he considered the band his property. "Bernie once got Brian James and Glen Matlock together and told them he was forming a punk supergroup with a Pistol, a Damned and a Clash. Glen asked: 'Who you got from The Clash?' and he just spluttered: 'I'm The Clash!'"

The Heartdrops, as they were now calling themselves, set to work rehearsing. "But we weren't allowed to make noise during the day," Labritain recalls, "so we'd spend all day painting and doing Rehearsals up, then about 5 or 6 we were allowed to start making a racket. It was seven days a week, full on."

In spite of the close proximity, the band were hardly close pals. According to Labritain there was little socialising – "nobody had any money to go down the pub". Simonon in particular was so viciously strapped for cash that he once ate the leftover flour paste he'd been using to stick up flyposters.

Early rehearsals included, according to Labritain, 1-2 Crush On You, Protex Blue, Bored With You, Deny and Short Walk To The Medicine Cabinet, which was quickly dropped. There were no 101'ers songs or, despite both Simonon's constant playlist of reggae and the band's later love of playing old reggae and R&B tracks, covers. Less surprising was a name change.

"Mick and Joe came into my record shop one day and said, 'We're not The Heartdrops anymore, we're The Outsiders,'" recalls Armstrong. "I remember going to a pile of records and picking out an album by the '60s garage band The Outsiders. They were crestfallen." Soon after, Simonon would come up with The Clash when he noticed the word cropping up a lot in the Evening Standard. "I think they did themselves a favour there," says Armstrong. "The Clash so suited the times and everything that the band were about."

Labritain was soon to find out just how much that name fitted as he became the next victim of what Clash associates termed 'friendly fire', the ceaseless internal politics for which they would become infamous. At a rehearsal attended by all the Sex Pistols bar Johnny Rotten, Labritain messed up a couple of songs. This infuriated Mick, as did Pablo's ignorance of obscure '60s garage bands.

"I was very nervous," recounts the drummer, "and on one song Mick said, 'Do this bit, do it like this record.' I didn't know what he wanted, and he was going, 'Ah God, he doesn't know!' and stormed off. The next morning I met Joe and he bought me a pint of beer, so I knew something was wrong. He told me, 'You're out.' Funnily enough, I went back to Rehearsals and had one last jam and it was great. Mick said, 'Why didn't you play like that last night?' But it was too late, I didn't measure up."

Simonon, Jones and Strummer wear their art on their sleeves at Rehearsal Rehearsals, 1976.

The speed at which events were unfolding was startling. By late June, Terry Chimes had already replaced Labritain, although the ousted drummer recalls seeing Jon Moss, later of Culture Club, sitting on the stool during one rehearsal. Chimes was far more suited to the task, a native East Ender who found that his ambition to be a rock star was matched by his new associates.

"This lot were hell-bent on success and very focused," Chimes said. "I realised that was all we had in common, but it was enough." Or so he thought.

THE NEWLY CHRISTENED Clash were also fast developing their image. As a side effect of renovating Rehearsals, their clothes had become paint-splattered like some Jackson Pollock experiment, which appealed to both Levene and Simonon. To Rhodes, who'd collaborated with McLaren on some of his Sex boutique T-shirts, clothes were political. Fortunately, Simonon was a genuinely gifted artist with a taste for subversion.

The image attracted the eye of Caroline Coon. "I was taking a photo of the band to go with a piece I was writing and wanted to capture these great paint-splattered clothes. I asked Joe to turn around and put his hands up against the wall and there on the back of his shirt was the slogan 'Hate and War'. It fitted perfectly."

After another fortnight of rehearsing, The Clash finally secured their first-ever gig, supporting the Sex

Pistols in Sheffield on 4 July 1976. Excited, the band were packing their gear into a van at 5am and on the road by 7. It wasn't an auspicious debut. Yet back in London, Rhodes deemed it time for The Clash's capital debut, and on 13 August, in front of a tiny invited audience, the band performed a showcase at Rehearsals.

"There was a little stage in the corner," recalls Roger Armstrong. "There was a curtain which the band were hiding behind, someone got up and announced them, and they came running on and just ripped into it like it was the biggest gig ever. Joe really had that wind-him-up, let-him-go element, regardless of the crowd. He didn't start that with The Clash, he brought that to them."

"They had absolute conviction," says Coon. "It was obvious that if they could hold it together on a personal level, artistically they were going to be magnificent."

Indeed, not everything about the band was quite as fully formed as Coon suggests. The Midnight Special bootleg album, from their public London debut on 29 August at Islington's Screen On The Green with the Sex Pistols and the Buzzcocks, shows that the band still owed a debt to pub rock and Mick and Joe's previous groups. Not everyone was impressed. Charles Shaar Murray wrote in the NME: "They are the kind of garage band who should be speedily returned to their garage, preferably with the motor running."

Simonon was so strapped for cash, he once ate the paste he'd been using to stick up flyposters.

Two weeks and one gig at the Roundhouse later, though, and the true Clash was rapidly emerging. Although Keith Levene didn't know it, he had played his last show as a member of The Clash at the Roundhouse. The main contention appears to have been Levene's lack of commitment to the cause, compounded by his love of sulphate. While the others indulged occasionally, weed and beer were their main vices when finances allowed.

"If you've got two musicians who want to get their songs played, they're not going to fuck around with someone who can't turn up for rehearsals, who is incapacitating himself," Coon states bluntly. "However brilliant a musician you are, if you're incapacitated you can't be part of the group, and the creative force is going to have to let you go."

The initiative again seems to have come from Jones. According to Terry Chimes, with Levene once more absent from rehearsals, the others agreed that they could do without three guitars and ditched him. The move surprised even Bernie Rhodes. He had always favoured Levene, and may well have been worried that, like Frankenstein, the monster he had created might just turn on him.

LEVENE'S DEPARTURE CREATED an easier atmosphere. Over the following weeks the band trimmed a number of makeweight early songs, replacing them with new numbers such as the Notting Hill riots-inspired White Riot. By the time of their appearance at the Punk Festival at Oxford Street's 100 Club in late September, the setlist had solidified into the basis of their debut album.

That 100 Club festival revealed another aspect of the group's public face, at the same time cementing punk's violent anti-social myth within the tabloids when Sid Vicious threw a glass at the stage during The Damned's performance, cutting a female fan's face.

For all their talk of riots and hate and war, The Clash were at heart music lovers not fighters, even though they had earned a reputation for confrontation after a dust-up between Simonon and Stranglers bass player JJ Burnel outside a Ramones gig just two months before.

"That violence stuff was all rubbish," says Armstrong. "None of The Clash were hard. The only genuinely hard men in those days were the two guys standing at the bar of The Roxy: Phil Lynott and Lemmy."

Just as the way forward now seemed clear for The Clash, one more spanner was thrown into their works. Terry Chimes, buckling under the combined pressure of daily rehearsals and Rhodes' hectoring, announced that he was leaving. The only person ever to leave The Clash rather than be fired, Chimes had joined because he saw in Strummer, Jones and Simonon a desire to succeed whatever the cost to those around them, but at just 19 years old he'd had enough. Rhodes had been wrong-footed again.

"When I left," says Chimes, "I thought Bernie would be happy. But he said, 'Look, you're the foil, whenever these guys come up with something, you say what the man in the street or the press would say. If they can get past you, they can get past the world.'"

While honouring gig commitments throughout November, Chimes's departure left The Clash drummerless, exactly where London SS had been just a year before. The one ace The Clash had up their sleeve was that they had just landed the support for the Sex Pistols' Anarchy tour, and that would catapult everyone into a totally different league.

Inspired by the beat poets and French Symbolists, Patti Smith's dedication to an uncompromising, bohemian life was total. But could her ideals survive rock stardom?

THE HIGH PRIESTESS

THEIR MISTAKE WAS to tell her she couldn't swear, because this was live radio and they had no bleep machine. Bourgeois conventions were as relevant to Patti Smith as an Elizabeth Arden makeover. Invited to appear on Harry Chapin's late-night slot on WNEW, which proudly billed itself as "New York's top alternative station", Patti was in no mood to mind her language.

"How alternative *is* this radio?" she sneered as Chapin opened up the microphone. Then, fired up on an unholy cocktail of outrage, exhaustion and rock'n'roll lifeblood, she began to free-associate the way she did on stage, tapping into some mysterious reservoir of disembodied poetics, speedfreak imagery and bullshit. "We have this total alternative to your alternative radio," she announced. "The radio that I represent…" – she fumbled for words that could capture the depth of her alienation – "it's like we're outer-space people."

It was November 1976, and Patti was on air to promote her second album, Radio Ethiopia. And that was where she was broadcasting from, she told the sleep-dazed Manhattan audience: they were listening to

WORDS: PETER DOGGETT. PHOTO: BOB GRUEN/STAR FILE

Radio Ethiopia and, by the way, "fuck the slang". That caught the attention of the station bosses, who made a mental note to cancel the planned radio broadcast of her New Year's Eve concert.

Who exactly was it aimed at, this free-form ramble about rock'n'roll and radio ethics? It was the same question Patti had been asking herself about the album, which had roundly failed to strike the same commercial or critical sparks as her highly acclaimed 1975 debut, Horses. At a London press conference the previous month, she'd been reduced to throwing food at the assembled journalists like a chimpanzee, and screaming: "I'm the Field Marshal of rock'n'roll! I'm fucking declaring war! My guitar is my machine-gun!"

At WNEW, the tide appeared to be turning in the same uncontrollable direction. "There's a lot of people that care about rock'n'roll and really believe in rock'n'roll," she declared, invoking the name of the music like a mantra. "I mean, a little club like CBGB, kids are emulating that club in Finland. All over the world there are these bursts of power and bursts of pleasure. Rock'n'roll is being taken over by the people again, by young kids again, who don't want to hear about your digital delay.

"They don't want to hear that they can't do an Eric Clapton solo, they just want to get out there and get down on a rhythm…" – her mind was tossing up images faster than her mouth could compute them – "they want to crawl up there like a dog, they just want to feel something. And it's these kids, you know, this is the art form" – she paused, as she realised that she had reached the hub of her argument – "this is the art of the future, and these kids, these stigmas to God, are gonna rise up."

IN ITS INCOHERENCE and zeal, it was as relevant a manifesto for punk as any. Patti's assault on linguistic decency aroused a teacup-disturbing brouhaha that eventually inspired her to pen a rant entitled You Can't Say Fuck In Radio Free America. But her rebel theatrics mattered less than the direct connection she had drawn between her own music and the punk rock being created 3,000 miles away in London. "Sometimes I get real mad and want to give Johnny Rotten a spanking," she admitted. "But I understand them; I think it's cool."

Anti-intellectual and rooted in social exclusion, punk was perhaps an unlikely destination for a woman whose soul was fired by artistic diversity and the limitless horizons of the imagination, and whose saints were the French poet Arthur Rimbaud, Bob Dylan and doomed Warhol acolyte Edie Sedgwick. Yet Patti Lee Smith had no problem relating to self-styled outsiders. She'd been

an eternal misfit from her early childhood until her arrival in New York in 1967.

"Everyone at school thought I was weird," she remembered later, "when all I was was romantic, not rebellious. But no one stared at me here. New York was like a huge cathedral. I could come here and hide. It's the only place that really accepted me."

There she fell into the company of her first kindred spirits – rock musician turned playwright Sam Shepard and photographer Robert Mapplethorpe. Winning parts in underground theatre productions, she soon plunged into Manhattan's demi-monde. She began hanging out with refugees from Warhol's Factory, addicts, visionaries and maverick spirits such as Gerard Malanga, with whom she was soon sharing poetry readings.

Her work was steeped in the rhythms of rock'n'roll and intimate identification with her idols. "I've always been hero-oriented," Patti admitted in 1973. "I started doing art not because I had creative instincts but because I fell in love with artists. I didn't come to this city to become an artist, but to become an artist's mistress. Art was never a vehicle for self-expression, it was a way to ally myself with heroes, because I couldn't make contact with God." Her heroes included "Brian Jones, Edie Sedgwick and Rimbaud, because their works were there, their voices were there, their faces were there".

"Sometimes I get real mad and want to give Johnny Rotten a spanking." PATTI SMITH

She and Shepard co-wrote, and performed, a rock-inspired play entitled Cowboy Mouth. By the early '70s she had begun to publish her poems via various small presses. Yet Patti Smith really came alive in front of an audience. Gawky, spiky, confrontational, sometimes gauche, never anything other than fully committed, she turned poetry into a form of performance art. In church halls, basement clubs and galleries, Patti would declaim her verse, unleashing floods of images, raiding inspiration from Rimbaud's disruption of the senses and Ginsberg's assault on the American mind.

At her side, matching her rhythm with jagged guitar chords or squalls of feedback, was rock critic Lenny Kaye. The spirit of East Coast rock'n'roll ran through his veins, yet Kaye shared Patti's willingness to stray beyond the boundaries of convention. "There was no one else doing anything remotely like us at that time," he says. "My contribution was being able to rise

(Right) Patti with Bruce Springsteen at New York's Bottom Line club, 1975, and (below) with Arista founder Clive Davis and Lou Reed, 1976.

(Above) Patti grabs a quiet moment in the run-up to a gig in New York City's Central Park, 1978.

to the moment, being able to respond to the spirit of the art and create instantaneously. That was what was wonderful about those shows – the improvisation, the freedom, the openness to the moment. That was what Patti and I loved in other people's music, and that's what we were able to create together ourselves."

Kaye introduced Patti to the magazine editors who were publishing her work, and during the early '70s her byline began to appear irregularly under impassioned reviews of Edgar Winter or her friend Todd Rundgren. She contributed verse to albums by Rundgren and Blue Öyster Cult (whose keyboard player Allen Lanier soon became her boyfriend).

Poetry and music remained her twin motivations, however. "At first it was just me and Lenny Kaye on electric guitar farting around at poetry readings," she recalled. "Then it gathered force." The pair began to appear along-side other outsider figures at Hilly Kristal's unassuming Greenwich Village venue, CBGB. Early in 1974, they added keyboardist Richard 'DNV' Sohl to their team, and recorded a debut single. Alongside a version of Hey Joe that mutated into a speculative rant about heiress, kidnap victim and (maybe) terrorist Patricia Hearst, the record included the remarkable Piss Factory. In four minutes, it not only documented Patti's miserable experiences as a factory girl in South Jersey, but also invented an intoxicating blend of jazz, poetry, improvisation and rock rhetoric that nobody has ever quite managed to build upon, not even Patti herself.

SHE WAS NOW obsessed by the dream of a purer form of rock'n'roll, a garage-punk frenzy that would favour feeling over technique, move like James Brown, and bite harder than Bob Dylan. It would even allow her to drop her poetess persona and become a rock'n'roller in her own right. "As soon as I took my guitar in my hands, I realised what it was I'd been looking for. It made me feel a quiet but noble power," she says.

As yet, she wasn't confident enough to stroke her instrument in public, so she and Kaye auditioned potential recruits who could handle guitar or bass. They had already freaked out prospective keyboard players by greeting them with stoned jive about wanting to push

the music "over the edge, man". The guitarists were subjected to a different ordeal, being forced to crank out versions of Van Morrison's proto-punk anthem Gloria until somebody cracked. If they gave up, they had failed the audition. But Czech-born musician Ivan Kral wouldn't quit, and landed himself the job. He accepted with one condition: he wanted to be a rock star, and so he needed to play with a drummer. Jay Dee Daugherty, whom she'd seen several times at CBGB, was Patti's first choice. Thus the Patti Smith Group was born, ready for a spring 1975 residency at CBGB with Television. (The latter's Tom Verlaine joined Lanier and Smith in a romantic trio later that year; Smith later immortalised the arrangement in the song We Three.)

Scenemakers and commentators flocked to the CBGB shows, expanding the reputation of Television and Patti's band way beyond the Greenwich Village underground. Eventually Arista Records boss Clive Davis appeared at the club, accompanied by Lou Reed.

Like everyone who witnessed Patti speaking in tongues over the band's righteous rock fury, Davis was entranced, and immediately offered her a multi-album deal.

No longer classifiable as mere poetry, Smith's incantations had now been structured into recognisable rock'n'roll form. But Patti treated her voice as a jazz instrument, building space into the arrangements for lengthy explosions of verbiage, some adapted from her books, others effectively extemporised night after night. The challenge for the band, and for Davis, was to translate this spontaneity into a record that would endure. To guide his maverick signing, Davis enlisted Velvet Underground legend John Cale as producer. "It's like A Season In Hell," Patti explained during the sessions, referencing Rimbaud's classic poem sequence. "John's a fighter and I'm a fighter, so we're fighting."

All of that tension and electricity, but none of the negativity, spilled on to Horses, Smith's incendiary debut album. NME critic Charles Shaar Murray, in an

Getting things off her chest with the Patti Smith Group: (from left) Ivan Kral, Lenny Kaye, Bruce Brody and Jay Dee Daugherty.

(Opposite) Reading from Witt, a volume of her poetry, at The Bottom Line, 1975.

epic, page-long review, recognised that the album "introduces an artist of greater vision than has been seen in rock for far too long". The album opened with Patti declaring "Jesus died for somebody's sins but not mine", and ended with an "Elegie" for Jimi Hendrix. The 40-minute journey between those two points incorporated classic rock motifs (Gloria, Land Of 1,000 Dances), tightly structured original material that matched those anthems for impact, and two lengthy flurries of free verse on which Smith sounded possessed by angels and devils in equal measure.

For Smith and Kaye, reworking rock standards was a statement of intent. "We thought of our albums as a call to arms," Kaye explains. "Like Patti always said, 'We created it, let's take it over, do something with it.' What people found in us was inspiration to a deeper degree. You don't want to write poetry like Rimbaud, in other words, but once you've read Rimbaud you want to create something of your own that has the same impact. And that's what we did to other people."

With her heroes, from Bob Dylan to Lou Reed, paying court at her shows, and the British music press welcoming her as a saviour, Smith had virtually achieved her lifetime's ambition with her first shot. Bootleg albums of her early live shows stoked her mythology even further, and the editor of the newly founded magazine Punk In New York treated her as a living encapsulation of his journal's raison d'être.

How do you follow a revolution? It was a question Patti Smith never satisfactorily answered. She began her second record, Radio Ethiopia, with Jack Douglas

In January 1977, two months after Patti's outburst at WNEW, the group were booked on their first arena tour, supporting Bob Seger & The Silver Bullet Band. Seger's music paid homage to the classic rock tradition, but wrapped it in a blue-jean, blue-collar conservatism that was a dry run for the way Bruce Springsteen would conquer the nation in the '80s. There was little generosity among his following for Patti Smith's punk ethos and poetic frenzy. On the first night of the tour, Patti goaded the Florida crowd by launching into an attack on the local people and their low-grade marijuana. On the second, an equally antagonistic audience witnessed a more crucial moment of drama.

JUST BEFORE THE tour, Patti had described how she literally whirled herself into dissociation of the senses every time that she performed Ain't It Strange: "I can go spinning off and get further and further and further into the Queen of Sheba's consciousness. It's different things every night – I get very angry or very afraid. Then I call out to God, like I challenge him. I shout, 'Turn around, God, make a move!'"

At Tampa, on 26 January 1977, God answered her call. As she explained later, "I was doing my most intense number. I spin like a dervish and I say, 'Hand of God, I feel the finger, Hand of God, I start to whirl, Hand of God, I don't get dizzy, Hand of God, I do not fall now.' But I fell." Reeling away from the microphone, Smith tumbled into the orchestra pit and fell head-first on to the concrete floor 15 feet below. "I did feel God's finger push me right over," she recalled. "I had to make a choice, just as I was losing consciousness, and I really felt like I was gonna die. Did I want a communication with God so intimate that I'd be dead, off the earth?"

As she lay twitching in the pit, blood flowing on to the concrete, onlookers were convinced she might be mortally wounded. In fact, she sustained broken bones in her face, fractured vertebrae in her neck, and severe lacerations of her scalp. Her legs were partially paralysed, and doctors warned that she might face a major operation to regain full use of them. Even her sight was affected by the nerve damage.

Patti was eventually informed that she could choose to recuperate with intensive physiotherapy, without going under the knife. Never a woman to underplay her own

"Everyone at school thought I was weird. All I was was romantic." PATTI SMITH

(a veteran of The Who, Lennon and Aerosmith) behind the control-board, as if consciously sacrificing Cale's spirit of adventure in favour of more orthodox rock techniques. But there was nothing orthodox about the lengthy title track, on which Patti not only reeled off an impenetrable prose poem but also unveiled her sub-primitive brand of rhythm guitar – soon a regular feature of her live shows. The rest of the album was more conventional, and impeccably recorded, hard rock, but little of the heady, almost mystical ecstasy of Horses was in evidence.

significance, she set herself the target of making a dramatic re-emergence on Easter Sunday. Combining divinity with the return of the prodigal daughter, she chose CBGB as the venue for her second coming, taking the stage with her neck in a brace, then casting the support aside in a gesture of faith and liberation.

Similar shows followed during the rest of the year, but Patti remained wary of resuming her major-league rock career. Instead she channelled her energies into completing a collection of verse, Babel, and mythologising her near-death experience into songs for her next album.

During her absence, punk rock transformed the British music scene. Whereas their American predecessors had intended the back-to-basics ethos as a clearing of the decks for a new exploration of creativity, UK punks took the street-kid rhetoric at face value, and turned rebellion into a restrictive formula. By midsummer, media suspicion surrounded every vestige of the old regime, and even recent heroes such as Patti Smith were now tainted by their links with the past. There was no room for The Beatles and the Stones in 1977, so The Clash declared – or, perhaps, for a woman who still worshipped Keith Richards, not Joe Strummer.

Sessions for Patti's third album began late that year, with Jimmy Iovine producing. He hooked her up with Bruce Springsteen, and the two artists – each a passionate disciple of a subtly different interpretation of rock history – began to edge towards a collaboration. During the endless gestation period for his own forthcoming album, Springsteen had composed the skeleton of a song entitled Because The Night. Smith was attracted by its immediacy, but wary of its commercial appeal.

Patti returns to CBGB in a neck brace after her near-fatal accident, 1977.

(Opposite) At Nassau Coliseum, 1977.

Yet she found the song a perfect vehicle for the romantic feelings inspired by her recent meeting with an American punk-rock icon: Fred 'Sonic' Smith of the MC5.

With its arena-rock structure and self-consciously 'new wave' guitar riff, Because The Night typified the music that came out of the Iovine sessions. When keyboardist Richard Sohl left the band after Radio Ethiopia, Patti had expressed the desire to leave his position vacant and become "the most unlistenable punk rock band of all". Instead they moved in the opposite direction. "Musically, we are getting more sophisticated," she admitted. "I'm getting more sophisticated, too, even though I don't want to... There's a part of me that doesn't want to grow at all."

STASIS WAS NO longer an option, however, for a woman who had considered the ultimate form of retirement and then pulled herself back from the brink. When the Easter album emerged in spring 1978, preceded by the hit single Because The Night, it was a commercial triumph. Patti's hardcore supporters in the press trumpeted its effective blend of improvisation and metallic swagger. But even they noted a sense of safety in the new music, a refusal to risk a footstep into the unknown.

For Patti herself, a return to arena stages, with their attendant dangers, was challenge enough in 1978. "I was a little afraid," she said later. "I was sweating, and I felt dizzy and weird. But I was curious to see what would happen. I thought I would be more conservative after my fall, but I think I'm crazier than ever. I have some fear, but it just doesn't outweigh my desire to be a maniac."

This edgy alliance between daredevilry and conformity was in evidence when the Smith Group arrived in Europe. At London's Rainbow Theatre, Patti celebrated her rebel status by booting an errant photographer in the head from the stage. But that was the only moment in the show where she threatened to lose control.

Although Kaye insists that "Arista always let us follow our own vision", the company was unsurprisingly keen to capitalise on the group's raised commercial stature. As tour followed tour, Smith must have recalled a credo she'd announced back in '73: "Repetition makes me nauseous." In public, the band maintained a collective sense of purpose; Smith even imagined a utopian future in which her singles would regularly top the charts, just

like the Stones in the '60s, at which point the revolution she hoped she'd inspired would be complete. But she couldn't escape the sense that she might already have achieved everything that was within her compass, and that nothing lay ahead but a stale, scripted reprise of her improvisational past.

And it was to her past that she returned when she invited her old friend Todd Rundgren to produce the fourth Patti Smith Group album. More than any of her previous collaborators, Rundgren was unable to avoid stamping his own personality on the records he produced. Wave sounded more like Fleetwood Mac than The Clash, thanks to AOR pop jewels such as

"I was curious. I thought I'd be more conservative after my fall, but I'm crazier than ever." PATTI SMITH

Frederick (she was now living with the MC5 guitarist) and Dancing Barefoot. Music business convention now demanded that the group undertake mammoth arena and even stadium shows, at which Smith's repertoire shared space with hamfisted attempts at rock anthems such as 5-4-3-2-1 and All Along The Watchtower, as if they had become a classic-rock tribute band.

Meanwhile, Patti's deepening relationship with Fred (they married in 1980) was sapping her will to continue. Two anarchic 1979 stadium shows in Italy, where the group were in danger of being consumed by their audience, hardened her desire to change. After the final show in Florence, she told the band she was quitting the road. There was one concert in her new hometown of Detroit the following June, and some half-hearted recording sessions, but effectively the group had disbanded.

Lenny Kaye takes a philosophical view of the band's career arc: "I've seen many rock'n'roll tales play themselves out, and I have to say that the tale of the Patti Smith Group has a certain perfection. From playing in front of a handful of people in St Mark's Church, to finishing in front of 70,000 people in Florence who were streaming across the stage, trying to take it over – well, you couldn't go any further than that. There was nowhere else to go." For Patti Smith, the "sea of possibilities" she'd announced as her playground on Horses had finally run dry.

The New York Dolls'
Johnny Thunders
showed London's
young upstarts what
real punk attitude
was all about.

A REASON TO BELIEVE

FOR THE GENERATION of kids who became punks, the New York Dolls' appearance on The Old Grey Whistle Test in November 1973 was an epiphany. Bob Harris, the show's normally benign host, infamously declared them to be "mock rock". His comment helped establish the 'them and us' divisions that would flourish between rock's old guard and punk's new guns.

Doll parts: the post-Richard Hell Heartbreakers in the UK: (from left) Walter Lure, Billy Rath, Johnny Thunders and Jerry Nolan, 1977.

The Bob Harris-troubling New York Dolls (with Thunders, far right) on the BBC's Old Grey Whistle Test, November 1973.

That night, the New York Dolls fired the starting pistol. Louche, loud and loaded, they flailed their way through cacophonous renditions of Looking For A Kiss and Jet Boy, moving like overwrought, inebriated automatons in a blur of backcombed hair, girly clothes and platform boots.

Watching the television in a student union bar in Wales, Joe Strummer couldn't believe his eyes. Down in London, Mick Jones was similarly galvanised, as was Glen Matlock. But it was Johnny Thunders' punk attitude that was truly iconic. Clad in a black leather motorcycle jacket with a skull and crossbones painted on the back, and playing a white guitar, the guitarist exuded maximum cool. Johnny Thunders didn't give a fuck better than anyone else.

His calamitous reputation was consolidated after that TV performance when the band travelled to Paris. At Orly Airport, Thunders threw up next to the press waiting for the band. They perceived Johnny's nausea, a symptom of his dalliance with heroin, as a manifestation of the Dolls' sickness.

As rhythm guitarist Sylvain Sylvain said: "It was all over the press. The Dolls arrive in France and they are degenerate, drug-addicted faggots."

Meanwhile, King's Road couturier Malcolm McLaren, who had fallen in love with the Dolls and followed them over from London, keenly observed their antics: "They were like the worst striptease rock act you can imagine. I loved their awkward, trashy vibe. I became a part of their entourage."

Amid the Dolls' usual capers, which included pissing off their record company with appalling timekeeping and drunkenness, the zenith of the European jaunt was a sold-out gig at the Bataclan club in Paris.

Chief roadie Peter Jordan sets the scene: "For some reason, all the bouncers were Samoan or Haitian and the whole audience was male. The audience started linking arms and doing this kind of runaround dance, like an early form of moshing. They were running round in circles, knocking each other over and yelling, 'Fuck you!' The bouncers started bopping the guys in the audience on the head with sticks. Somehow Johnny got involved and somebody got smacked in the head. It was a typical punk rock show."

Onstage, Sylvain Sylvain kept a wary eye on the situation: "A couple of guys in front of Johnny started to spit at him. Johnny spat right back. Then it escalated from spitting to kicking and they threw something at him, so he picked up the microphone stand – you know how they have a heavy round base – and threw it right in their faces. After that, this guy and all his buddies went for us and we had to run off. Of course, everyone remembers, 'Wow, the Dolls started a riot', but it was bad. Somebody could have got killed. If they'd have caught up with Johnny, I don't think they would have let him go."

The gig was abandoned. All those dreams they'd had – about being mobbed by fans, like The Beatles or the Stones – evaporated as the Dolls beat a hasty exit.

JOHNNY THUNDERS WAS born Johnny Genzale, a shy, if spirited, kid of Italian heritage. Raised in Queens on the outskirts of New York, he'd gone to church, loved his mum, hated school and excelled at baseball until he got thrown off the team for refusing to get his hair cut. For someone who hated

"The Dolls were like the worst striptease rock act. I loved their trashy vibe." MALCOLM McLAREN

authority, the only other avenues open to him were delinquency and rock'n'roll. He chose both and never looked back, dying in suspicious circumstances in a New Orleans boarding house on 23 April 1991, aged 38. Romantics say he was found holding his guitar; cynics, that he was murdered for his drugs and cash.

Genzale began playing music in 1971, when he was 18. The group included Arthur Kane, guitarist Rick Rivets and drummer Billy Murcia. Johnny had started off on bass but always had a hankering to play guitar and practised whenever he could. His mentor was Arthur Kane. "I promoted him from bass to guitar and put myself on bass because I knew that way we would have something," says Kane.

Genzale was delighted. However, as serious as he was about the music, he was equally aware of image, which camouflaged his shyness. He sought out a new name befitting his ideal of a dream guitarist, a hybrid of sight and sound that was loud, flashy and electrifying. He toyed with calling himself Johnny Volume before settling on Johnny Thunders.

Joined by singer David Johansen, the New York Dolls, as they called themselves, brought Babylon to the Bowery when they made their live debut playing a Christmas show for the city's homeless. Shortly after the gig, Rick Rivets was bounced out of the band and replaced by Billy Murcia's best friend, rhythm guitarist Sylvain Sylvain. By early 1972, the Dolls were playing rent parties and any place brave enough to book them.

The venues included a gay bath house. "We did these two very weird shows," Arthur Kane remembered. "It was like there was no audience because all these guys stayed in their cubicles having sex. Everyone in the group had taken MDA; I think I was selling it at the time. It was like LSD without the heavy thinking but it makes you stumble around, hallucinating.

"We weren't sure how to dress, so the first night we went feminine, and I wore hot pants. They didn't appreciate the femme look. The next night we wore leather and chains, and everyone came out of their cubicles to watch us."

The band's breakthrough came when they landed a 17-week residency in New York's Mercer Arts Center, which housed several theatres named after authors and playwrights. Holding court in the Oscar Wilde room, the New York Dolls gave free licence for everyone to be themselves.

Sylvain: "It was freaky. There was one guy me and Johnny named 'Clothes Tits' 'cos he'd always wear an open, shiny-black vest and have clothes-pins on his nipples. There were two Tibetan girls covered in tribal tattoos, one of whom became Billy's girlfriend. All the drag queens had glitter in their beards and wore lipstick. The umbrella man dressed up in nothing but discarded umbrellas he'd found on the street, and there was Flop Top, who covered himself with the ring-pulls of soda and beer cans."

IN SUMMER 1972 Andy Warhol's Interview magazine declared: "The Dolls have been getting a lot of people in New York up off their decadent asses and making them dance." Taking inspiration from Bo Diddley, Eddie Cochran, Otis Redding, The Rolling Stones, T.Rex and The Shangri-La's, the group developed their own raucous brand of dirty bubblegum blues. They cared not a jot for propriety as long as they and the audience had a good time.

Rhythm guitarist Sylvain Sylvain was the most musically accomplished, the perfect foil for Johnny

Thunders' exhilaratingly traumatised Chuck Berry/ Keith Richards power-chord distortions.

"Johnny once said I taught him everything he knew, and my retort was, 'Johnny, you better come back for some more lessons!'" laughs Sylvain Sylvain. "He was a great musician. When he first joined me and Billy Murcia in Billy's mom's basement, it was because we thought he was the coolest – he had all the chicks, and we thought if he's in the band we'd have his run-off."

The New York Dolls conquered their home turf, drawing the likes of David Bowie, Lou Reed and Alice Cooper to gigs, while inspiring countless bands to get out there and do it – including Kiss, who took their moniker from the Dolls' Looking For A Kiss. However, despite snaring a team of top managers, nobody wanted to sign them. So the Dolls' managers hit on the idea of sending the band to England, where rock outrage was better tolerated, in the hope of finding a deal.

In the winter of 1972, the group arrived in London for a short English tour. The highlight was a 7 November support slot to Rod Stewart And The Faces at the 8,000-capacity Wembley Pool. Neither cowed by the size of the venue nor daunted by wolf-whistles, the Dolls whipped up a storm. For Sex Pistol-to-be Glen Matlock, Johnny's performance was memorable: "They played a few numbers and Johnny broke a guitar string," he recalls. "But he didn't have a spare guitar. Can you imagine playing Wembley without an extra guitar? So 8,000 people had to wait while a roadie borrowed a string from The Faces, and Johnny put it on and tuned up at full volume. Then they started the number again, he broke the string again and we had to go through it all again. People started booing and yelling, but they didn't give a shit."

AFTER THE SHOW, Kit Lambert, The Who's manager and the boss of Track Records, took the Dolls out to dinner. Lambert wasn't the only one courting the band: Virgin impresario Richard Branson and Charisma Records' Tony Stratton-Smith were also making overtures. While their managers weighed up the offers, the group sampled the local pharmaceutical delicacies. Drummer Billy Murcia was turned on to the delights of 'Mandies' (Mandrax, the UK brand name for Quaaludes) mixed with alcohol.

Murcia bid adieu to his fellow Dolls and went to a party in Kensington. On the other side of town, the Dolls' managers sat down with Kit Lambert, who offered them £100,000. As the New York Dolls' future was being discussed, Murcia was passing out. His hosts put him in a bath of cold water in an attempt to revive him, but he drowned. The drummer was just 21.

Murcia's death sent the Dolls spinning like skittles. They returned to the US too shaken to even contemplate the future. "When we came back I didn't have a clue about what we were going to do," says David Johansen. "It wasn't like, 'What are we going to do?' It was, 'Well, we aren't going to do anything.' We were like brothers in a way. It was heavy."

Briefly, they considered disbanding, but by staying

"I taught Johnny everything he knew. He got the blame for it all, but I did it all." JERRY NOLAN

L.A.M.F.

together they could at least keep the spirit of the band intact. Robbed of their innocence, the New York Dolls entered a second, more hardcore phase, particularly in the case of Johnny Thunders. Crucially, Billy Murcia's replacement – tough-talking former gang member Jerry Nolan – was to exert considerable influence on Thunders.

Nolan was a no-frills drummer of Herculean strength who'd played with Suzi Quatro and Wayne County. His seasoned aptitude brought the Dolls up to fighting strength. The record industry, meanwhile, remained frosty, with the sole exception of Paul Nelson. A former journalist who worked in A&R at Mercury Records, Nelson mounted a concerted campaign to sign the band. Eventually, in March 1973, Mercury proposed a two-album record deal.

Produced by Todd Rundgren, the Dolls' self-titled debut album was released in the summer of 1973. Reviewing it for NME, Nick Kent noted: "The New

PHOTO: ANDRE CSILLAG/REX, ERICA ECHENBERG/REDFERNS

York Dolls are trash, they play rock'n'roll like sluts and they've just released a record that can stand beside Iggy & The Stooges' stupendous Raw Power as the only album so far to fully define just exactly where 1970s rock should be coming from."

Meanwhile, Thunders and Nolan were growing closer. Seven years his senior, Nolan pulled rank at the commencement of the Dolls' first major US tour.

"We got into a big fist fight in the back of the limousine and I kicked the shit out of him," explained Nolan. "Ever since that day Johnny was like my son. He loved me for it. Every once in a while he would push and I would let it get so far then I'd say, 'No more, boy, no more.' I happened to know Johnny real well. I knew his type. Maybe it was the neighbourhood I grew up in. I taught Johnny everything he knows; he got the blame for it all, but I actually did it all."

And so the New York Dolls' delinquent duo forged their alliance around a growing taste for heroin. In 1973,

though, relatively little was known about the long-term effects of the drug. It still had the alluring qualities of the semi-obscure while providing a vicarious connection between the street and rock stardom.

Johnny Thunders: "I was very young and innocent when I started using heroin, and I thought I knew it all. But I didn't, and I'd never have [stopped] even if I did. I had nobody to warn me off. I tried it and I liked it, and in some ways I don't regret ever having used it. I loved taking drugs, right? I thought I was having a real good time, taking drugs and playing rock'n'roll."

BY THE TIME the New York Dolls embarked on their second tour of England, Johnny Thunders was primed for self-destruction. While the Dolls' return trip further stoked their nefarious reputation and ensured a dedicated follower in Malcolm McLaren, it offered only a brief respite as the band hurtled towards decimation, with Johnny valiantly leading the charge into the void, as he ignited the collective pre-punk imagination.

With a teasing irony, the band called their second album Too Much Too Soon. Produced by The Shangri-Las' mentor George 'Shadow' Morton and released in the spring of 1974, the delightfully fractious record sold marginally less than their debut album. Most bands would have pulled back from the brink. But, aside from their increasingly excessive predilections for liquor and narcotics, the group's main songwriting team – Johansen and Thunders – had become distanced once the guitarist shifted his loyalty to Nolan.

Always the peacemaker, Sylvain became resigned to the situation: "There was nothing wrong with the Dolls that couldn't be fixed, but everybody stood their own ground. Johansen blamed Johnny, and Johnny was like, 'Fuck you, you've got a huge ego.' And Jerry was behind the lines, but yelling Johnny on: 'Yeah, you tell him.'"

The group also had to contend with a record company that unceremoniously dropped them, and managers concentrating on the up-and-coming Aerosmith.

The Dolls influenced countless bands but they couldn't save themselves. Making a last-minute rescue bid, McLaren attempted to revive their career with a 'communist' makeover in early 1975. Dressing the band in red patent leather and hoisting the communist flag behind them, the new direction turned out to be a political and sartorial disaster.

Unabashed, McLaren and the band set off on a backwater tour of Florida that resembled a rock'n'roll version of Deliverance. McLaren: "We were travelling by car and it was pretty redneck down there. It was KKK land. We'd hit a town and get stopped by a group of guys who'd threaten to call the sheriff if we didn't get out of

Pink rocker: Johnny Thunders in London, April 1977.

(Opposite) The Mk II Heartbreakers on tour in the UK.

the car. Clearly, you did not want to step out of the car; you just pushed your foot right down on the accelerator and sped out of town and on to the freeway as fast as you could, without stopping. These people were crazy. You could get the shit beaten out of you or end up in a swamp, 10 feet under."

With not a stitch to wear but army fatigues and red leather, nowhere to stay but a godforsaken trailer park, not enough love left between band members and no more drugs, Nolan was the first to bail out. He was swiftly followed by Thunders. Returning to New York,

the pair recruited former Television bass player Richard Hell for their new band, The Heartbreakers. Joined by guitarist Walter Lure, they worked up a set of furiously paced songs about girls and drugs, including heroin anthem Chinese Rocks.

Photographer Roberta Bayley captured the defining moment of the Hell line-up with a session in which the band all appeared to have gushing gunshot wounds. The accompanying slogan – "Catch Them While They're Still Alive" – was dreamed up by their new manager, Leee [sic] Black Childers, who had served

The Heartbreakers bring their raw US rock to London.

(Right) Johnny takes a beer break on the Anarchy tour, 1976.

with David Bowie and Iggy Pop. Hell attempted a foolhardy takeover coup but hadn't bargained on Nolan's fierce opposition.

Nolan: "Richard wanted to do all the singing and figured he'd get rid of Johnny, but little did he know – we got rid of him."

HELL'S REPLACEMENT was Boston-born Billy Rath, yet The Heartbreakers soon reached a dead end. Some blamed Thunders for the Dolls' break-up and didn't want to see him get a second chance. Meanwhile, The Heartbreakers' love affair with heroin and self-destructive tendencies frightened off record companies.

"I didn't really have much argument for American record companies, because it was before the Sex Pistols," explains Childers. "I couldn't very well say, 'Oh, but that's good that Johnny calls the audience motherfuckers and they spit at the audience and walk offstage after two songs and curse', because there was no precedent to prove that anyone would want to buy records by someone that horrible.

"I was just stonewalled... particularly with Johnny. He had taken, not entirely deservedly, most of the bad publicity from the Dolls."

For over a year The Heartbreakers worked the gig circuit from CBGB to Max's Kansas City and back again. Just as they faced the bleak prospect of another

rock fans, punks included, were still enamoured with the USA and the iconography of a million movies: motorbikes, jukeboxes and leather jackets. Thunders was the all-American anti-hero in the bruised and track-marked flesh. Drawling about street gangs and smack, The Heartbreakers wooed the bands and music press with tall tales of low life.

Glen Matlock met The Heartbreakers at the Anarchy Tour rehearsals. "They looked very New York, dressed up like Italian spivs," he recalls. "Musically, they blew us away with how tight they were. I remember saying to Jerry Nolan, 'I really liked your set. What's that song Chinese Rocks about?' And he said, 'Heroin, boy', like I was an idiot, but heroin wasn't around at that stage. I firmly believe there hadn't been heroin on the punk scene until The Heartbreakers turned up."

Although most of the dates on the Anarchy Tour were cancelled, The Heartbreakers decided to stay on in England and take their chances at getting a record deal. Their first gig in London was a sold-out show at Dingwalls. "It was magnificent," recalls Childers. "You couldn't have got another person inside there with a crowbar! I just thought, 'Oh boy, we're going to be the next Beatles.' Of course, the last Beatles weren't wildly self-destructive junkies..."

Meanwhile, the Sex Pistols were busily following the Johnny Thunders guidebook to punk etiquette – spitting, swearing and vomiting at Heathrow en route to a gig in Holland. It worked an absolute treat, ensuring plenty of outraged newspaper headlines. But while there may have been an element of play-acting with Rotten and crew, Johnny Thunders was the real deal.

Nonetheless, as Glen Matlock discovered, Thunders always had a heart. "Johnny was a really sweet person," he explains. "He was very shy and all those problems with drugs were a way of covering it up."

It was a high price to pay. In the end, when his habit began to alienate people, Johnny the punk king stood accused of being, well, a punk. That very first Christmas The Heartbreakers spent in London, they'd attended a party thrown by journalists John Ingham and Caroline Coon. Afterwards the band had been reproached for running up the phone bill, stealing and using drugs.

Well, wasn't that what bad boys were supposed to do? And why would anyone have expected anything less from Johnny Thunders? After all, they'd been warned...

> ## "I thought, 'We're going to be the next Beatles.' Of course, they weren't junkies." MANAGER LEEE BLACK CHILDERS

New York winter without a record deal, McLaren phoned offering The Heartbreakers the opportunity to join the Anarchy Tour alongside the Sex Pistols, The Clash and The Damned. They hadn't heard of the bands, but they didn't care. As Childers quipped: "We would have toured with Barry Manilow!"

Thunders arrived in London as punk's first superstar and didn't disappoint. In 1976, the majority of English

dressed to kill

How two London clothes shops and a handful of would-be fashionistas changed the way rock stars and their fans looked forever.

Mohair Jumper

These rattily knitted punk perennials harked back to McLaren's days as a beatnik. In SEX, however, they cost a then-prohibitive £30.

VIRTUALLY EVERY ELEMENT of punk's style, attitude, politics, musical tastes and even personnel emanated from two tiny clothes shops on Chelsea's King's Road 30 years ago.

Those two shops were Acme Attractions at 135, in the basement of Chelsea Antique Market, and, at number 430, SEX, situated at its most westerly point, World's End. But who was that guy in a leopardskin waistcoat, dreads and shades wreathed in a haze of weed at Acme's counter? Don Letts, Roxy DJ, award-winning filmmaker, future member of Big Audio Dynamite and then-boyfriend of the other assistant, the gorgeous Jeanette Lee, who would later join PiL.

Acme's accountant was Andy Czezowski, who would manage The Damned and launch punk's first venue, the Roxy. Its owners, Steph Raynor and John Krevine, opened the first high-street punk store, BOY, and managed early punk band Chelsea.

"Acme was more than a shop. It was a club, a lifestyle, a forum for talent," says Letts. "It reflected the way London was going – it was about multi-culturalism."

Among those who teetered down Acme's staircase to the sternum-shuddering rhythms of dub reggae were John Lydon, Mick Jones, Billy Idol, Sid Vicious, and Patti Smith. Another frequent visitor was Bob Marley, attracted not only by the availability of spliff but also the charms of Jeanette Lee.

Anarchy Shirt

Created by Vivienne Westwood, who took her cue from Jordan's home-bleached shirt. The Seditionaries classic bore slogans such as "Only Anarchists Are Pretty" and armbands with swastikas or the encircled anarchy 'A'.

WORDS: PAUL GORMAN. THANKS TO ONLY-ANARCHISTS.CO.UK

Bondage Trousers

The unexpected inspiration for these were the fatigues worn by US marines. Westwood customised them with added fetish elements such as restrictive zips.

Tits T-shirt

As worn by Paul Cook and Siouxsie, McLaren took the image from a tourist souvenir T-shirt he'd bought in the US.

Leather Jacket

An item that dated from the pre-SEX Too Fast To Live Too Young To Die days. The Ramones wore this classic, zip-fronted design on the cover of their debut album.

Brothel Creepers

A hangover from when 430 was a '50s emporium, these proved incendiary in the Punk vs Ted wars.

Label

In 1976, the SEX shop mutated into Seditionaries, from whose fashion lines this label is taken.

MALCOLM MCLAREN
VIVIENNE WESTWOOD
SEDITIONARIES
PERSONAL COLLECTION

MADE IN ENGLAND
0207-022 Size
Shoe No. 3976

Acme's inclusive nature was reflected in its range: '60s suits, skinny ties and tab-collared shirts for modernists; '50s peg slacks and 'Tommy Steele' jackets for retro-stylists; fluffy jumpers, Big Smith painters' jeans and plastic sandals for wedge-haired soul boys, and Brighton Beach Riot and John Wayne Gacy T-shirts and plastic trousers for punk's spiky-haired first wave.

ACME'S ATMOSPHERE WAS at odds with the hard-edged environment of SEX. In the '60s this site had been hippie magnet Hung On You and later Mr Freedom, where Tommy Roberts sold pop-art fashion to Mick Jagger, Peter Sellers and Elton John. Among Roberts' regulars were a penurious couple, perennial art student Malcolm McLaren and sometime supply teacher Vivienne Westwood. One day McLaren, then known as Malcolm Edwards, purchased a pair of quilt-topped D-ring blue suede brothel creepers at Mr Freedom. "Those shoes were probably the most important things I ever bought," McLaren said. "It was a symbolic act to wear them."

Roberts proved to be something of a mentor. His stewardship of Ian Dury's Kilburn & The High Roads provided a blueprint for managing the Sex Pistols, but in 1971 Roberts drew McLaren's attention to the fact that the latest incarnation of 430, Americana outlet Paradise Garage, was faltering in a mist of debt and drug-associated business problems. In November, McLaren, Westwood and friend Patrick Casey deposed Roberts' former partner Trevor Miles and installed themselves in the back room of the shop as Let It Rock.

Early pictures show McLaren in Ted garb while Westwood sports lurex pedal pushers, fluffy jumper and a spiky, dyed hairstyle which is believed to have made an impact on early visitor David Bowie, then planning a new look to complement his upcoming album The Rise & Fall Of Ziggy Stardust & The Spiders From Mars.

Selling Teddy-boy jackets, straight and narrow-cuffed trousers and original '50s records, McLaren describes the shift from art study to fashion as "like jumping into the musical end of painting". Decked out like a '50s suburban sitting room complete with jukebox, Let It Rock soon engulfed the store. "It was like entering the set of a B-movie – there were old Teds, dwarfs and generally disfigured people hanging around," says Steph Raynor.

Within 18 months, McLaren and Westwood had tired of their regular clientele and refashioned 430 in homage to Britain's early-'60s 'ton-up' boys. Now it

"I think kids have a hankering to be part of a movement that's hard and tough, like the clothes we're selling here." MALCOLM McLAREN, 1975

was called Too Fast To Live Too Young To Die, with studs'n'chains biker jackets, custom-made zoot suits and black sleeveless T-shirts emblazoned with motorbike insignia and slogans.

Among the strangest creations was the T-shirt with VENUS spelt out on the front in studs and tiny rubber tyres over the shoulders, which were also festooned with horsehair, while the nipples were covered by peep-hole zips. There was another that featured the letters R-O-C-K in bleached chicken bones purloined from a local takeaway. Alice Cooper bought one of these during his first British tour, while other customers snapping up the ready-made stagewear included the New York Dolls, Iggy Pop, The Sensational Alex Harvey Band and Lou Reed.

(Above) 430 King's Road, Chelsea; a Seditionaries loose-knit mohair jumper; and (right) a SEX mail-order catalogue.

BY THE SUMMER of 1974, when Saturday boy Glen Matlock started to talk to shop regulars Paul Cook and Steve Jones about forming a band, the restless McLaren had experienced Manhattan's sleazy underbelly as de facto manager of the disintegrating New York Dolls. Fired by his experiences, he reopened 430 as a fetish and bondage outlet.

Over the shop front, four-foot-high pink rubber letters spelt out SEX and on the lintel was spray-painted with 17th-century clergyman Thomas Fuller's dictum: "Craft must have clothes but truth loves to go naked." Inside, the pervy lingerie, rubber and leather costumes and outrageous T-shirts hung from gym exercise bars, while the rubber-draped walls and ceiling were peppered with quotes from the SCUM (Society For Cutting Up Men) manifesto as set out by Valerie Solonas, the militant feminist who shot Andy Warhol.

There were also Situationist aphorisms, including the question "Does passion end in fashion?" inscribed by 430 acolyte Bernie Rhodes, who later suggested "Passion is a fashion" for a militaristic shirt worn by his charge Joe Strummer.

The shop assistants included Chrissie Hynde (a struggling musician who had not long given up her job as an NME writer) and the extraordinary Jordan, the rubber-stockinged fashion plate who would later star in the film Jubilee and manage Adam & The Ants.

In the early summer of 1975, McLaren, wearing a shirt that bore the words "Be Reasonable Demand The Impossible", told Street Life writer Rick Sky: "I think kids have a hankering to be part of a movement that's hard and tough and in the open, like the clothes we're selling here."

As the clientele coalesced around the Sex Pistols, who settled on their line-up in September 1975 and played their first gig two months later, so punk's protagonists came into focus: not just Hynde and Jordan, but also Sid Vicious, who became another assistant, while the customers ranged from the Bromley Contingent and Mick Jones to the generation who became movers and shakers in the '80s pop world: Adam Ant, Boy George, Steve Strange and Banarama's Siobhan Fahey. It was also the first place Nancy Spungen sought out on her arrival in the UK.

McLaren and Westwood's pathological contrariness was underlined when another facelift in December 1976 unveiled 430 as Seditionaries: Clothes For Heroes. The new name was etched on to a small brass plaque fixed on the anonymous, frosted-glass exterior, while inside all was post-apocalyptic courtesy of David Connors and Ben Kelly, who would later design The Haçienda. With a grey industrial carpet, the walls displayed a giant upside-down view of Piccadilly Circus as well as images of bombed-out Dresden. Jagged holes were poked into the ceiling, through which blinding arc lights shone.

Shopping at 430 had always been a forbidding, almost anti-retail experience, yet the popularity of punk meant that it now had crowds of kids there, and the frontage was often kicked in and/or sprayed with graffiti. It lent the shop a besieged atmosphere, just as the Pistols were being physically attacked on the street and banned from playing live.

By now BOY had opened at 135 King's Road, peddling zippered, burnt and torn versions of the gear being sold in Seditionaries. Similar shops proliferated: in nearby Beaufort Market X-Ray Spex's Poly Styrene, Banshees manager Nils Stevenson and rock'n'roll fashionista Lloyd Johnson all operated punk stalls, while Boy George was selling winklepickers at Shades in Chelsea Antiques Market.

WESTWOOD AND MCLAREN decided to refashion 430 once more as World's End (which it remains to this day), giving the designer Roger Burton a brief that drew on Expressionist landmark The Cabinet Of Dr Caligari, Alice In Wonderland, Dickens' The Old Curiosity Shop and 18th-Century galleons. As they moved into new romanticism, 'punk' clothes became available to all, via Miss Selfridge and the classified pages of the music press.

These days, knock-off Cowboys T-shirts, Destroy muslins and tartan bondage trousers are to be found for sale in shops from Trash & Vaudeville on St Mark's Place in New York to Rellik in London's Golborne Road, although neither Westwood nor McLaren has ever shown the slightest inclination in claiming copyright infringement on what is now a worldwide multi-million pound trade in their astounding designs.

"In the shop's various incarnations I made clothes that looked like ruins," McLaren wrote in his foreword to my book The Look. "I created something new by destroying the old. This wasn't fashion as a commodity; this was fashion as an idea."

And what an idea – so revolutionary that it continues to reverberate three decades later.

Malcolm McLaren (right) and partner Vivienne Westwood created a style revolution.

Past Perfect

Bob Gruen took his first photographs at the 1965 Newport Folk Festival when Dylan 'went electric'. Hanging out on the Greenwich Village folk and rock scene, by the early '70s he had forged a special relationship with John Lennon and Yoko Ono, and took pictures of the former Beatle wearing a New York City T-shirt that would become iconic. A friendship with the New York Dolls led him to the CBGB scene, then, via their one-time manager Malcolm McLaren, to London, the Sex Pistols, The Clash and beyond…

Killer combo

Steve Jones' guitar and amp, October 1976

Early on, this simple set-up of Les Paul plugged directly into a Fender Twin is all the Pistols guitarist needed to achieve his awesome live sound. Both guitar and amp had originally belonged to Sylvain Sylvain of the New York Dolls, whom Malcolm McLaren briefly managed at the end of their career.

The model

Debbie Harry, CBGB, 1976

Blondie were still regarded as something of a joke on the New York underground scene when this picture was taken. A few months prior, journalist Charles Shaar Murray had concluded: "Blondie [sic] will never be a star, simply because she ain't good enough."

The sin crowd

Max's Kansas City, 1976

Opening its doors in 1965, Max's became a haven for New York artists, sculptors and scenesters, including Willem De Kooning and Robert Rauschenberg. This shot, with Wayne County centre-stage, was taken one Sunday afternoon.

Well heeled

The Stilletos, 1974

After a stint as one of two female vocalists in late-'60s folk-rock group The Wind In The Willows, Debbie Harry joined The Stilettos, an outfit fronted by three girls that also included her partner Chris Stein. When The Stilettos split in August 1974, Debbie and Chris formed Angel & The Snake, which then morphed into Blondie.

That's all, folks

The Sex Pistols, January 1978

Taken backstage before the band's last-ever gig – at San Francisco's Winterland on 14 January 1978. The mural was commissioned by promoter Bill Graham.

I love rock'n'roll

Joan Jett, 1978

Having survived chick-rock new wavers The Runaways, managed by wigged-out music-biz legend Kim Fowley, Jett went on to become an international solo star. This shot was taken at infamous rock'n'roll haunt the Sunset Marquis hotel in West Hollywood.

Mob handed

New York Dolls, 1974

Gruen had met the Dolls in 1972, and shot them throughout their career. Here they forsook their tranvestite chic for a gangster look. "It was illegal to be homosexual," says Gruen. "It wasn't hatred or fear, it was the law."

Flip your wig

Wayne County, 1974

Wayne – later Jayne – County, the New York underground's favourite cross-dresser, performing at Club 82. Born Venoy Wayne Roger in Dallas in 1946, he'd arrived on the scene in 1972 via his first group, Queen Elizabeth.

One-way ticket

The Ramones, 1976

'Da bruddas' taking the subway
to Manhattan from their home
suburb of Queens. They couldn't
afford guitar cases at the time,
and carried their instruments to
rehearsals in plastic carrier bags.

Freak show

Sid Vicious, Baton Rouge, Louisiana, January 1978

The bass-player on an airport bus for the fourth date of the Pistols' ill-starred US tour. To Sid's left is one of the minders hired to keep the band out of trouble – and protect the $1m surety Warner Brothers had put up to obtain visas.

Slashed

Alan Vega, Suicide, 1978

When New York art-punk duo Suicide supported The Clash on their summer '78 On Parole tour, they were regularly subjected to a hail of glasses and bottles. At Crawley Leisure Centre on 8 July, a skinhead climbed onstage and punched Vega in the face.

Endgame

Winterland, San Francisco

The scene of the Pistols' last gig, the Winterland was a cavernous, tubular hall with, on that night, a totally inadequate PA system. The group made their last stand at midnight, following sets from the Bay Area's key punk bands.

Up in the air

Johnny and Sid, USA, 1978

The Pistols' deadly duo enjoying in-flight refreshments. Later on the US trek the two old pals opted to take the tour bus across country, while the rest of the group flew.

All for one

CBGB glitterati, 1976

In the lobby of the New York Palladium on New Year's Eve: (from left) David Johansen, Lenny Kaye, Dee Dee Ramone, Patti Smith, Jay Dee Daugherty, Tom Verlaine, John Cale.

In 1975, Gary Valentine was a struggling poet/lyricist, living in an abandoned storefront in New York. Here he recalls how he became Blondie's first bass guitarist.

TOUCHED

KODAK

KODAK SAFETY FILM 5063

6   6A   7   7A

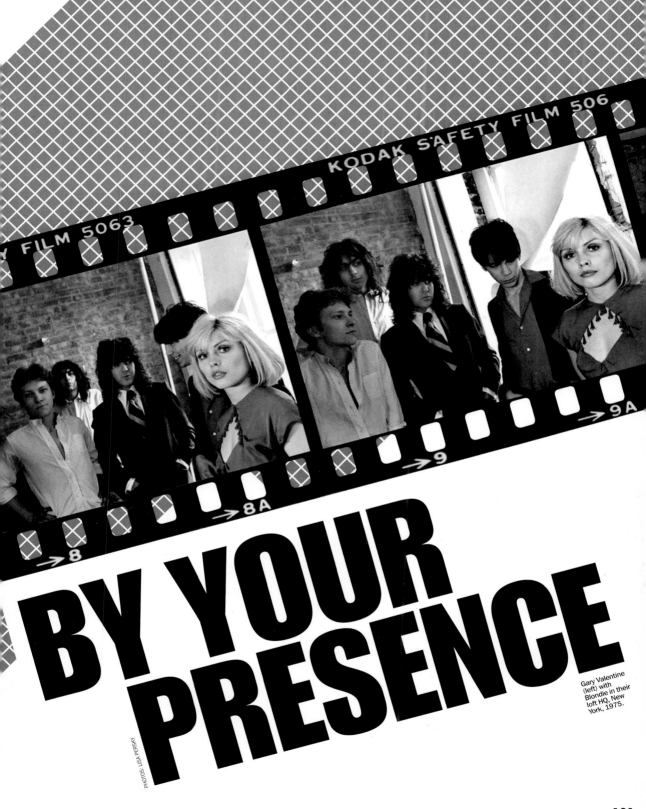

KODAK SAFETY FILM 506

FILM 5063

→ 8

→ 8A

→ 9

→ 9A

BY YOUR PRESENCE

Gary Valentine
(left) with
Blondie in their
loft HQ, New
York, 1975.

PHOTOS: LISA PERSKY

101

Chris Stein (left) and Debbie Harry in their pre-Blondie band The Stilettos, 1974.

(Inset) Before finding fame with Blondie, Harry tried her luck as a folk singer, waitress and Playboy Bunny.

THE FIRST TIME I met Chris Stein and Debbie Harry was in 1975. I was 19 years old, had left home the year before, and was living in a storefront on East 10th Street, in New York's East Village. The neighbourhood boasted junkies, prostitutes, East European immigrants and gangs of Hispanic kids. Back then it was a sort of no-man's-land, but nowadays yuppie moms wheel their prams through the reclaimed streets without a second thought. If you throw a rock in any direction, you're bound to hit a Starbucks, or a branch of Gap.

I moved to New York from my parents' house in New Jersey. A series of misadventures, culminating in my underage girlfriend becoming pregnant and me being arrested for it (the autobiographical material behind my song X-Offender, Blondie's first single), led my parents to give me an ultimatum: change my ways, get a job, think about returning to university and forget about rock'n'roll. I packed a bag and left. A friend had sublet the storefront from a friend of his who had converted it into a studio. There were mounds of unwashed laundry, a couch that was more holes than couch, a dilapidated stereo, ashtrays overflowing with cigarette butts, and stacks of greasy dishes. "Perfect," I thought. My hero at the time was Henry Miller and my plan was simple: I was going to become a poet.

My friend was eccentric. He divided his time between working for the Manhattan Transit Department, studying the Bible for hints about the end of the world and dreaming about being a rock star. He also squeezed in a lot of drugs. He wore eye-liner too, a leftover from the glitter days of the New York Dolls and Club 82, an old drag club on East Fourth Street which for a brief time a year before was the centre of the New

York underground scene. We had a vague plan to start a band, and one item in the storefront helped: an old piano. Practically every other key on it was broken, but this didn't matter. I taught myself how to play and started writing lyrics instead of poetry.

Most of the time I was hungry. I had barely enough money to cover my rent. It was the kind of life you're supposed to lead if you want to write or paint or be any kind of artist. At least that's what I told myself those days I hadn't eaten, when I tried to quell the pains in my stomach by drinking warm water, a trick I picked up from the French writer René Daumal. It didn't help Daumal much: he died of tuberculosis at 36. Luckily for me, something happened in the summer of 1975.

CLEM BURKE, whom I knew from high school and who had been drumming in bands since he was a kid, had started playing with a group in New York. I had seen Clem play for years and we had become friends. He always had some sixth sense about what was going to be the Next Big Thing, and more times than not he was right. He knew about David Bowie before any one else, and in '73 was already

I vaguely remembered: Club 82, to me, was a melange of the Dolls, drag queens, transvestites, a brief encounter with Lou Reed and David Bowie, too many Tequila Sunrises and an unfortunate whiff of amyl nitrate. I think I saw them on the same bill as Wayne County.

Yeah. Sure. I remember.

He told me the name of the place – White's Pub. If I wanted to go, I should be there when he got there.

I HAD ALREADY been to CBGB on the Bowery to see Patti Smith and Television, and I had observed Richard Hell prowling the East Village with a perpetual sneer cut into his face. Like him, I had taken to wearing shades all the time. I picked up the habit from peering at Ian Hunter albums and old Dylan photos, and what I gained in imperturbable cool I lost in eyesight.

In those days there weren't many places for unsigned bands to play. Max's Kansas City hadn't reopened yet and Club 82 had lost its cachet when glitter dried up. Walking around Second Avenue and St Mark's Place, I'd see little flyers for Television or Patti Smith on streetlamps. But they were just a small part of the self-advertising that goes on in any big city. In that early summer of 1975, things were quiet on the rock'n'roll front. Hence Blondie busking in the depths of downtown Manhattan.

I don't remember much about the show. The place was practically empty. What I remember of the audience is a handful of barflies occasionally letting out a frank appraisal of the singer. If they didn't always appreciate the material, at least they liked her looks. It was only later I found out they got the gig because Debbie worked there as a waitress.

My memories of Debbie from that night are vague. But I was impressed by guitarist Chris Stein's voodoo attire. He was covered in skulls, pentagrams, crossbones and swastikas, this last item a bit odd for a Jew. He wore dark eyeliner, his nails were long and black (he never used a plectrum, and played his guitar

"The guitarist's a real nut, but the singer's sexy."
CLEM BURKE EXPLAINS BLONDIE TO GARY VALENTINE

walking around with lipstick or his eyelids painted red, a dangerous thing in New Jersey.

It was a coup to have a place in the city, and he was always dropping in, bringing grass or a bottle of wine and a handful of new records. Most of the time we had Ziggy Stardust, Fun House or Highway 61 blaring, and we'd sit and talk about how we were going to be bigger than The Beatles. Clem was still in college, and occasionally he'd ask me to write a paper for him. His band was playing in the Wall Street district. Did I want to come?

"Yeah, sure. What're they like?"

"Oh, sorta campy. The guitarist's a real nut. But the singer's sexy. We do some weird songs"

"Yeah. What're you called?"

"Blondie. You saw them once at Club 82. They were The Stilettos then."

as if it were a banjo), and his hair fell around his rouged face in gypsy ringlets.

Also there that night was bassist Fred Smith. When he left Blondie to replace Richard Hell in Television, it probably seemed a chance he couldn't pass up. After all, Blondie then were little more than a joke. Television were getting press. Verlaine's surreal lyrics and switch-blade guitar were grabbing critics' attention. Blondie had little more going for them than Debbie's looks. It was a good move for me, because soon after Clem asked me if I wanted to play bass with the band.

AFTER HANGING AROUND at a couple of gigs, they knew who I was. Clem had told them I was a poet and that I wrote songs – my repertoire on the clapped-out piano was growing – and I guess I looked the part. The fact that I couldn't really play the bass was a minor detail. The whole idea behind the early New York scene was that you didn't have to depend on established rock performers to provide your musical sustenance. If you had the nerve to get up onstage and bang away, you could do it yourself. Clem said they'd have a bass at the rehearsal space – I didn't have one.

Debbie would pull out a frying pan, yawn and make scrambled eggs for Chris and me.

(Left) Blondie in 1975, with (clockwise from top) Debbie Harry, Gary Valentine, Clem Burke, Jimmy Destri and Chris Stein.

(Right) Cosy: chez Harry and Stein.

The place was uptown, in an office building on West 37th Street. What I remember most from that first jam was realising how attractive Debbie was. Not that I hadn't noticed this before. But sitting across from her in a small, brightly lit room was different from seeing her in a dive like White's Pub. I knew that I was looking at a very sexy woman.

Clem was supportive and avuncular, jollying me out of my natural shyness, telling them about my poetry and songs. Chris lit a joint and handed me the bass.

"Whaddya know?"

"Er…"

"Can you play A and D?"

"Yeah."

"OK. You know the Stones' Live With Me?"

I nodded.

"Awright."

We went to it. Chris had a scratchy, plucky way of playing, as if his fingers hit two different chords simultaneously, one banging into the other. I ploughed into the bass, figuring it out with a kind of join-up-the-dots approach. Debbie let the chords churn around for a while before coming in. Casually, in thin T-shirt, ripped jeans and tennis shoes, she sang.

"I got nasty habits…"

"I bet she does," I thought.

"C'mon now, honey, donchu wanta live with meee…"

An hour later we stopped. Finally Chris said, "OK, you can play." Clem got off the drums and moved over to the piano.

"C'mere," he said. "Play one of your songs."

I put down the bass and sat at the upright. I hit a C, got my pitch, and sang something I had just come up with. They nodded.

"OK. Sounds good."

"So?" Clem asked.

"So he can play. So he's in."

"Debbie?"

"Yeah. Sure. He sounds great."

"Cool," I said. I was officially in a New York rock'n'roll band.

A lot happened after that audition. My friend at the storefront announced he was moving to a kibbutz in Israel. I had to find a new crib. Rehearsals were going well, and I was getting better on bass. There was no way around it. I took a deep breath and knocked on my parents' door.

That lasted a few weeks. The fact that I was playing in a band didn't go down well, and they didn't care for me crawling into bed at 4am after a gig. I received another ultimatum, packed another knapsack and left.

For the next few nights, I crashed at the rehearsal space. Eventually the subject of my plight came up at a rehearsal.

"Debbie," Chris said. "Gary doesn't have a place to live."

"Shit."

Then a thoughtful moment.

"Well, I guess he can live with us."

Chris and Debbie lived in a tiny one-bedroom flat above a grocery store on Thompson Street. There was hardly enough room for the two of them. Every vertical surface was covered in photographs. A bulletin board had flyers for The Stilettos, an Elvis record cover, a photo of Debbie in her Chevy Camaro, the inevitable skull and cross-bones, a Rolling Stones button with Brian Jones. Crucifixes, magical talismans, voodoo dolls, images of Warhol, The Velvet Underground and junk art Chris picked up from the trash: the bric-a-brac of the streets found its walk-in display case in that small flat.

My other vivid memory is of shivering most of the first night I spent there, crashing on a small couch amid amplifiers, speaker cases and guitars, because I was too shy to ask for a blanket after Chris and Debbie had gone to bed.

MEMORIES: DEBBIE MAKING coffee in the morning. Bleary-eyed, rats'-nest hair, she'd fall out of their bedroom wrapped in a housecoat, then pull out a frying pan, yawn and make scrambled eggs for Chris and me. Most times I had been up already for a few hours, reading, or quietly plucking one of the guitars.

She'd kick us out every now and then, to have the place to herself. Chris would roll a joint and we'd hit the streets, usually heading across Houston to the East Village. I wore his hand-me-downs – black peg-leg pants, a white leather jacket. I even got a new pair of shades using his Medicare card.

By then we'd played a few gigs, recorded a demo and I had had my trial by fire. My first performance was at a dive called Monty Python's, on Third Avenue and 12th Street. It was the only time I ever suffered stage fright and played with my back to the audience. In the early days, different bands would support one another, turning up to what might otherwise be empty gigs, like people on a desert island taking in one another's washing.

We played a lot of small gigs in those early days – bachelor parties, weddings, forgettable dives with names like Brandy's and Broadway Charlie's. The idea was to get money to eat. Most people think a musician's life is about sex and drugs and rock'n'roll, but most of the time it's about food. After a show we'd hop into Debbie's

Camaro and go to Dave's Pot Belly, an all-night coffee shop in Greenwich Village, and stuff ourselves on cheeseburgers, fries and milkshakes. If the take wasn't good, there was Smiler's Deli, on Seventh Avenue and Sheridan Square, for less sumptuous fare, like chicken salad sandwiches and chocolate milk. For special treats, Debbie went to Chinatown and brought steamed buns filled with pork and sweet sauce.

In July we debuted at CBGB's Festival Of Unrecorded Rock Talent, playing with the Ramones and Talking Heads, and in August shared a bill with the latter. We were known as the band that would open for anyone, and to a degree this was true. We simply weren't that impressive. Debbie would forget lyrics. Chris would look at his guitar as if it had just materialised out of thin air. The only one of us who could keep things together was Clem. We rehearsed at a loft on Third Street owned by Arturo Vega, who later became an art director for the Ramones. But after a few weeks he lost interest in us and we had to find a new place. Meanwhile, the Thompson Street flat was getting too small. It was time to move on.

We landed in an illegal loft space above a liquor store on the Bowery, two blocks from CBGB. A friend of Chris's had got a lease on the place and rented us a floor. The friend, Benton, was a peculiar individual. Thin as a rail, he was an artist of sorts, but spent most of his time

Home and away: at CBGB, 7 June 1976 and (inset) on the tourbus in 1977.

We simply weren't that impressive: Debbie would forget lyrics...

wearing biker gear and fantasising about the Hell's Angels. (During the end of our stay there, on a PCP binge, Benton asked an Angel to beat him; he obliged.) Sometimes he wouldn't leave his room for days, and his floor was dotted with Coke bottles filled with urine.

The loft was unheated; I spent one Christmas Eve (my birthday) burning a stack of Hendrix posters to stay warm. Our furniture was dragged in from the streets and was filthy. Outside, the sidewalk was covered with winos and down-and-outs; often we struggled to push open the door in the morning because a bum had camped out

there the night before. One winter morning, we discovered one had frozen to death; someone suggested hauling the body inside, but luckily an ambulance arrived. (Benton had got his hands on a series of Tibetan paintings, one of which was a cheery scene of a group of monks eating one of their fellows.)

An eerie statue of a nun stood in front of a fireplace. A cross was painted on her forehead and rosary beads hung from her hand. The fireplace itself was covered in occult formulae. Benton was fond of Aleister Crowley, meditated on the Tarot and in inspired moments read aloud from Diary Of A Drug Fiend. Between this and Chris's voodoo fascination, the place had the air of a bad Satanist film. Chris said the loft was haunted and that he could feel poltergeists.

One time an off-duty policeman arrested me. A friend of ours was acting in The Tempest, and Clem, Benton and I had gone to a matinee at the theatre in

Chelsea. Walking back, we shared a joint. A madman grabbed me, shouting, "No! No! This can't happen. Not in my neigbourhood!" I had no idea what he was talking about. In those days people smoked openly, figuring that the police had better things to do. He never said he was a policeman, showed no badge or ID, just flashed a set of bracelets and tried to cuff me. I fought him off, but he chased me into the street. Finally, he grabbed my shirt and threw me to the asphalt, my head hitting the deck.

We spent the next three nights in three different jails. It was Friday; the courts didn't open until Monday. My head pounded from its recent meeting with West 18th Street. I couldn't see. The police had taken my glasses and had refused to give me painkillers. And I was hungry. Worse still, we had a show at Max's Kansas City

Chris and Debbie were convinced Patti Smith had a vendetta against them.

that Monday night and there was no guarantee we'd be released on time. Throughout, Clem kept up a mantra of, "Shit, man, this sucks", which Benton would counter with his single maxim for a philosophy of life: "Learn to love it." The cops didn't know what to make of us.

We spent Monday in a holding pen, waiting for our case to be heard. Chris and Debbie got a public defender. He told us not to worry. We weren't. Finally we were brought before the judge, five minutes before he left for the day. The arresting officer admitted he hadn't identified himself as a policeman. Case thrown out. We made the soundcheck at Max's. The best thing of all was that I was interviewed by New York Rocker magazine.

AROUND THIS TIME, Jimmy Destri joined the band. He had come to our gigs at Mothers, a gay bar on 23rd Street across from the Chelsea Hotel. Jimmy had played with a group called Milk And Cookies. He brought his Farfisa organ to the loft and it sounded right.

One of the first things we did together was the music for Vain Victory, a play by Jackie Curtis, one of the Warhol crowd. Chris and Debbie always aspired to that set, and thought it was a coup when Debbie got the part of Juicy Lucy. The party after closing night was a smash. Lisa Persky, an actress who also wrote for New York Rocker, had been invited, and in the taxi uptown she sat on my lap and we made out. At the party I got loaded and we

On the verge of stardom, Debbie poses outside CBGB in 1977.

(Inset) Flyers for one of Blondie's 1976 shows.

decided to go to her studio. The elevator down was a bit abrupt, and when I hit the street I heaved. She huddled me into a taxi, and when we finally got to her place we ran into her father, who had dropped by for a visit. I later wrote (I'm Always Touched By Your) Presence Dear, Blondie's second hit, for Lisa.

Clem went to London for a six-week adventure; we took the opportunity to write songs. The first album grew out of this time. When Clem returned from

England he brought back the first Dr Feelgood album. We threw a party at the loft and invited everyone. We had more people there than at any of our gigs. Johnny Thunders, Jerry Nolan, Hell, the Ramones, The Miamis, The Marbles, The Dictators, Talking Heads, Suicide. Conspicuous by their absence were Tom Verlaine and Patti Smith, who didn't mix much with other bands. Chris and Debbie were convinced Patti had a vendetta against them. The paranoia drove them to succeed.

Clem played the Dr Feelgood album over and over. The stripped-down R&B inspired everyone there that night, and not too long after the torn shirts of early Television would turn up in the Sex Pistols' aesthetic, shipped back to us via Malcolm McLaren.

BLONDIE'S RISE TO fame began with those first shows at CBGB with Jimmy Destri, in February 1976. For the first time, Blondie sounded like a real band and started building up a following. It was a struggle, but, looking back, the rest seemed to follow as a matter of course. At 20, it's immensely gratifying to see people in different cities across the country wearing peg-leg pants and skinny ties just because you do. That's what happened in LA, where we played with the Ramones and Tom Petty, in San Francisco, and later across the States after the first album, Blondie, was released and we opened for Iggy Pop on a nationwide tour.

The same thing happened when we toured the UK with Television in spring 1977. That was my favourite time with the band. I was an Anglophile, and to find myself playing London, Manchester and Glasgow was a dream, even if I did fall off the stage in Bristol. But in July I left the band, moved to the West Coast and pursued other goals, one of which was fronting my own group, The Know.

My life with Blondie wasn't over yet. Almost 20 years later, after I had moved to London and was working as a freelance writer, I got a call from Chris Stein. It was an odd sensation hearing his voice again, but what he asked was less expected still. He wanted to put the original band back together. Was I interested? I had just returned from a tour of Eastern Europe, where I had played guitar in a gypsy band. Heading to New York to play pop music again wasn't the first thing on my mind, but I was intrigued. I decided to give it a try.

In November 1996, I landed in New York. Jimmy Destri met me at JFK and we drove to Chris's loft in TriBeCa. After the initial shock of comparing grey hairs and paunches, things settled into familiar routines, the way it is around family. Later that day Debbie showed up and we remembered a few old times. Maybe you can't go home again, but it sure is interesting seeing your old roommates 20 years on.

The Story Of CBGB

It began as New York's outlet for country, bluegrass and blues, but soon became a breeding ground for the rebellious sound of punk.

10 December 1973
CBGB opens.

Hilly Kristal (club founder) I'd been running my own club, Hilly's, in the West Village, but I had problems with the junior mafia. So when the East Village became the place for poets and musicians to rent loft space, I found an old derelict bar under The Palace Hotel. It stunk of dirty old men, vomit and urine. I had to fumigate it.

Alan Vega (vocals, Suicide) He [Hilly] had a good room in the back where the stage is now. You could buy a pitcher of beer for a quarter. So it had nothing but Hell's Angels and the bums from the Bowery in there.

31 March 1974
Television make their CBGB debut.

Hilly Kristal One day I was putting up the awning for CBGB when [Television's] Tom Verlaine and Richard Lloyd walked by, and we talked about the club I was starting. I didn't give it another thought until a week later, when this non-stop talker, Terry Ork, comes in and he's their manager. He told me they were a wonderful band, and he persuaded me to put them on. So they came in and they were just horrible.

Gary Valentine (bass, Blondie) I wasn't yet playing for Blondie when I first saw Television at CBGB. But the great thing was realising how badly they played. It let me know there was hope for me as a musician.

Hilly Kristal My first response was, "No more!" But Terry insisted Television were going to practise really hard, and said he had another band from Queens – the Ramones – and they could play. It wasn't costing me anything because I was usually closed on Sundays, so we tried again with both bands a few weeks later.

28 April 1974
Television and the Ramones play at CBGB.

Hilly Kristal The Ramones were even worse than Television. Their equipment kept breaking down and they were constantly yelling at each other. They only had a few songs, but they would never get all the way through any of them. It would take over an hour to play them by the time they'd had all the fights.

Richard Hell (bass, Television) The scene started snowballing. CBGB was where things were happening. Television were unique. There was not another rock'n'roll band with short hair. There was not another rock'n'roll band with torn clothes.

Gary Valentine There was a pool table where people hung out beside the stage. I was shooting pool once when Dee Dee Ramone walked by and started throwing the balls around. He said, "I guess you think I'm acting like an asshole?" and I replied, "No, Dee Dee, I don't think you're acting at all." His friends had to hold him back.

> ## "Linda Ronstadt came to hear the Ramones. She flew out the door holding her ears." HILLY KRISTAL

Richard Lloyd (guitar, Television) Patti Smith started coming to see Television play at CBGB. Everybody knew that Patti was nuts for Tom [Verlaine].

5 May 1974
Television play CBGB, supported by The Stilettos.

Hilly Kristal The Stilettos had three girls up front – one was Debbie Harry. She was very shy, but absolutely beautiful. She and her boyfriend Chris Stein left and formed Angel, then that turned into Blondie. The rival club, Max's Kansas City, closed down for 10 months and CBGB was starting to get someplace by December 1974.

COMPILED BY: JOHNNY BLACK. PHOTO: © GODUS

17 January 1975
Television and Blondie play CBGB.

Gary Valentine Outside CBGB was a great scene. You could look at the line and there'd be Johnny Thunders, Richard Hell, Talking Heads. All the members of future bands were the audience.

14-15 February 1975
Patti Smith plays her first CBGB gigs.

Hilly Kristal Jean Friedman, Patti's manager, came to see me. She asked if I could fit Patti in and have Television open. Patti was great. She was getting a better response than Television. She was already known as a poet, so when she came it brought in people like Andy Warhol and Allen Ginsberg.

20 March 1975
Patti Smith and Television begin a five-week residency.

Patti Smith It was the greatest atmosphere to perform in. It was conspiratorial. It was physical, and that's what rock'n'roll's all about – sexual tension and being drunk and disorderly.

20 June 1975
Talking Heads make their debut.

David Byrne (vocalist, Talking Heads) CBGB was the kind of place where you'd sit at the bar and when your time came you'd casually walk over and get on stage.

Hilly Kristal David performed with a jerky motion that reminded me of a chicken walking around without a head. Talking Heads were amazingly visual.

David Byrne When you were done you'd walk off, wipe the sweat off your head, then walk back to the bar and have a beer.

Tina Weymouth (bass, Talking Heads)
The first time we played CBGB was the second time we'd ever performed and we started getting publicity quickly. The other bands didn't like it and were very unfriendly… Our crowd was very different to the Ramones' and Television's.

16 July – 2 August 1975

The CBGB Festival Of The Top 40 Unrecorded New York Rock Bands features the Ramones, Blondie, Television, Talking Heads, Mink DeVille, The Shirts, The Heartbreakers and more.

Hilly Kristal I decided to do my own festival. I couldn't afford the New York Times but took huge ads in the Village Voice and SoHo News. It was three weeks with two weekends. It was hugely successful. All the writers who had just

been in town for the Newport Jazz Festival stayed and came to CBGB. And they spread the word. The Ramones were signed to Sire, and people suddenly realised there was all this talent in New York and it never had an outlet before. Linda Ronstadt and her entourage came slumming to hear the Ramones and see what all the fuss was about. I got them right up front, but they lasted less than five minutes. She flew out the door holding her ears.

March 1976

Wayne County, the cross-dressing frontman with the Electric Chairs, responds to heckling from 'Handsome' Dick Manitoba of The Dictators by hitting him with a microphone stand.

Bob Gruen (photographer) I was standing in the back of CBGB; there was

this commotion, but we didn't know quite what was going on.

Scott Kempner (guitar, Dictators)
Wayne County would yell something out, and Dick would yell something back to engage him, not to heckle him.

Wayne (now Jayne) County I kept hearing, "Drag queen, fucking queer!" I yelled back, "Stupid fucking asshole."

'Handsome' Dick Manitoba (vocalist, The Dictators) The taunting was going back and forth, and then he interpreted a move that I made as violent.

Andy Shernoff (bass, The Dictators)
Wayne picked up his microphone stand and smashed it down on Dick's shoulder.

Bob Gruen They dragged Dick Manitoba out – literally, two guys were dragging him. He was limp between their shoulders, with blood pouring out of the side of his head.

Excited punters wait for the next band onstage, 1977.

4 June 1976

The album Live At CBGB's is recorded over a weekend, featuring Mink DeVille, The Shirts, Laughing Dogs, Manster, Tuff Darts and others.

Hilly Kristal It was very disappointing that Talking Heads decided not to be on the album. I never learned why – maybe because they were about to be signed by Sire. The other big disappointment was that Blondie were not together enough to make a good live recording.

25 July 1976

The Dead Boys make their CBGB debut.

Maureen Nelly (CBGB bartender) When the Dead Boys happened, the club changed. It became punk. Pre-Dead Boys it was Television, Talking Heads, The Shirts – which had a more under-ground-poet-beat sort of feeling. Then, when the Dead Boys happened, it was the whole English punk scene with the Sex Pistols.

Gyda Gash (musician) From the end of 1977 on was like a death period. It was the beginning of the end, and you could just feel it.

19 April 1978

Johnny Blitz, drummer of the Dead Boys, is attacked outside CBGB.

Michael Sticca (Dead Boys associate) We were standing on Second Avenue hailing a cab. This car comes along and swerves towards us, like it's going to hit us… All of a sudden, like, these five fucking guys get out of the car…

Johnny Blitz Two minutes later, one of the girls comes in to CBGB and says, "Michael's in trouble." So I run outside and he's surrounded by about five guys with baseball bats, and of course, I dive

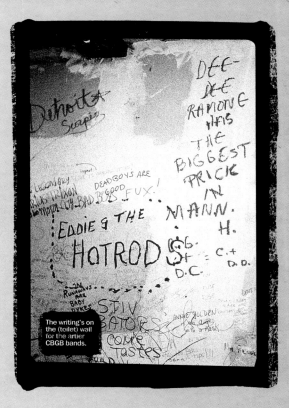

The writing's on the (toilet) wall for the artier CBGB bands.

in without thinking, and a fight breaks out. So I pull a knife, and next thing you know, I'm chasing a guy down the street with my knife and I get one of them. Then I get it with a baseball bat… they sliced me up pretty good.

13 December 1981

Sonic Youth play at CBGB.

Hilly Kristal We carried on into the '80s with the same policy: showcasing young bands that played their own material. We put on The B-52's and Sonic Youth, but suddenly there were 20 clubs in New York doing the same thing as us. We introduced experimental and hardcore things on Sundays, where we'd have people like Agnostic Front or Bad Brains. We ran that for two or three years until these bands started breaking things, so I had to stop it.

12 February 1991

Smashing Pumpkins play CBGB.

Hilly Kristal In the '90s, alternative rock became the mainstream, but we were still trying to bring along the new bands. We had Smashing Pumpkins about 30 or 40 times. We had people like Soul Asylum and Goo Goo Dolls.

4 March 2005

It is reported that CBGB may have to close in August if its landlord, The Bowery Residents' Committee (a homeless services agency), succeeds in its plan to double the venue's rent to $40,000 per month. The New York mayor's office receives over 100,000 emails supporting the club.

10 August 2005

CBGB gets a stay of execution when judge Joan Kenney refuses to allow its eviction on the basis of unpaid rent Later in the month, a CBGB support rally in Washington Square Park, Manhattan is attended by artists including Blondie and Public Enemy.

1 September 2005

CBGB's lease expires and the club is served with an eviction notice.

Hilly Kristal Despite what Judge Kenney said, we lost out in the appeals court, so I was put in a position where I'd have to take everything from here and re-create the club somewhere else.

8 December 2005

Hilly Kristal announces that he has agreed to quit the club's Bowery home by the end of next October. In recent months, the rent has rocketed from $19,000 to $35,000 a month.

Hilly Kristal It has been a traumatic year, but we have financial backers who are prepared to help me move to a new location in New York. We're also looking at opening up a CBGB in Las Vegas. Same kind of club, same philosophy, but maybe a little more spectacular.

peek-a-boo

Macabre and musically inept, Siouxsie & The Banshees were punk's untouchables. But behind the goth-fetish chic lay an enduring talent.

Siouxsie and friend at the Buzzcocks/Clash/Sex Pistols gig at the Screen On The Green, Islington, London, 29 August 1976.

IN THE EARLY HOURS of Thursday, 6 October 1977, a bottle-blond young man, his leather-jacket studded with the legend SIOUXSIE on the back, took several cans of spray paint to the front doors of 15 London-based record companies. His message was simple: SIGN THE BANSHEES. DO IT NOW.

This act of cultural terrorism was reported in the gossip pages of the music press, which gleefully added that one corporate victim, CBS, had ordered its immediate removal. It would be another eight months, though, before another bowed to public pressure and whipped out their chequebook.

Were Siouxsie And The Banshees, the last bastion of punk purity, truly untouchable? That's the question Sounds put to Andrew Lauder, then in the process of launching Radar Records as a 'new wave' imprint under the auspices of Warner Brothers. "That was the vibe," he replied. "I suspect it was true."

While the identity of the band's most courageous supporter was later revealed as Les Mills, an early fan-turned-roadie who went on to manage The Psychedelic Furs, the reasons the Banshees struck fear into the heart of the mainstream record business were far more complex. Costumes adorned with swastikas and fetish accoutrements created an awkward clash of symbols. They were poseurs, intellectuals, art students. Too radical, too shocking for 1977, too "last year's thing" for '78. There was always one reason or another to keep Siouxsie And The Banshees at arm's length.

In many ways, this unspoken exclusion order worked in their favour, for few rock bands have ever worn their outsider status so impeccably. Guitarist John McKay summed it up neatly in December 1978, shortly after the acclaim heaped on The Scream, the band's eagerly awaited debut album, had vindicated the Banshees' sign-us-if-you-dare stance. "We feel alienation all the time," he deadpanned, "which is why we're in this band. Alienated from society, alienated from the rest of humanity."

"Punk was already becoming staid and cliched," says Marc Almond. "But there was something decadent and provocative about the Banshees. They were disdainful and enigmatic, and that's what made them attractive."

Austere, untouchable and uncompromising, the Banshees embodied all the radical rhetoric of early punk. When critic Paul Morley wrote a staunch, self-styled "Defence of Siouxsie And The Banshees" early in 1978, he refused to define them as a rock group, preferring instead the grander, more conceptual "20th century performers". Rock was, declared one of the more outré T-shirts of the era, "for arse-lickers". Everything about Siouxsie And The Banshees suggested they were still on a mission to destroy the milieu, rotten to the core with complacency, cliche, the weight of history.

"To me, punk sounded like skiffle," said Phil Oakey, of The Human League, who toured with the early Banshees. "The theme was social commentary, protest songs almost, and when we first heard The Clash and The Damned it sounded like Buddy Holly-era rock'n'roll with tougher lyrics. The Banshees were different. They created something that's not been seen before or since. They weren't an identikit punk band. That would have been completely against who they were and where they came from."

BORN SUSAN JANET Ballion on 27 May 1957, at Guy's Hospital in London, Siouxsie Sioux sprang from suburbia. Chislehurst on the Kent borders, to be precise, a half-hour train journey to the heart of London. Her parents had met in the Belgian Congo, where her father, a bacteriologist, had 'milked' snakes for their serum – a peculiar occupation that sat comfortably with the band's later voodoo vibe.

Though hardly deprived, her upbringing was marked by a struggle between convention and the dangers, or even possibilities, of a world beyond it. At first, like every child desperate to fit in, the pre-teen 'Susie' was embarrassed by the family's flat-roof residence ("a sick house", she later said), the woefully unkempt front garden, even her difficult surname. Later on, though, she learned to feel "proud of the difference".

A lengthy spell in hospital provided the defining moment. Just weeks after the sudden death of her alcoholic father in spring 1972, she was rushed in bleeding and in agony, an effect of ulcerative colitis, a debilitating condition prompted by hyperactive antibodies. It was while recuperating from a blood transfusion and difficult operation that she witnessed David Bowie's infamous performance of Starman on Top Of The Pops.

"Bowie was incredible," Siouxsie told me in 2003. "The skinniness, the alienation, the otherworldliness… He was definitely the man/woman of the future, a springboard to accentuate your own individuality." The teenage loner was suitably inspired: "I enjoyed being the freak in a middle-class suburb," she says.

Susie saved hard for the occasional Biba dress, and conserved her energies for the showy delights of the West End gay scene, which she'd discovered through her go-go-dancing elder sister. After leaving school, she took lessons in theatrical make-up for fun, and a secretarial course at Orpington College to keep her mother happy. And she fell in with a small, exclusive group of friends based in nearby Bromley.

Later dubbed "The Bromley Contingent" by the music press, this loose-knit bunch of thrill-seekers was defiantly nonconformist.

(Above) The Banshees' live debut at the 100 Club Punk Festival, 20 September 1976: (from left) Siouxsie Sioux, Steve Severin, Marco Pirroni and Sid Vicious.

(Right) In Transit: (from left) Kenny Morris, Severin, Siouxsie, John McKay.

Siouxsie and the Banshees

Hong Kong Garden

And by spring 1976, they formed the flamboyant hard-core of early Sex Pistols fans. One key character was the 15-year-old 'Berlin', his name a homage both to Warhol's Factory superstars and to early '70s Cabaret chic. He clearly remembers the effect that 18-year-old Susie had on him and his Bromley pals the night she waltzed into a party hosted by Severin (real name Steven Bailey) and his mate Simon Barker.

"They'd invited this girl they'd met at a Roxy Music concert, who was outrageous and glamorous, and there was an excitement that she might actually turn up," he recalls. "About 1.30am, she walks in with her friend Myra, and the whole room crackled. She wore a gold and black Chinese dress, fishnets and these pink, transparent stilettos from SEX. Her hair had blonde spiky bits around the fringe, and she wore the-atrical make-up with little swastikas on her cheekbones. She was glamour incarnate."

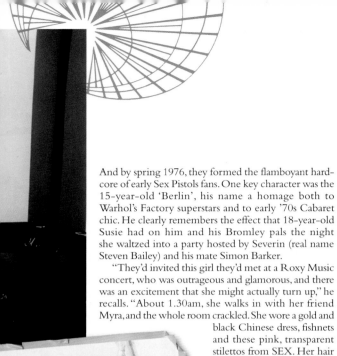

Days later, Berlin was on the 227 bus from Bromley North to Chislehurst, his striped T-shirt, red plastic sandals and outsize gold belt a loud distraction from his callow attempts at make-up. "I got off at this little parade of shops and she came screaming round the corner in a flared '50s skirt from

"Sid Vicious hated us. He called us a bunch of poseurs, and in a way he was right." STEVE SEVERIN

Swanky Mode, a bodice, stilettos and full make-up." It was still mid-afternoon. "We went back to her house, where her mum served us pate on toast with Earl Grey tea. It was kind of formal except that she was being really naughty. Afterwards, we decided to go to SEX."

"My first memories of Sioux is when she used to come into Let It Rock [renamed Sex in 1975] when I worked there," recalls Glen Matlock. "She was one of a crowd who'd trawl up and down the King's Road from ACME Attractions to Malcolm's shop on a Saturday afternoon. They were a bit different from the rest – a bit

glam rock, a bit Velvet Underground, a bit Roxy Music. The forerunners of punk - The Bromley Contingent."

Simon Barker had been the first among the Bromley set to see the Sex Pistols, when they played at nearby Ravensbourne College Of Art on 9 December 1975. By spring 1976, Barker and Steven Bailey had become regulars at their shows. And one night, Sioux - who'd previously seen John Cale, Lou Reed, Hunter/Ronson, Roxy Music and not much else – went with them. "It was amazing, great theatre," she says. "I'd never seen a band intimidate and repel an audience like that before."

BY THE TIME of the Pistols' May 1976 100 Club residency, a gang of Bromley regulars had begun to show up, their number increasing over the summer. When the Pistols hit the Screen On The Green, Islington on 29 August, they were in danger of being upstaged by their extravagant suburban supporters. The bizarre spectacle that was Siouxsie, an eye-catching clash of bare white flesh and black rubber fetish-wear, her breasts and swastika armband provocatively displayed, was further evidence of the extraordinary effect the Pistols were having.

As the idea of punk as a movement took hold, it was inevitable that some of the Pistols' earliest fans would take the do-it-yourself aesthetic at face value and form their own bands. One night at Louise's in Soho, when Malcolm McLaren was fretting that he'd lost a support band for the forthcoming 100 Club Punk Rock Festival, Siouxsie blurted out: "We'll play." Taking a cue from Cry Of The Banshee, a Hammer Horror film shown on television a few nights earlier, a new band was born.

When Siouxsie And The Banshees debuted, on 20 September 1976, with a bottom-of-the-bill appearance at the first night of the festival, they'd had just one aborted rehearsal and a vague notion that they were going to 'play' The Lord's Prayer until they got thrown off the stage. The makeshift band - Sid Vicious on drums, (future Ant) Marco Pirroni on guitar, Steven Severin on bass and singer Siouxsie – became the archetypal "Can't play but we'll give it a go" punk-rock stage invaders. Their impro-vised performance may have been greeted with beery bonhomie, but the legend persisted: the Banshees, swastikas'n'all, were truly untrained and untouchable.

"The gig established that sense of bloodyminded-ness," reckons Marco Pirroni. "We're gonna go up there in a packed club, having never rehearsed, having never written any songs, having never tried to write any songs, and just play. It really was, 'We don't give a fuck.'"

Even some among their fellow Pistols enthusiasts regarded the Bromley Contingent with contempt. "Sid Vicious hated us," says Berlin. "He called us a bunch of poseurs, and in a way he was right. All we did was stand

around, give off attitude and look incredible. After all, what is posing besides standing there being yourself and presenting your creation?"

HAVING BRAVED THE limelight once, Sioux and Severin, who'd grown close since the summer, realised that posing from the stalls had its limits. "From the beginning, I'd harboured a dream of being a musician," Severin admitted, "but I never saw any way of doing it." Siouxsie had even recorded a version of The Velvet Underground's What Goes On, backed by another Bromley boy Billy Broad (alias Idol) on guitar, to take with her to auditions she'd find in the music press classifieds. Invariably, they wanted some ballsy, Janis Joplin or Maggie Bell type. Invariably, she was eminently unsuitable.

Right from the beginning, her voice was as startlingly inventive as her costumes. "Steven played me a tape of some songs where she'd sung along to a couple of records, *[Bowie's]* John, I'm Only Dancing and maybe Rebel, Rebel," recalled Simon Barker, "and it was incredible. She sung exactly as she later did in the Banshees. It was purely her own style. She wasn't influenced by anybody. And in that respect, the voice completely mirrors her personality."

Just as the band would. But first, Sioux had her five minutes of tabloid infamy after the punk witch-hunt that followed the Pistols' 'fuck'-word frolics on LWT's Today show. Two days later, on 3 December 1976, the Daily Mirror outraged the nation with a front-page shot of her, bottle-blonde, thumbing her braces, a star painted over one eye, next to the headline: "SIOUXSIE'S A PUNK SHOCKER". In another piece, Severin – sporting two-tone hair and handcuffs, his torn T-shirt mutilated with paint, paperclips, safety pins and curtain runners – told The Sun: "Our clothes reflect hard times. They're also a revolt against things like Mick Jagger's diamond-studded teeth."

The band began gigging in earnest on 24 February 1977 with a 20-minute set supporting Johnny Thunders' Heartbreakers at the Red Deer in Croydon, and very soon were having public slanging matches with more laddish punk combos like The Damned.

1977 witnessed a torrent of guitar-swinging punk opportunists, many of whom quickly snagged record deals. But three bands proved too hot to handle: The Slits, Adam And The Ants and Siouxsie And The Banshees. The Slits were perceived as unruly women, the Ants as overly obsessed with Nazi chic. The Banshees' reputation was tainted by both perceptions.

A piece written by Jane Suck in Sounds in June 1977 did much to typecast the Banshees. Under an "Outrage Is The Game, Siouxsie And The Banshees Is The Name"

heading, the writer claimed the band "reckon Belsen was a gas!". While gallows humour had been a keen feature of punk's early taboo-bashing sensibility, the Banshees were now becoming sensitive that their shock tactics were being misconstrued. "We're not Nazis," they complained in a follow-up letter, "and we are getting pissed off for being shunned because of misquotes by sensation-seeking reporters."

For a band that neither had, nor sought out, friends in the music business, the patronage of faded glam star Marc Bolan was strangely perfect. He plugged them in his Record Mirror column, and spoke about producing them and getting the band exposure on his television show. But his death in a car accident at the end of September 1977 cruelly closed that particular chapter. That same month, NME's Julie Burchill was putting the knife in, gloating that Siouxsie would

"We heard Hong Kong Garden and we all went potty. It was a brilliant record." GEORGE McMANUS, POLYDOR RECORDS

never surpass her "Sun centrespread". The Banshees aroused strong opinions.

In December, Sounds put Siouxsie on the cover of an issue that fanfared "New Musick". She was, the magazine boldly decided, "The Ice Queen". Vivien Goldman's article proved the point. "I could never be a nurse, helping old people with bedpans and all that shit," Siouxsie told her. "I don't like a lot of people. I think everyone should help themselves." She claimed she laughed when her father died, and that she hated the idea of being worshipped by an audience: "That's so false." Worst of all were the record labels. "Look at all these arseholes that are signed up," she spat. "That's proof."

(Above) The Banshees at Polydor's London offices, March 1979.

(Right) Doing a little research at north London's Roundhouse.

But as Les Mills' graffiti campaign suggested, the band had been busy acquiring a hardcore following through regular gigging and a fast-improving set. Although another suburban boy, drummer Kenny Morris, had joined in time for the new line-up's debut gig in Croydon, they didn't find the right guitarist until 11 July 1977, when John McKay made his debut at the Vortex.

ART STUDENTS WITH great faces, Morris and McKay shared Sioux and Severin's conception of the band as an innovative, iconoclastic work of art. Morris's remarkable voodoo vibe was as much Glitter Band stomp as it was a refinement of Maureen Tucker of The Velvet Underground's cymbal-free style. Meanwhile, Sioux was issuing instructions to the equally gifted McKay. "I played him the soundtracks to Psycho and The Omen," she told me in 2003, "and said that was the sound we wanted. I wanted music to be exciting, but with a sense of fear, of uneasiness to it. We didn't want the guitar to sound like a guitar. It had to sound like stabbing violins, and he seemed to be into that."

United in their siege mentality, and in their commitment, Siouxsie And The Banshees shrugged off financial hardship and knocks in the press. "We were such a tight unit," Morris said, "and it was lovely when it was like that. John and I both felt like we'd met our kindred spirits. It was like, 'How could this possibly be? Aren't we lucky.'"

Eventually, on 9 June 1978, the Banshees secured the contract they wanted. According to Polydor Records' head of marketing, George McManus, the SIGN THE BANSHEES graffiti played its part in securing the label's interest. But, he reckoned, one song clinched it. "We heard Hong Kong Garden and we all went potty. It was an absolutely brilliant record."

The Banshees sealed the deal with a sell-out gig at the Roundhouse. New songs such as Jigsaw Feeling, driven by one of Severin's skull-pummelling basslines that did so much to define the band's sound, and the labyrinthine Switch, reinforced the idea that this was the era's most gifted, challenging band.

Hong Hong Garden charted, just as Polydor hoped it would, as did their debut album The Scream, one of the most critically acclaimed records of 1978. In a piece written by Pete Silverton for Sounds at the end of the year, the Banshees were dubbed "The Most Elitist Band

In The World". It was true: no other contemporary group sounded so uncompromising, or struck such a devilishly handsome pose.

"Did we feel like the ultimate rock band? Yes, absolutely," Severin told me years later. "It was the best-looking band I'd ever seen too. Those early pictures now look so iconic. The difficulty was following up that first success, how to step up the pace and get into the big league. Some people can and some people can't."

The haste with which the Banshees recorded their second album, September 1979's Join Hands, which included a reworking of The Lord's Prayer to flesh out the material, had left Kenny Morris and John McKay seething. "It was absolute shit," Morris said later. The pair were also concerned that manager Nils Stevenson was increasingly calling the shots – and inevitably siding with Sioux and Severin. On 7 September, right at the start of a huge nationwide tour, the pair quit the band.

The flashpoint had been a signing session at a record shop in Aberdeen. After a row over the sale of promotional copies of the new LP, the pair walked out, returned to their hotel rooms to pack, then took a cab to the nearest airport and flew off into total obscurity. Sioux and Severin were livid. "You have my blessing to beat shit out of them," she announced later that evening at Aberdeen's Capital Theatre, where the pair performed an impromptu version of The Lord's Prayer backed by support band The Cure.

McKay and Morris's departure brought an abrupt close to the first, dramatic chapter of the Siouxsie And The Banshees story. But in many ways it marked a new beginning. Chastened by the experience, Sioux and Severin rebuilt the Banshees with drummer Budgie and guitarist John McGeoch, and during the early 1980s they became the most successful of all the bands with roots in the punk era. They spawned an entire subculture, too, with Siouxsie lookalikes sprouting up everywhere, and a wave of 'goth' bands – led by Joy Division and The Cure – emerging in their wake. After much success, even in America which had proved bullishly resistant to punk, the Banshees finally called it a day in July 1995.

"To call them punk or goth is really only part of the story," says Marc Almond. "They've always been innovators. And they've influenced everyone from Massive Attack to Björk, PJ Harvey to The Cocteau Twins. Like the Velvet Underground, Siouxsie And The Banshees sum up an era, and yet transcend it too."

the writing on the wall

Brash, basic, difficult to ignore – flyers and posters gave glorious expression to the punk scene's do-it-yourself ethic.

11,18
100 OXFORD S

T. J. DAVIDSON presents
A HIGH ENERGY PUNK NIGHT
THE DRONES
&
GENERATION X
FROM LONDON
PLUS FULL DISCO
on FRIDAY, 17th DECEMBER, 1976
at the HOULDSWORTH HALL
Commencing 7.30 p.m.   Tickets 75p

LESSER FREE TRADE HALL
FREE TRADE HALL–PETER ST MANCHESTER
£1.00   TUESDAY 20th JULY 7.30pm £1.00
SEX PISTOLS
WITH SLAUGHTER
AND THE DOGS
BUT BUZZCOCKS
TICKETS AT FREE TRADE HALL £1.00 BOOKING OFFI

GOD BLESS **television** + KEEP THE
one two many mornings...
BUZZCOCKS
MACAL
PERFORMANCE AT TH
LESSER F

WARNING
SLAUGHTER & THE DOGS
WILL TEAR APART!

Roll up, roll up…

Linder Sterling cut up magazines to promote the Buzzcocks, Jamie Reid mixed up type styles for the Pistols – and one designer omitted a vital vowel…

ARTWORK BY LINDER

POSTERS FROM: PAUL BURGESS, MATTHEW NORMAN @ MANCHESTER DISTRICT MUSIC ARCHIVE

121

"ONE, TWO

NEVER MIND THE BOLLOCKS HERE'S THE

HERE'S THE

GOD Save THE QUEEN

Sex Pistols

THREE, FOUR!"

A short, sharp shock: The 20 Best British Punk Singles.

1 God Save The Queen
Sex Pistols
MAY 1977

God Save The Queen burst upon the world with the intention of stirring up a storm mysteriously failed to reach Number 1. There were even rumours of a fix by trade body the BPI when the Jubilee week chart put Rod Stewart on top. So the music industry's long march to political respectability continued; but punk and the Sex Pistols were trapped in a cul-de-sac. As the song said: "No future"; the group were vilified, banned and physically attacked. Like the House Of Windsor, the Pistols faced years of mixed fortunes, marked by premature death and the faint aroma of underachievement, but also lingering affection in the British psyche.

2 New Rose
The Damned
NOVEMBER 1976

It's striking to note that Britain's first punk record was a teenage love song. The Damned had no agenda and none of The Clash's ideological top-dressing. They revelled, instead, in the sheer pleasure of noise and the classically retro values of teenage pop. Dave Vanian's mumbled introduction "Is she really going out with him?" was a quotation from The Shangri-Las' Leader Of The Pack, while the B-side was a cover of The Beatles' Help!. Released a couple of weeks before Anarchy In The UK, New Rose was an invigorating racket. The breathless rush of a new affair was a wonderfully apt overture for punk itself.

binned the band. Musically, the single remains a landmark. The bubbling stew of provocative ideas in the song was supplied by Malcolm McLaren, Vivienne Westwood and graphic artist Jamie Reid, brilliantly distilled by Rotten and soundtracked with violent panache by the band and producer Chris Thomas. As the debut release by the figureheads of British punk, Anarchy… opened deep divisions. The day this record came out, you were either with the resistance or the collaborators.

4 White Riot
The Clash
MARCH 1977

 The 1976 Notting Hill Carnival witnessed a spectacular eruption of civic tensions as the police fought running battles with black youths. The rioters found a couple of pale-faced recruits in Joe Strummer and Paul Simonon, who hurled bricks and tried to
po
fo
of

charge, taken at the same carnival, would soon adorn The Clash's first album.

5 In The City
The Jam
APRIL 1977

 The Jam's image of sharp suits and shiny shoes meant the inner-London clique who ruled punk rock viewed the band with suspicion. It didn't start that way – teenage out-of-towner Paul Weller, from Woking in Surrey, had written In The City as a declaration of his love for the London punk scene. But when The Jam released the song as their debut, Weller was already disillusioned. As it turned out, the group had no need of in-crowd endorsement; this nervy rush struck an instant chord in the desolation of the provinces. For sheer attack, The Jam rivalled any 'official' punk act, while Weller's career would prove the sturdiest of them all.

6 Complete Control
The Clash
SEPTEMBER 1977

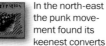 The title made

unauthorised single. But it's the added boom of reggae producer Lee Perry that lends an even more epic texture to the ranting.

7 Spiral Scratch EP
Buzzcocks
JANUARY 1977

 When punk reached the North of England it began to take on unpredictable new forms. Manchester was the first provincial city to develop a thriving punk scene of its own, largely inspired by a Sex Pistols visit that Buzzcocks Pete Shelley and Howard Devoto helped organise. The key track of this EP was the sardonic Boredom, laced with a humorous detachment and stiffened with the pop vitality that Shelley would soon become proficient in.

8 Don't Dictate
Penetration
NOVEMBER 1977

 In the north-east the punk movement found its keenest converts

9 Neat Neat Neat
The Damned
FEBRUARY 1977

 Although its lyric comes close to being disjointed gibberish, the very meaninglessness of Neat Neat Neat supports the claim that The Damned were a truer punk group than either the Sex Pistols or The Clash. Their entire first album, from which the track is taken, was recorded by Nick Lowe in less than a day. Released as the follow-up to New Rose, Neat Neat Neat was even more stripped down than its predecessor. The Damned soon became commanders of punk's pantomime wing, but tracks such as this were a testimony to the tightly drilled band of belligerent little bastards they remained at heart.

10 Oh Bondage, Up Yours!
X-Ray Spex
OCTOBER 1977

The London punk movement was a small army of reinvented

11 Something Better Change

The Stranglers

JULY 1977

There were two kinds of punk band: the sort that was inspired into existence by seeing the Sex Pistols, and the sort that made a shrewd sideways move when they saw how the wind was changing direction. Clearly in the latter category, the elderly Stranglers overcame their lack of authenticity by out-yobbing every young band in town; Something Better Change was rich in rhetorical anger. But if The Stranglers were old hippies, they were born at Altamont, not Woodstock.

12 Eddie And The Hot Rods

Teenage Depression

NOVEMBER 1976

Despite their youth and ferocity, Eddie And The Hot Rods appeared on the scene too early to be considered punk. And by the time it arrived they showed no inclination to take part. They were really a bluesy rock'n'roll band from the same Canvey Island stable as their mentors Dr Feelgood. But Teenage Depression is their punkiest moment, in the same goosed-up Eddie Cochran spirit that galvanised the Pistols.

13 We Vibrate

The Vibrators

NOVEMBER 1976

The larky name betrayed The Vibrators' pre-punk mentality: they were from the pop conveyor belt of producer Mickie Most's RAK label and gave the impression of old lags who could play this stuff standing on their heads. Having made the necessary trips to the barber's, they emerged with breezy knockabout numbers such as this, a knowing pastiche of early 1960s dance craze numbers like The Loco-Motion. Bubblegum punk by men who could barely take the whole thing seriously.

14 Your Generation

Generation X

SEPTEMBER 1977

Tony James had been among the pool of players who gave rise to The Clash and The Damned, while Billy Idol was an ace face in the 'Bromley Contingent' of early Pistols fans. But by the time they formed Generation X, the pair's commercial yearnings were obvious, and they were the first punk band who looked made for Top Of The Pops. Your Generation is punk rebellion in a shrink-wrapped package.

15 One Chord Wonders

The Adverts

APRIL 1977

Much to the band's discomfort, guitarist TV Smith's songwriting was eclipsed by the allure of bassist Gaye Advert, one of British punk's few female pin-ups. Smith composed One Chord Wonders in 20 minutes, giving it a stomping neo-glam appeal, while its cheerful assault on muso values makes for the perfect punk statement: a celebration

16 Whole Wide World

Wreckless Eric

AUGUST 1977

Stiff Records specialised in acquiring those waifs and strays, such as Ian Dury and Elvis Costello, whose careers were made possible by punk without being quite punks themselves. Wreckless Eric was another. This is the howl of a lonely romantic, dreaming of love with 'totty' on sun-kissed beaches. You could admire his poetic desperation without really fancying his chances.

17 Where Have All The Boot Boys Gone?

Slaughter And The Dogs

SEPTEMBER 1977

Whereas the punk mainstream would soon put on primary colours and become 'new wave', the purist fringes kept the faith. Some took the proletarian, brutalist path pioneered by Manchester's Slaughter And The Dogs. It's not a pretty thing, this garbled lament for skinhead glory, but you'd trust it to charge across no-man's land in a hail of bullets.

18 Shadow

The Lurkers

JULY 1977

As Johann Strauss was to the waltz, so The Lurkers were to the pogo. Shadow is a Ramones-style bash, built around a riff of limited ambition, and a favourite for the perpendicular dance style evolved by punks to accommodate their rhythmic shortcomings and confined floor-space. It's often the simplest life-forms that are hardest to eradicate, and The Lurkers are known to be gigging still.

19 Right To Work

Chelsea

JUNE 1977

Life took on a sombre hue for Gene October when his band-mates Tony James and Billy Idol left Chelsea to form Generation X. In the best traditions of show business, he picked himself up and penned this defiant tirade. Many mistook it for an attack on capitalism, but October's wrath was actually directed at trade union 'closed shop' policies. In his deserted state he identified with workers who were denied their livelihoods.

20 Lookin' After No. 1

Boomtown Rats

AUGUST 1977

Isolation from the London scene enabled Dublin's Boomtown Rats to undergo an opportunist punk makeover in privacy. Like Paul Weller, singer Bob Geldof was an object of suspicion among the tastemakers, but Top Of The Pops allowed the Rats to leapfrog critics and reach the public directly. For many, Lookin' After No. 1 was the first punk they encountered, and it defined the chart-punk style: catchy, fast and brattish.

CHAPTER TWO

NEWSDESK

UNK AKES OFF!

K ROCK moves from
ground to overground
month when the leading
sh bands follow up their
singles with their own
tours with top
erican bands who are
ing in.

E DAMNED, whose first
ngle, 'New Rose' (coupled
with Lennon And
McCartney's 'Help') has just
been released by Stiff, have
 already scheduled several
dates through November on
their own. In addition, they
will be special guests on the
FLAMIN' GROOVIES'
British tour which starts on
November 11.

The Damned's single sold
4,000 copies last week and in
order to make it available
quickly throughout the
country Stiff have signed a
special one-off deal for the
manufacture and distribution
of 'New Rose' with United
Artist.

Stiff's A&R manager
Tyrone Contract told
SOUNDS this week:
"We have placed the Damned
single with United Artists
company as they were the only
company who would keep the
original Stiff logo, label and
catalogue number and distribute the record in its original
picture sleeve." The deal
takes effect from this Wednesday.

The Damned headline the
following gigs on their own
through November: London
Hope And Anchor 2, Canter-
bury Kent University 3, Nor-
wich Keswick College 13,
London Finchley Manor Hill
Secondary School (with
Slaughter And The Dogs and
Eater), Liverpool Eric's 26
and Manchester Electric
Circus 28.

Between November 3 and
11 the Damned will start
recording their first album
which will be released by Stiff

SEX PISTOLS: T

although no dat
fixed.
And the band a
guests on
GROOVIES' Britis
which begins at Red
ham Bowl on Novem
tour continues at Li
Eric's 12, Birmin

MALLARD

CLOVER
MEAL TICKET

DARTS
EX Rocky Sharp
Tuesday, September 14th Free
ISAAC GUILLORY
Wednesday, September 15th Free
CALICO
Thursday, September 16th Free
THE DERELICTS

WORDS ST ALBANS CITY HALL

EDGAR BROUGHTON BAND
plus SKY plus VAMBO

RING 01-855 7777
to Advertise

MAN IN THE MOON 392 Kings Road SW3

SQUIRT
adm. 60p
BURLESQUE
PACIFIC EARDRUM
adm. 75p

SPECIAL WEEK AT THE ROCKGARDEN

CIMARRONS
(OUR FIRST REGGAE NIGHT
FEATURING ONE OF THE BEST)

GONZALEZ
SAT. SEPT 11 £1.75

LEE KOSMIN
BAND

SURPRISE SISTERS

Fergus

His First Single
GOTCHA NOW
IS ON PALADIN
PAL 7

THE NASHVILLE Room
Corner Cromwell Road/North End Road
(Ads West Kensington Tube) 603 6071

Thursday, September 9th   Free
BOWLES BROTHERS
Friday, September 10th Saturday September 11 £1.00
The Sensational
MEAL TICKET
Sunday, September 12th   60p
From the USA
TRAIN
Monday, September   Free
NAT'S WOO

Pistols sign EMI deal

E SEX ISTOLS,   the   A&R manager of EMI, Nick
ing Bri   'wave'   is a group
record   that p
o-ye   and
ear   a li
riday   iness
Pisto   the   up
recording a single, 'Anarchy In   'That's   they
                                     wouldn't sign the group; they took
                                      all too personally. But what other

THE BEGINNING OF THE END

Within 18 months, punk had reached a commercial peak. But with record labels cashing in and the Pistols and Damned splitting up, the dream was rapidly turning sour…

i'm a mess

Sid Vicious began life as Simon John Ritchie, a contradictory bundle of pop-star ambition and psychotic tendencies. How did he go from loose cannon to Sex Pistol?

IN THE BITTERLY cold winter of 1975/6, a year before they were to perform together in the Sex Pistols, the future Sid Vicious and Johnny Rotten shared a squat together in Hampstead, north London. Built in the 1880s, and hidden away from view like a deformed royal scion, New Court comprises two imposing tenement blocks looming over a small grass square. According to locals, the flats have a dark history involving suicides, murders, fights. In the 1970s, after some well-connected drug dealers moved in, they became a popular hangout for dissolute aristos and rock-star druggies, including Marc Bolan.

New Court's darkness seemed to be pervasive, creeping into visitors and inhabitants. It was here that Sid Vicious, then known as John Beverley or 'Spiky John', was said to have strangled a cat and slashed his arms with the lid of a tin can. It was also where he probably first used heroin.

"I didn't like going up there," says Jah Wobble, alias John Wardle, the third of the unholy trinity of 'Johns' – Lydon, Beverley, Wardle – whom punk would soon make famous. "It had a weird force. I think I only visited twice. There were stories of kittens being thrown out of windows – I was told that Sid did it. And there was a story about Sid mugging an old lady. It was a rumour, but I couldn't say he wasn't capable of it."

There are other, contradictory stories about Sid at New Court. Lindy Poltock, who would later marry The Clash's road manager, Johnny Green, lived there. She recalled the old ladies at New Court adoring Sid. Apparently, he would always stop for a chat and carry their

shopping bags up the stairs. She thought him vulnerable, but very intelligent, very witty, very good company.

It was a view shared by many. "He was the last person you'd call dumb," says Mike Baess, a good friend of Sid's during 1975 and '76. "There are a lot of tall stories circulating these days which make Sid out to be tougher and more frightening than he really was. He was a big softie at heart."

But the truth was that, even if he didn't kill a cat, he repeatedly smashed a kitten against a wall after it had pissed on his bed (a friend finished the poor thing off; Sid couldn't bring himself to do it). What's more, he almost certainly roasted a guinea pig alive and robbed at least one old lady at knifepoint.

Even before he ever became a star, it seems, Sid had a knack of keeping people guessing about who and what he really was.

THERE CAN BE little doubt that Sid's death in 1979, from a heroin overdose in a New York apartment after allegedly killing his girlfriend, Nancy Spungen, elevated him into punk's greatest icon. Today, he's one of the chosen few who enjoy a symbolic relationship with his age: nihilistic, senseless, empty, vain, talentless, iconic. He's a gift for students of postmodern theory, who find his myriad identities, instant celebrity, self-inflicted wounds and fascination with Nazis endlessly meaningful, but the man behind them elusive and one-dimensional. But somewhere at the bottom of it all, when you peel off the layers of myth, Sid Vicious was an extremely contradictory and complex human being. Jah Wobble knew Sid well, and understands implicitly why his old pal has become a Brit-Art conceit.

"Sid was all about image," he explains. "He was one of the pioneers of dumbing down. It's certainly related to existentialism and the whole postmodern thing. Not really being part of anything or having an identity. It was fucking annoying, actually. With John Lydon there were always moments to reflect about stuff you liked. With Sid there was no real empathy, he hated everything."

Sid was born Simon John Ritchie in London, on 10 May 1957, to parents Anne and John. His father, a former grenadier guard, left the family in the early '60s. Anne was by all accounts something of a beatnik. and took Simon to live in Ibiza for a short time. The boy quickly became accustomed to an unsettled life. Back in England, Anne married a middle-class Kentish man called Chris Beverley, who died of cancer soon afterwards, in 1965. Before the death of his stepfather Sid was earmarked for a place at a posh boarding school. Instead, in 1968 he ended up at Sandown Court, a rough secondary modern in Tunbridge Wells, the town where Sid and his mother lived for four years.

Silly thing: Sid at Kingsway College, autumn 1975, and (inset) on tour with the Pistols in the US, 1978.

(Previous page) In Penzance on the SPOTS (Sex Pistols On Tour Secretly) trek, September 1977.

When he was 12 or 13 Sid rebelled. An awareness of his dysfunctional home life may have been one reason. His search for an identity led him to become an incorrigible attention-seeker and general nuisance. Something of a loner, he became disruptive in class and lost all interest in schoolwork.

"He became a pain in the arse, basically," says Colebrooke. "It was funny for the first lesson every day, but then it quickly got boring. One day, Simon managed to carve his initials about a quarter-inch deep into an old desk in the science lab. He must have used a knife. He was quite proud of that."

There were more alarming incidents. In his last year at Sandown Court, he got into a fight with a fellow pupil. A crowd gathered outside the school to watch Sid beat up his opponent. While other kids would be content with meting out a split lip or bloody nose, Sid kept on and on. A passing motorist was concerned enough to stop and pull the boys apart. Sid took a swing at him as well.

Colebrooke and his friends were unsettled by Beverley's latent ferocity. He was never a bully, but he was clearly someone not to be messed with. He had an unpredictable temper. He was also slightly mysterious. Besides the fact that he kept ferrets, and didn't have a dad around, no one knew much about Sid's life outside school, least of all that his mother, Anne, was a junkie. Taking heroin since the early '60s, she was by the early '70s an intravenous user.

WHEN JAH WOBBLE met Sid in 1974, the Pistols' future bassist was 17 and living with his mother in a council tower block on Queensbridge Road in Haggerston, east London. They'd moved back to the capital a couple of years previously, and were constantly being re-housed. At the time Wobble was attending Kingsway, a further education college in Kings Cross, which catered for day-release apprentices, wayward kids belatedly sitting their O levels (like Wobble) and arty A level students. There, Wobble had befriended an acerbic Hawkwind fan from Finsbury Park called John Lydon and his strange, lanky mate.

Wobble remembers Sid, a year his elder, as good fun and sparky. He was now calling himself by his middle-name, John. The three Johns bonded, Wobble says, because of their lively personalities, lower-class backgrounds, keen intelligence and nose for trouble. They

"Sid was all about image. He was one of the pioneers of dumbing down." JAH WOBBLE

"When he first arrived, he was very well behaved and didn't stand out," recalls classmate Jeremy Colebrooke. "He was bright and quite good at football. I remember him as tall and thin and almost Chinese-looking. He had jet-black hair, a round face and slitted eyes, which were deep brown with a darkness around them. His mother must have been quite arty and bohemian for the time, because Simon always ponged of garlic, which was highly unusual back then."

all loved music and getting drunk. More significantly, perhaps, they were outsiders. According to Wobble, "We shared a deep dissatisfaction about the world and most of the people in it."

Barely old enough to get served in pubs, Wobble was shocked when he visited Sid's flat. "I remember going round there with Lydon," he says. "Sid and his mum were openly using needles. Sid was shooting up amphetamines. I was 16 years old – I'd never seen anything like that before. Shooting up drugs with your mum! It wasn't bohemian. It was gloomy, a certain sort of gloom you get around heroin and class-A drugs." Sid, who used Vaseline to slick back his hair, slumped backwards after taking his hit and left a greasy trail on the wallpaper.

The experience had a depressing effect on Wobble. These days a scholar of the occult, he explains that Haggerston is on the fringes of east London's marshlands, associated in ancient times with pagan rites; to this day, he says, the area maintains a strange, occultish vibe. His trip to the Beverleys' flat spooked him. It also shows just how messed up the young John Beverley was. His was exactly the kind of alienated, dysfunctional, high-rise existence punk would soon come to symbolise. It's tempting to think that Sid was already condemned.

Lydon and Beverley had previously been at school together in Hackney. They were both Bowie, Eno and Roxy freaks, and by all accounts looked extraordinary: John with his long, dyed-red hair and Sid dressed head to toe in black.

Though Sid was yet to enroll at Kingsway, he latched on to its social scene. He hung out in the common room, smoking joints and goofing around. Simone Stenfors, later a punk scenester, met him at a Hallowe'en party in October 1974. "He looked completely different to everyone else. He wore black and looked like Johnny Depp in Cry Baby. I fancied him immediately. He was very shy. Now I realise that I probably petrified him. He didn't have a girlfriend. He never had a girlfriend."

"Sid always knew how to look good," adds Mike Baess, who studied at Kingsway. "His role models must have been the leather-era Elvis and James Dean. He was the sort of bloke everyone looked at when he came in the room. I think he knew he had that power and deliberately cultivated it. He gained our respect by being so different."

MIKE BAESS AND John Beverley – who gained his 'Spiky' epithet after adopting a proto-punk crop in early 1975 – started hanging out together. They shared a passion for Roxy Music, Pink Fairies, John Cale, Eno and Syd Barrett-era Pink Floyd. Every Saturday, they'd meet with other friends in Portobello Road under the Westway and go

shopping for bootlegs (Sid would steal his), then meet up on Sunday afternoon at The Roundhouse. It appears Sid also had a soft spot for jazz-rock: he loved to get stoned with a pal called Mandy Pete and listen to Weather Report and Stanley Clarke.

Mike Baess's description of Sid at this time is quite charming: he seems to have been the slightly dopey, loveable oaf you glimpse in some Sex Pistols footage. He was out of control, but still harmless. Mike stresses that he "never paid for anything, he just blagged his way through life. He didn't give a fuck, which was fantastic. He would always nick his dinners from the canteen – if the dinner lady shouted out, 'Oi! Come back and pay!', he'd shout, 'Fuck off!', then run away. But he always got away with it. He was antisocial but almost to a comical degree.

"Sid was actually very bright. There was an intellect at play there that never really surfaced. It never had a chance to. But you couldn't pull the wool over his eyes or spin him a yarn. He was wise. Sometimes you'd look into those

(Right) Sid with "Gimme A Fix" scrawled on his chest, Dallas Longhorn Ballroom, 10 January 1978.

(Below) With his mother Anne Beverley after being released from jail, New York, October 1978.

"Sid looked completely different to everyone else – like Johnny Depp in Cry Baby." PUNK SCENESTER SIMONE STENFORS

brown eyes, and see someone who knew no fear. It could send a shiver down your spine."

Towards the end of 1975, Mike Baess saw a dramatic change in 'Spiky John'. The date, interestingly, coincides with his best mate John Lydon's induction into the Sex Pistols. As a kid who thrived on what psychologists term 'negative attention', it's possible he resented being left on the sidelines – especially since he was by then as much a fixture as Rotten at Malcolm McLaren's SEX boutique, and arguably the more obvious frontman.

Now living at New Court, he was taking increasing amounts of speed, which made him unpredictable and aggressive. Jah Wobble remembers Sid's 'fuck you' carapace hardening. He began picking fights in pubs that he knew he'd lose. Perplexingly non-sexual, he still had no girlfriend, casual or otherwise. "I don't think he knew how to talk to girls," argues Baess. "But I don't

think he was gay. He preferred attention from older, maternal figures."

For Mike, one incident more than any other illustrates Sid's transition from fun-loving idiot-savant to nasty bastard. "A mate of mine called Chris had a party in Oxford. This was in October 1975. A load of us went up by coach. Sid brought along some powder he tried to pass off as speed. It was actually *[the domestic cleaning agent]*Vim. Some guy bought some, took it and had to be taken to hospital. They had to pump his chest to revive him. That wasn't funny. That was horrible. I was there – it happened."

Soon after, Mike bumped into Sid one night in the dingy alleyway behind New Court. Sid boasted that he'd just mugged an old lady, then produced a flick-knife and a small leather lady's purse full of money to prove it. Was it a wind-up? Baess doesn't think so. He was genuinely scared by Sid's threatening manner. It seemed that when he was on drugs (chiefly mainlined speed), which was increasingly often, Sid no longer could differentiate between what most of us would describe as amusing delinquent behaviour and unacceptable, cowardly acts of violence. It was around this time that he acquired the name Sid Vicious. Depending on whom you believe, this was either after Lydon's pet hamster or Beverley's love for Syd Barrett. Whichever, each new name change seemed to signal not so much a reinvention as another incremental step towards his self-obliteration.

NO FATHER FIGURE, junkie mum, itinerant childhood, breadline existence… it was hardly the foundation of a content and fulfilled personality. Also, when someone seeks negative attention, they often have to up the ante to generate the same intensity of response, leading them to behave ever more outrageously.

This, indeed, is what happened with Sid throughout 1976, when the spotlight cast on the Sex Pistols, and Lydon in particular, threatened to leave him in the shadows. His impulse to command centre-stage revealed itself, quite literally, at the Pistols' gig at the Nashville on 23 April. Kate Simon's photos show Sid, resplendent in gold lamé Elvis jacket, poised to join the stage-front punch-up started by Vivienne Westwood. As the Pistols' Number 1 fan, he's standing so close to the stage as to be almost on it.

Sid at the 100 Club Punk Festival with (from left) Viv Albertine, Siouxsie and Steve Severin, 20 September, 1976.

(Inset) Ready to ruck during the Pistols gig at the Nashville Rooms, 23 April 1976.

By the summer, the hottest that century, he'd taken steps to form his own group, Flowers Of Romance. With his instinct for originality and striking imagery, he formulated the idea of an all-girl backing band with him as frontman. The initial line-up featured Sarah Hall on bass, Viv Albertine on guitar and Palmolive on drums (the latter pair would go on to form The Slits). The group rehearsed in the basement of 42 Orsett Terrace,

mostly because Sid was lazy and got bored quickly. One evening after a practice, he and Paloma fell into conversation about politics. "He made a statement about liking Nazis and being a racist," she says. "I told him why I disagreed with his point of view. Soon after that he kicked me out of the band."

Paloma accepts that Sid may simply have been acting provocatively. It wasn't unusual for him to say idiotic things for effect. But he also clearly shared punk's fascination with the Third Reich and Nazi imagery. "My perception was that he was a kid who was childish and rebelling against everything," she says. "I think the whole thing with the hate and anger of punk was it took him further than he wanted to go. There was a dark force there that was pushing him on. We were all playing with it, we liked to show off and look mean, but you have to be careful you're not taken in by it."

IN SEPTEMBER, SID was co-opted to play drums in the fledgling Siouxsie And The Banshees, hastily assembled to kick off the infamous punk festival at the 100 Club. In under a week, Vicious was accelerated from punk fan to bona fide group member. This clearly wasn't enough attention. The following evening, while watching The Damned, he threw a glass tankard against a pillar, blinding a girl in one eye. He was arrested by the police and beaten up. In one moment of gross stupidity, Sid became as famous to music press readers as his pal Johnny Rotten.

During his subsequent week-long incarceration at Ashford Remand Centre, Sid suffered from nightmares and attacks of paranoia. He forbade his mother to visit him, lest the other inmates – presumably genuine hardcases – think him a mummy's boy. Vivienne Westwood ill-advisedly sent the 19-year-old a copy of Helter Skelter, the story of the Manson Murders. Isolated and scared, Sid grew another outer layer.

On his release, Vicious bedded down at The Clash's rehearsal space in Camden Town. He found he'd become a kind of punk superstar – and martyr. Still desperate to front a group, he tried to revive The Flowers Of Romance. But by now many of his friends, including Jah Wobble, found it impossible to penetrate his goofy-obnoxious exterior. He was edging towards his final phase as a heroically confused and misanthropic lunatic.

The theatre for his complete self-destruction was presented in March 1977 when he was invited to join the Sex Pistols following Glen Matlock's departure. "I remember thinking, 'I can't wait to see how this works out!'" laughs Jah Wobble. 'But it wasn't funny. There was a darkness about McLaren, that manipulation… it wasn't good. I never had that same connection with Sid that I had with Lydon. But, y'know, Sid was our mate."

'Sid was determined to get noticed. He wanted to be in a band. We all did.' PALMOLIVE, THE SLITS

the squat where Palmolive, a Spanish emigré, lived with her then boyfriend Joe Strummer.

"I'd seen Sid at the pub gig with the big fight," recalls Palmolive, who's long reverted to her real name, Paloma. "He looked really mean and was determined to get noticed by being obnoxious. He wanted to be in a band – we all did. His voice wasn't very good but his strength was his punk image. He could be funny, but he was also unfriendly and moody."

The Flowers Of Romance rehearsed three or four times, attempting Ramones covers, Sid originals and also a number by the singer's favourite crooner, Frank Sinatra – possibly My Way. Little headway was made,

STRANGE RECEPTION

Television were the most defiantly arty and cerebral of New York's punk class of '76. But the vision and iron will of their leader, Tom Verlaine, would exact a heavy price.

WORDS: IRA ROBBINS. PHOTO: GOOLS

TELEVISION ENDED as they'd begun, with a show at a small Manhattan club. Having arrived on the New York under-ground scene four years earlier, they split on 29 July 1978 without telling anyone. "Actually, we'd broken up a couple of weeks earlier," recalls guitarist Richard Lloyd. "There was no mention made at the show, but I knew that was it. It was a relief at the time."

It was a fitting farewell from a band that had largely kept to itself, putting maximum effort into the music while displaying minimal concern for anything outside it. "The band was heartfelt," says Lloyd. "We knew it was the swansong, so there was something extraordinary being given for the fans but they didn't have the wistful-ness of knowing it was the last."

The band began with a cover of the 13th Floor Elevators' Fire Engine, with singer Tom Verlaine using made-up lyrics. Facing a rowdy audience, the group followed with Glory, the unreleased Grip Of Love and Foxhole. Each had room for a guitar solo or three – either one of Tom's quivering wires or Richard Lloyd's furious outbursts, or both together.

The band then rolled out a long Ain't That Nothin', a tightly wound Friction, a delicately unveiled Prove It, and Marquee Moon, a spiralling dialogue of guitars. Fred Smith pulsed out a two-note bass heartbeat, smoothly connecting the unpredictability of the two front men to Billy Ficca's jazzed-out drumming. After 15 minutes of brilliantly sustained drama and a roaring coda, the song ended. Television proffered more unre-corded gems – Kingdom Come and a psychedelic twist on the Stones' Satisfaction. One eyewitness says, "When they finished, there was dead silence in the room. Then, slowly, the applause and screaming started."

Television didn't leave much to weigh down shelves – only 1977's Marquee Moon and 1978's Adventure (not counting one authorised live album and 1992's self-titled reunion). It's likely that Marquee Moon has never been in more than 100,000 American homes. Yet its creators set a standard that has rarely been matched since. It's amazing what could emerge from a Bowery dive.

BORN TWO WEEKS before the start of the '50s and raised in Delaware, Tom Miller decided to ditch classical music for jazz after hearing John Coltrane and Albert Ayler. He started to perceive the possibilities of improvisation, so long as it was on saxophone. He hated the sound of jazz guitar, only warming to the instrument after Motown-loving twin brother John played him The Four Tops' Shake Me, Wake Me (When It's Over).

"Up until then, the guitar was a stupid instrument to me," recalled Miller, now better known as Verlaine. "Those records made me think the guitar could be as good as jazz." His first attempt at rock'n'roll was a short-lived group with drummer Billy Ficca. Then in 1966 he ran away from home with best friend Richard Meyers, a Kentucky reprobate who attended Miller's Delaware boarding school. They planned to hitch to Florida but only got as far as Alabama, where a roadside campfire attracted the authorities. To Richard's disappointment, Tom meekly went back to school and then college. Meyers became a poet and publisher in New York.

Within a few months, Miller dropped out of college in Pennsylvania and spent nine months "taking drugs

> ## Patti Smith described Verlaine's guitar-playing as "a thousand bluebirds screaming".

and growing up". He followed Meyers to New York in the middle of '68. It was a tense time in NYC as students took over Columbia University, but Miller was searching for music and poetry, not urban renewal. "We hung out together all the time," recalled Meyers. "We'd stay up all night writing poetry together on an old typewriter."

Meanwhile, Richard Lloyd was beginning his own adventure. Born in Pittsburgh and raised in Greenwich Village, he played piano and drums before picking up guitar. Moving to New Jersey, he lasted a year before taking off in '69 for LA, where he "hung out at record company freebies and fell into glamorous Hollywood swimming pools", and met rock stars. When he returned to New York in '71 he was a bottle-blond punk.

If Miller was the musician and dreamer, Meyers was the schemer, and it was his idea, after they saw the New

(Top) Television play CBGB, 1976: (from left) Fred Smith, Billy Ficca, Tom Verlaine, Richard Lloyd.

(Inset) Manager Terry Ork grabs Verlaine fan Patti Smith.

(Previous page) The band in St Mark's Place, New York, autumn 1977.

York Dolls at the Mercer Arts Center, to form a band. Tom showed Richard how to hold a bass and which notes to play. He located Billy Ficca drumming for a blues band in Boston, and told him he was needed in New York. They dubbed themselves the Neon Boys and sought a second guitarist. One candidate was a local delinquent called Douglas Colvin. Verlaine later reported that the future Dee Dee Ramone didn't know one chord from another and asked, "How can people call me hard to work with?"

Chris Stein of The Stilettos, the precursor to Blondie, allegedly tried out as well, but probably played better than they did. Giving up the search, the trio recorded six songs on a basement four-track in 1973. A few years later, an almost unrecognisable version of Love Comes In Spurts and the jazzed-up garage rocker That's All I Know (Right Now) were belatedly issued on a single. Both were Meyers' compositions; Tom's three songs from those sessions remain unreleased.

In autumn 1973, Miller played a solo electric show on audition night at the Reno Sweeney club. Meyers was acting as his manager. Terry Ork, who managed the

movie-stills store where Miller and Meyers worked, introduced Tom to a guitarist who was living in Ork's loft. Lloyd: "As soon as Tom started playing, I knew something in his approach was correct. And I knew I could augment it." A week later, the two guitarists played together in Tom's apartment. Ficca was recalled and the quartet was finally assembled. Ork bought them gear and let them rehearse at his house. That made him their manager.

"It was like running away from home," recalls Lloyd. "It was exciting, like joining the circus." Meyers came up with the name Hell for himself and Television for the group. Miller rechristened himself after the 19th-century French Symbolist poet.

TELEVISION FOUND THEIR first venue by going to see Suicide play at the small Townhouse theatre just off Times Square. They rented the place on 2 March 1974 and, in a never-repeated fit of obviousness, performed in front of TV sets. Verlaine's post-mortem was simple: "We've got to rehearse a lot more. This sounds horrible."

Three weeks later, Verlaine and Lloyd stopped by the latest happening bar on the Bowery. Hilly Kristal hoped

CBGB would attract solvent customers to skid row by presenting live country music, bluegrass and blues. The pair swore their band would fit the bill, so Kristal booked them for that coming Sunday, 31 March. The drinking age in New York was still 18, the Number 1 song on New York radio was Terry Jacks' Seasons In The Sun and admission to CBGB was a buck.

Within six months, Television were a sensation. And so was CBGB. Lloyd remembers "a lot of [shows] with humungous tuning marathons and broken equipment", but the press went mad. So did the glitterati, who loved the Dolls but were ready for something younger (even though Television were slightly older than the Dolls). David Bowie, Paul Simon and Lou Reed visited. Gene Simmons of the not-yet-famous Kiss looked at their proto-punk clothes and called them "messenger boys".

Patti Smith, who knew Hell from poetry circles and Verlaine from a laundromat, wrote a review in the Soho Weekly News. This she then recycled into a sexually charged note to Verlaine — famously describing his "swan-like" neck as "the most beautiful in rock'n'roll" and his guitar-playing as "a thousand bluebirds scream-ing" — that ran in Rock Scene magazine. By the time her article appeared, Smith and Television had done a joint residency at CBGB, and Tom and Patti had become a power couple, collaborating on a book of poetry and her first single.

Asked about their relationship in 1995, Verlaine was non-committal. "We hung out for a couple of years. It's hard to remember. I think almost every woman artist I've ever met has this ideal of being in a partnership-working situation with a man that men don't seem to share."

Smith wasn't the only person hot for Television. Debbie Harry of Blondie said Richard Hell had "so much sex appeal it could lead anyone, male or female, into groupiedom". Legs McNeil and Gillian McCain's celebration of the NY punk scene, Please Kill Me, quotes at least three men who adored Richard Lloyd.

It didn't take long for the record industry to come calling, excited but deeply uncertain of the commercial potential. Buzz was honey, but not the same as money. The only important act to rise from the city's under-ground to a major label since the Velvets was the Dolls, and they had sizzled without selling.

Television's initial suitor was Richard Williams of Island Records, who co-produced their first demos in New York with Brian Eno in early '75. Verlaine emerged from the experience convinced of two things: that he would have to supervise the band's recordings in the

(Below) Up against the wall, 1977.

(Opposite) Verlaine at the Record Plant recording Adventure; the early line-up with Richard Hell (left).

"Tom wouldn't record any of my songs. I was basically a shadow."
RICHARD LLOYD

future, and that the bassist had to go. Hell says all he can remembers is "the horrible tension which goes with being in any situation where Tom has power. He wouldn't record any of my songs. It'd gotten to where I was basically a shadow, and I left the group shortly after."

Verlaine's shyness hid an iron will, a matching creative ego and a focused work ethic at odds with Hell's onstage conduct. Hell found performing "total catharsis, physically and mentally. I used to go wild. Tom told me to stop moving. He said he didn't want people to be distracted when he was singing."

The band was listing dramatically to one side. Heroin and alcohol were further diminishing Hell's usefulness in the group, although Lloyd and Ork were also using.

Shortly before Hell's departure, Television opened for the New York Dolls at Manhattan's Little Hippodrome in March 1975. The gutter glamsters were days away from breaking up and had fallen in with a Brit with ambitions to be a music business Svengali – Malcolm McLaren – who swathed the Dolls in red patent leather and put them in front of a Chinese flag.

DOLLS GUITARIST JOHNNY Thunders' unemployment coincided with Hell's, so they formed punk's first junkie supergroup, The Heartbreakers. Hell: "I felt completely betrayed. Not only had Verlaine been my best friend but I'd had as much to do with what made the group interesting as he did. He went beyond tactlessness into the most awful blind self-centred condescension and warped meanness."

Verlaine already had a replacement in mind – Blondie bassist Fred Smith (not to be confused with Fred 'Sonic' Smith, late husband of Patti). Smith, however, felt an allegiance to Blondie: "I told Tom no the first time he asked." But things weren't going well for Blondie, and when the offer to join Television was repeated, Smith said yes. "Blondie was like a boat that was sinking and Television was my favourite band," he says. Debbie Harry acknowledges in Please Kill Me that she was "pissed off. Boy, did he make a mistake."

Says Smith: "My leaving was probably the best thing that happened to Blondie. And to Television." Lloyd says Smith "became the stable element that allowed a lot of the interplay, to let the gears not look like a watch that had sprung, but to look like a very interesting group of gears moving."

"We plugged away every day," says Smith. They eventually graduated from Ork's to a Midtown space they shared with Patti Smith, where they recorded Little Johnny Jewel on a four-track tape recorder. Each man played in a separate room. "We were all expert engineers," Fred quips. "We'd hear each other through the walls. Tom played guitar directly into the tape recorder and over-dubbed a one-note piano thing." Terry put the song out on Ork Records in August 1975.

"I don't know how many copies [we pressed] – maybe 500 at first," says Smith. "Then we got a review in Penthouse, and suddenly we got orders from Canada, everywhere, and we were stuffing envelopes." The single sold something like 20,000 copies. The song, which some believe is about Tom's twin brother, was for years a highlight of the band's set.

Lloyd, however, objected vehemently to the choice of single. "My personal view then was that it was not the best chance for us, and Tom was adamant that it was. Seeing as we were at loggerheads, I pulled out." He quit the band. "About two months later, we ran into each other in a restaurant and we started talking," says Lloyd. He rejoined. "I couldn't influence Tom, even by quitting. He's a person with a will that's not amenable to anything. There was nothing to be done about it. It was still my band too, and I wanted to be in it."

The homemade hit attracted major labels. Seymour Stein, who would sign the Ramones and Richard Hell to Sire, told Lloyd, "I could make you into The Grateful Dead. You won't sell a lot of records, but you'll sell them consistently for 30 years." Says Lloyd dryly, "It didn't sound very appetising."

They also auditioned for Atlantic's Ahmet Ertegun, who declared, "I can't sign this band. This is not earth music." Lloyd: "I took that as a very high compliment."

Patti Smith, whose fixation with Arthur Rimbaud lent a literary logic to her coupling with the name-taker of his mentor and lover, tried to get Television on to her label, Arista, and persuaded Allen Lanier of Blue Öyster Cult – her other boyfriend – to produce their demo. But it was Karin Berg, head of publicity for Elektra/Asylum, who finally brought Television in from the cold.

Danny Fields, the former Elektra staffer who signed The Stooges and MC5, tipped her to Television. Ork arranged a private showcase at CBGB, and Berg was bowled over. She couldn't believe the band was unsigned, and quickly convinced her boss to remedy that.

By the time they signed the deal in July '76, both the Ramones and Patti Smith had released debuts. But Television hadn't wasted their time. "We used to rehearse six or seven days a week," recalls Lloyd. "Those songs that ended up on Marquee Moon had been through the wringer umpteen times." Determined to produce themselves, they still needed someone to guide them through the recording process. Verlaine called Andy Johns, an Englishman who had engineered records for Led Zeppelin and The Rolling Stones.

Johns spent his first night in A&R Studios setting up the drums alone. The next day, says Lloyd, "Andy played back some stuff he had recorded. And, by God, out of the speakers came John Bonham's drum sound! Billy was like, 'It sounds pretty good to me,' and Tom was like, 'No, no, no. You've got to undo all of this. We want dry, small sounds, not this.' Then Andy went, 'Oh, this must be like a Velvets thing, right? It's a New York thing, right?'"

Exactly why Verlaine believed "small and dry" was Television's sound has never been explained, but he prevailed. Marquee Moon was recorded and mixed in three weeks. Smith says, "I think most of the songs sounded pretty much like they sounded live – except in tune."

BY TODAY'S STANDARDS, Marquee Moon was a Dogma '95 field recording. Verlaine played a little piano. Lloyd double-tracked his solo, note for note, on Elevation, which also used a harmoniser on the chorus so it sounds as though Verlaine is singing, "Television, don't go to my head." The 10-minute title track, an early acoustic ballad of Tom's, was completed in one take that Ficca thought was a rehearsal.

From the opening See No Evil's sinuous guitar figure, Marquee Moon cuts deep into alien territory. In the colour-xeroxed Robert Mapplethorpe cover photo Television look like stock new wavers, their deadpan stares and casual clothes a visual cliche of the '70s. But the record was strung tight, potently dramatic and unfailingly original. Verlaine's singing, compared by Rolling Stone to "an intelligent chicken being strangled", was offhand yet had Dylan's intuitive raw intensity. The spare production made obvious just how much thought and invention went into its details. The sound of punk was strum and run, but the LP had a compelling undertow.

Guitarwise, Verlaine and Lloyd could mix and mingle notes and chords as if four hands were controlled by one mind. Each had a distinctive style – Verlaine was prone to spasmodic hyper-strummed one-string freak-outs, Lloyd was more controlled. "The electric guitar had become such an unoriginal-sounding instrument. Hearing [Marquee Moon] was such a throw-down to me," says U2's The Edge.

Marquee Moon appeared in the US in February 1977. The album stayed stubbornly on store shelves in the US, despite a tour opening for Peter Gabriel. "The band wasn't badly received," Verlaine said. "But you're playing for somebody else's audience." A single of Marquee Moon, its 10 minutes divided unequally across two sides, peaked at Number 30 in the UK. That brought Television to Europe for a three-week trek headlining over Blondie. "We found our equipment pushed to the front of the stage, where Television wanted me to confine my movements to a small space so that Tom Verlaine could stand strikingly and sombrely alone in a very large space when he came on," complained Debbie Harry in Blondie's autobiography, Making Tracks.

Verlaine was not impressed with the English music scene. "People were giving me records. They all sounded the same. The sound was copped from The Ramones, and the lyrics, the attitude, were taken from Patti Smith." His disdain found a mirror in The Damned, who flew to LA to open a show for Television in April 1977 to find

> **Verlaine's singing was compared by Rolling Stone to "an intelligent chicken being strangled"**

their services were no longer required. They responded with Idiot Box, a vague but vindictive attack, complete with sloppy musical parody, on Music For Pleasure.

When Television started to record another album, the only unrecorded numbers they chose from their stage repertoire were Foxhole and I Don't Care (renamed Careful because The Ramones already had a song by that name). Lloyd says making the LP, Adventure, "was more arduous for me. Tom was using the studio as a place to find something. I loved working with Andy [Johns on Marquee Moon]. It was a real rock'n'roll experience. The second album was a lot more workmanlike and sober."

Recording in New York stretched from September through December. Work was interrupted when Lloyd developed endocarditis and landed in hospital. Ork arranged a sickbed photograph of him to explain the album's delay. The widening of the group's sonic ambitions – the album was recorded in four separate rooms, with a different drumkit rented for

"Sorry I can't make the recording session…" Richard Lloyd recovering in the Beth Israel Hospital, New York, 1978.

instrumental guitar of 1992's Warm And Cool, on which Ficca drummed. Lloyd began a long professional relationship with Matthew Sweet; he also released two more solo records.

AND THEN, IN 1992, Television unexpectedly existed again. A third album, the low-key but substantial Television, on which Verlaine split the difference between 1978 and 1992, with Lloyd, Smith and Ficca providing subtle ballast, was followed by their most extensive tour to date, taking in the UK's Glastonbury festival and Roskilde in Denmark. They played Japan for the first time and undertook a long US itinerary. "It was pretty easy to come back," says Lloyd. He calls the album "OK" but "liked the tour. Jazz musicians do that all the time – they have a quartet and then they go and do other things and then they return and then that quartet exists. And then it doesn't."

The band's second finale came on 14 March 1993, at the Academy in Manhattan, two blocks and 19 years from the Townhouse. It was no secret that they were calling it quits this time, but the band still had the magic. Older, more skilled and less excitable, they matched the memory and honoured their previous work by accepting what they were, and what they were not. They made their point and retired with dignity intact.

Television still holds a force over its five principals to this day. They are a town with a dark secret. Lloyd's observation that "for listeners, a rock band is not just four people, it's this other thing" is equally true of the men who make the music.

Verlaine once said: "Television is something I never talk about. It just doesn't interest me." He has never been a voluble spokesman for his artistry. "I like thinking of myself as invisible. Unfortunately, it's not the way the music business works."

The Television story is still not over. The band Tortoise, who were curating the All Tomorrow's Parties festival on the English south coast, persuaded them to perform in April 2001. The group also booked shows in London, Spain, Chicago, Dublin and Seattle, turning a one-off into a mini-tour. Television have returned to the road every year since, playing festivals and solo gigs in Europe, America, Japan and Brazil.

They have yet to release new material – but they have written new songs and intend to cut them. Stay tuned.

each cut – complicated the process. But the group was tighter, and ready for a challenge. "To me, the songs don't sound that far away from the material on the last album," said Verlaine. "There aren't many overdubs."

It has a smoother tone than Marquee Moon, as if they had less to prove and more to say. A lot of fans and critics were disappointed, and the playing and singing does lack the debut's tension, substituting catchier tunes suspended in a sophisticated, laconic cool. But the album is true to Television's virtues and articulates them with clean production. The pop melodies of Glory go handsomely with the folkish lilt of Days. Only the Stonesy Ain't That Nothin' rivals the rock edge of Foxhole – and neither song raises the mercury-like Friction or Prove It.

Adventure was released in April '78, and sailed up the UK chart to Number 7. But in America it did nothing, and by August the band no longer existed. The break-up has been blamed on Tom's personality and the loss of record company support, but Lloyd said: "I don't believe the break-up had anything to do with anything. If I had been asked, I'd have stayed, but I'm happy to be out."

After the split, Verlaine and Lloyd each made solo albums for Elektra; Smith played on both. Ficca joined The Waitresses (and several other groups). Tom "decided to go to the movies for two years", then returned – with Smith always on hand – to make a progression of increasingly atmospheric albums on their way towards the artful

Generation X play London's Marquee club, where they had a residency in September 1977.

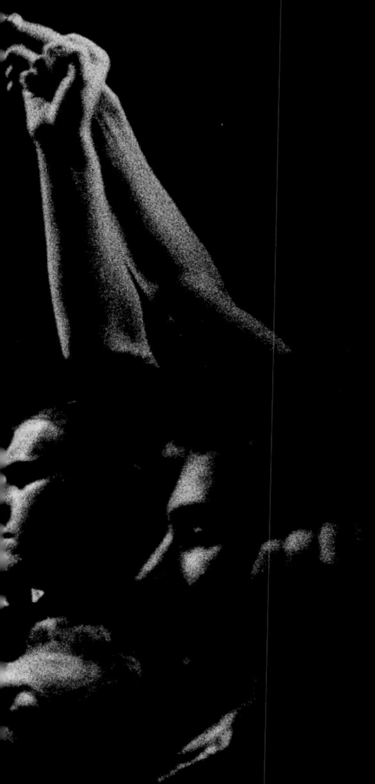

PRETTY VACANT

Dismissed as rebel wannabes, Generation X survived countless traumas only to see singer Billy Idol conquer the world. Alone.

ON 1 DECEMBER 1978, Generation X pulled up outside Birmingham's Aston University to play a concert with The Cure. The glamour-puss punk band, fronted by Billy Idol, were met with disturbing news. The promoter told them local Hell's Angels had "invited themselves" to police the gig. In the late '70s, outlaw biker culture in the Midlands was at its height. Each town had its own club, and turf wars were bloody affairs, fought with hammers, knives and, occasionally, shotguns.

The group barricaded themselves in the dressing room. Peering out at the ranks of bearded heavies, they had visions of a punk Altamont. Pretty-boy guitarist Bob "Derwood" Andrews was petrified. He'd been hospitalized the previous year in Leicester by an airborne beer glass. Another Birmingham

gig had been abandoned when the skinhead/punk audience invaded the stage and attacked the group.

"I wasn't a fighter, I was a musician," explains Derwood. "I was cowering in the toilet."

Halfway through the third song, what drummer Mark Laff describes as "a great big fucking greaser" appeared stage left. "I shat myself," he says. "Our security guy stepped aside to let him pass. He sauntered over to Billy and punched him in the head."

Idol, the platinum blond reviled by the punk hardcore for being both good-looking and middle-class, lay on the deck out cold for a few seconds. Then he leapt up, curled his lip at the Angels, clenched his fist in his trademark manner, and carried on singing.

It was an early indication that Billy Idol was made of stronger stuff than anyone had previously supposed. Within 18 months, Generation X would crumble amid heroin use, nervous breakdowns and, possibly, witchcraft. But Billy would survive to become the richest and most famous English punk rocker on the planet.

Back in Birmingham, after the show the bikers swarmed around the dressing-room, helping themselves to drinks. One oily giant put his arm around a shaken Idol and offered words of comfort. "Youse was lucky, mate. Normally, he chains people he don't like."

"Our security let the Hell's Angel walk past. He sauntered over and punched Billy in the head. I shat myself." DRUMMER MARK LAFF

IN FEBRUARY 2005, Billy Idol is sitting in a five-star hotel suite on London's Marylebone Road, sipping from nothing stronger than a glass of water. There's something of Brian Jones about him; the compact, boyish frame and oversized doll-like head. His reputation precedes him: '80s MTV icon, ex-heroin casualty, Harley Davidson nut who nearly lost a leg in a bike smash, occasional Hollywood film star, cartoon rocker.

He's likeable and painfully candid. Quick to lapse into caricature, he will sneer, raise his fists, and talk about "Billy Idol" in the third person. He seems pleased that a new generation of music fans, too young to be prejudiced by Generation X's reputation as punk softies, regards Ready Steady Go, Kiss Me Deadly, Valley Of The Dolls, and Dancing With Myself as some of the finest songs to come out of new wave. But did it bother him, being a detested punk pin-up?

"I didn't care," he rasps in his cracked Keith Richards voice. "I was getting all the pussy, so I didn't give a shit what a bunch of ugly geezers who ain't getting any were saying. Was Billy Idol gonna make himself more ugly so he wouldn't get any girls? We got a lot of stick, but it was also what kept us going and kept our identity. The thing

was to front out the audiences. You had to stand there and rub the blood into your face. The Iggy Pop rules."

Before punk claimed him, Billy Idol was a well-spoken, bookish teenager called William Broad, born on the fringes of London in 1955. He spent his early years in New York, where his father was working. "When I got back to England, I was called 'The Yank,'" he says. "I was an outsider in America, then an outsider over here." Billy read English at Sussex University. When his arty Bromley pals – Siouxsie Sioux, Steve Severin, and Simon Barker – alerted him to the Sex Pistols in April 1976, he had long hair and John Lennon-style reading glasses.

The Bromley Contingent became the Pistols' biggest fans. The group viewed suburban Billy with amusement. One night, he turned up in a brand-new Austin Princess. Having pulled two girls, Idol bombed off toward Ladbroke Grove, only for Glen Matlock, who was tailing him, to rear-end Billy's car. "What have you done?" Idol howled in despair. "My dad will kill me!"

Idol wanted to form his own group, and in July 1976

The first Generation X line-up: (from left) John Towe, Bob 'Derwood' Andrews, Tony James and Billy Idol, July 1977.

(Right) Billy and Tony with Mick Jones and, behind, Sniffin' Glue's Mark Perry, The Vortex, 1976.

PHOTOS: KATE SIMON, RAY STEVENSON

"Billy and I were clearly middle-class in a movement created by Bernie and Malcolm McLaren to look working-class," Tony explains. "We were the guys who had been to university. But Bernie had toughened me up."

IN SEPTEMBER 1976, James and Idol joined a group called Chelsea. Tony and Billy took control, ditched the group's 30-year-old singer, Gene October, and started playing their own material as Generation X. The band – named after Charles Hamblett's book on '60s youth culture – was completed by Bob 'Derwood' Andrews. By day, Derwood, then only 17, worked at Kensington Palace as a gardener. At night he rehearsed with a hard-rock covers band called Paradox. Billy spotted Derwood at Paradox's first-ever gig, at Fulham Arts Centre on 4 December 1976.

Billy: "I noticed this young kid on guitar. I thought, 'He's really good!' He was playing Hendrix, Led Zep, Black Sabbath. I was trying to call him over – 'cos we were a load of punks, he thought I was trying to beat him up. He auditioned the next day."

"I went down there and Billy was on guitar," recalls Derwood. "What they were doing was fucking brilliant. Really fast, so pure... Then I got up and played with Billy singing, and it clicked."

The group performed at the opening night of the Roxy Club in Covent Garden on 21 December. "It was really exciting," says Derwood. "Billy and Tony had a vision. Back then, though, Billy was this nice, softly spoken, middle-class boy. He used to get my sister to teach him Cockney rhyming slang. Like Pygmalion in reverse. My Fair Billy!"

Generation X caught the eye of Sounds' John Ingham, one of the first journalists to champion punk. "Tony and Billy were very likeable," explains Ingham. "What attracted me was that they were articulate; they had ideas and knew how to express them. I told them I'd be their manager.

"We were sitting in this room I rented in Notting Hill, listening to Low and The Idiot. This was when I realised Tony had a skill – he was saying, 'Listen to the mix, listen to the kick-drum, listen to what he's doing with it.' His understanding of music was very detailed."

The group decided they should combine elements of classic rock – The Who's Live At Leeds, Iggy's Raw Power, early Led Zeppelin – with the stripped-down punk format. Derwood was encouraged to freewheel on guitar. Visually, they opted for black leather and, later,

to his parents' place one afternoon," recalls Tony James. "There was an instant bond. Billy and I sat and played some Lou Reed songs, the Stones' It's All Over Now."

Tony James was about to graduate from Brunel University with a maths degree. In 1975, he and Mick Jones had formed The London SS, under the tutelage of future Clash manager Bernie Rhodes. When the group fizzled out, Rhodes abandoned Tony.

Tony's homemade, culturally vibrant T-shirts: volumetric Léger blocks of colour, a gun-wielding Patty Hearst... Yet, right from the start, the press loathed them.

"The first interview we did with NME, they crucified us," groans Tony. "Me and Billy had got the clap off the same girl, and in those days the antibiotics meant you couldn't drink for two weeks. We did the interview in the pub and had orange juice. The headline was 'The Terror Of The Orange Juice Punks'."

Out on the road, their image resulted in hailstorms of beer glasses and gob. Yet record companies saw them as potential gold dust. In July 1977, Generation X signed to Chrysalis. The advance for the first album was £75,000 – for the fifth, if they got that far, it would rise to £1 million. Predictably, in Derwood's words, none of them would "ever see a fucking bean".

"The first interview we did with NME, they crucified us." TONY JAMES

Today, Mark Laff lives in a smart house on the outskirts of Brighton, the legacy of the sizeable fee MTV paid in 1993 for a one-off Generation X reunion. In the hallway is a framed photo of the group on Marc Bolan's TV show, recorded a week before Bolan's death. A working-class lad from Finchley, Laff looks uncannily like Keith Moon, his hero since he was a schoolboy.

Laff, once a candidate for the Clash drum seat, joined Generation X in June 1977, replacing original drummer John Towe. His explosive, Moon-like fills were exactly what the group wanted; he, in turn, loved the music. "Derwood was fantastic," says Laff. "Billy was a treat to look at. Tony was very authoritative, maybe annoyingly so. They thought the Keith Moon thing was the way to go, play over everything, which is what I did."

Tony wrote the lyrics – fixating on youth culture and revolution (Your Generation, Ready Steady Go, Wild Youth) – and Billy wrote the music, brazenly cribbing ideas from Pete Townshend's Who licks. "Before Billy turned into Coco The Clown he was a musical genius," states Derwood. "He would show me stuff on his acoustic that I wouldn't think of in a million years."

The connection with The Who took an unexpected twist when Keith Moon turned up at their rehearsal place in Chalk Farm with Monty Python's Graham Chapman. Moon took the seat for I Can See For Miles, Shakin' All Over and Summertime Blues. Thrilled, the group arranged to give the drummer a guided tour of the punk scene. They wound up at the Vortex on Wardour Street, but the night ended badly when Pete Townshend, who'd turned up to meet Moon, hit Mark Laff.

Laff: "Townshend was a sod. I said I'd heard him on the radio saying he saw no future for The Who live. He stood up and screamed, 'TV! Radio! Gigs! Stand up and fucking fight me then!' It was fucking horrible."

IT WASN'T JUST the press, punk audiences and their heroes that took exception to them. The band's first singles were made with Sweet and Bay City Rollers producer Phil Wainman. Sessions for the debut album were abandoned after Wainman thought Laff's playing too wild. He insisted they hire a session player. Tony James argued the group came as a non-negotiable unit. The standoff caused a major rift between John Ingham and Tony. "It was admirable on one hand, but on the other you think, 'Oh Christ!'" sighs Ingham. "You're never going to have a hit single with an out-of-time drummer. I thought Tony was being an idiot, so we fell out." Eventually the album was re-recorded with Buzzcocks/Stranglers producer Martin Rushent. Ingham, fed up with his irascible charges, quit and moved to the US.

Generation X's self-titled debut appeared in March 1978 but stalled at Number 29. The group focused on live work, delivering incendiary performances, but nothing ever went smoothly. One incident sums up the enveloping weirdness. On 20 May, they were scheduled to appear on the TV show Revolver, hosted by Peter Cook.

Royal Festival Hell: Gen X on London's South Bank with second drummer Mark Laff (far left), 1978.

(Right) Billy lights up a friend, Eric's, Liverpool, 1978.

"We'd done a gig at Barbarella's on the Friday and the show was on the Saturday," recalls Mark Laff. "I was rooming with Billy. He'd pulled this bird and done his business, and said, 'You fancy a go?' I said, 'Thanks, Bill, but we've got a live TV show tomorrow, so I'd rather get some sleep.' But this girl didn't want to leave! There was a big argument in this horrible little hotel room. The road crew came to help us get her out. Then she dropped her knickers and said, 'Come on! I'll fuck the lot of ya! I'll split you up, just like I did the Pistols.'"

The next day their TV spot was nixed due to technical problems. "We looked at the audience and there was this girl again, staring at us madly," says Laff. "It was bizarre!" Searching for an explanation for the bad luck, Billy was convinced someone had cursed them – his next-door neighbour in Notting Hill was a witch.

The problems didn't let up when, in August, sessions began for a second album. Tony had suggested Ian Hunter, his hero from Mott The Hoople, as producer. Derwood felt they were being railroaded into making a "boring '70s rock record". Idol thought the sessions "lacked energy. We should have been making a punk record." Laff recalls Billy and Tony "bitching at each other". Mark's drumming was again an issue.

The pressure took its toll on Tony. "I got very ill," he says. "We were in the studio, and I started shaking. It was nervous exhaustion. I bumped into Keith Moon, who said, 'Don't worry, old boy, my doctor will sort you out.' He was the one later struck off for misconduct. He prescribed three Valium plus a massive sleeping pill each day. I felt like I was living underwater."

The press crucified the album, Valley Of The Dolls, for being "overblown". It spawned two hit singles, the pummelling King Rocker and

149

GENERATION X

K.WEST

AIR CONDITIONED OFFICES
APPROX 12 SQ.FT
TO LET

ALLSOP
&CO
21 SOHO SQUARE 01-437 6977
LONDON W1

BASEMENT
800 SQ.FT 1ST FLOOR
ALL ENQUIRIES
Tuckerman
01·799 5511/2

TELEPHONE

Bowie-ish Valley Of The Dolls. Meanwhile, Idol and James decided to amp up the glam factor, with Billy transforming into a kind of new wave Alvin Stardust with eyeliner, beckoning glove movements and pursed lips. "Billy and Tony were preaching new music, new attitudes," says Derwood, "but they wanted to be pop stars. I didn't, and I don't think Mark did either. Down the pub, friends would say to me, 'You looked a right cunt on Top Of The Pops.'"

During sessions for an aborted third LP, Derwood left when Tony and Billy wouldn't let him contribute ideas. Tony was increasingly autocratic. "We were all out drinking and doing drugs, and he'd be in his room reading New Scientist," says Derwood. "He knew about the

By now, Billy was transforming into what Laff calls "a kind of… entertainer". He began seeing Hot Gossip dancer Perri Lister, taking him further into the realms of flamboyant costumes and showmanship. His entourage included drug-buddies Steve Jones from the Sex Pistols and ex-Rich Kid Steve New. His drug addiction eroded his friendship with Tony. "Billy was in a different orbit," explains James. "We virtually stopped speaking."

A new line-up emerged with James Stephenson on guitar and former Clash man Terry Chimes on drums. The group shortened their name to Gen X. Idol took to wearing a cape and a leather codpiece. After Dancing With Myself stalled at Number 62 – twice – Idol left for a solo career in America in 1981. He didn't even tell his songwriting partner. The English student turned hophead rock star had his own agenda.

Idol: "The manager wanted us to go to America but I don't think Tony liked

"The manager wanted us to go to America. I bought a Gretsch guitar, a cheap trunk and the rest I spent on heroin." BILLY IDOL

Big Bang theory but didn't have a clue how to hold a band together."

Mark Laff: "I knew I was finished when I walked into Chrysalis and saw Tony and Billy in the boardroom talking to the directors. It seems they wanted to try something new. Pretty soon after that I was out of the band."

TONY JAMES IS perched on the sofa in his London home, once occupied by Sir Arthur Conan Doyle. "I was so focused, I didn't realise people were getting pissed off," he admits. "We wanted to go international and be pop stars. We had the songs and the look. I realise now that Derwood was a very creative guitar player, but as far I was concerned it was me and Billy who wrote the songs."

In late 1979, Tony suggested the group employ Kiss's manager, Bill Aucoin, "a man who understood the TV age". Aucoin hooked them up with Giorgio Moroder's engineer, Keith Forsey. Months of contractual wrangling ensued. The enforced hiatus brought about the biggest development in the group's decline: Billy started using heroin. "I spent all my £25 wages on drugs," he grins. "Good stuff. It got me."

the idea. The record company gave me $1,000. I bought a Gretsch guitar and a cheap trunk – the rest I spent on heroin. I arrived in New York with loads of spots on my face."

"I didn't see him for another year," says Tony. "Then he knocked on my front door in Maida Vale. He was holding a white label of White Wedding. I wanted it to be terrible, but it was great. I knew then Billy would become a huge star."

"We worked hard to make Generation X a success," reasons Billy Idol today. "But things always fell apart for one reason or another. We were a great group, though. I'm really proud of what we did."

The Bollocks

An East End street kid, Dennis Morris was still a schoolboy when he began taking photos professionally. In 1973, aged just 14, the talented young lensman was invited by Bob Marley to chronicle the Wailers' 1973 UK tour. His classic shots of Marley led the reggae-loving Johnny Rotten to recruit him as the Pistols' semi-official lensman in 1977, allowing him unprecedented access.

Kohl comfort

Punks at The Vortex, summer 1977

The Vortex opened its doors in July 1977. Situated at 201 Wardour Street in Soho, it became the chief punk hangout after the closure of the legendary Roxy club in nearby Covent Garden.

All hung up

Johnny Rotten backstage at the Marquee, 5 July 1977

This shot was taken during the filming of the promo video for the Pistols' third single, Pretty Vacant.

Sweet and sour

**Johnny and Sid,
December 1977**

After a nine-date visit to Holland,
which had been hastily arranged
partly to get Sid away from his drug
dealers, the Pistols returned to
England for their Never Mind The
Bans tour. The title was all too apt
– half the original eight bookings
were cancelled and this would turn
out to be the band's final UK
excursion. Here the old Hackney
school pals tuck into a Chinese
takeaway on the tour bus.

My aim is true

Sid Vicious, July 1977

Morris cornered the bassist in
Rotten's hotel room one morning
during the group's Scandinavian
tour. The photographer said
afterwards that it was "the first
time I got to know him".

We don't care

**Sex Pistols, the Marquee,
5 July 1977**

The Pretty Vacant video shoot. The
group refused to mime, preferring
to perform the track live. The
result, says Morris, "was chaos".

Oh bandage!
The Vortex, 1977

Fan opts for Invisible Man headgear and paint-spattered shirt – on an evening when Roxy Music sax player Andy Mackay was sufficiently curious to turn up.

Smash it up
Sid's hotel room, 1977

The group refused to allow Sid's girlfriend Nancy Spungen to tour with the group. As a result, he'd indulge in "an orgy of drugs and booze". Destruction ensued…

Double-crossed

Live in Sweden, July 1977

Although he'd been attacked by
knife-wielding thugs in Islington
the previous month, Rotten retains
his sense of humour in Sweden.
Here he's sporting what Morris
calls his "Bryan Ferry look".

Love kills

**Sid Vicious and
Nancy Spungen,
16 December 1977**

Banned from the bus she may
have been, but Nancy was able
to get to this gig at Brunel
University in Uxbridge, 12 miles
to the west of London.

Sick and tired

**Johnny Rotten,
Brunel University,
16 December 1977**

The first date of the Never Mind
The Bans tour was held in the
university's gym and was marked
by audience violence. Here, during
the soundcheck, Johnny Rotten
tries to grab a quick 40 winks
before the hordes descend.

Banana twits

**Paul Cook, Steve Jones
and Roadent, 1977**

Roadie Steve Connolly, alias
'Roadent', defected to the Pistols
after a year with The Clash.

the art of .
noise

Jamie Reid was the man behind the Sex Pistols' influential cut'n'paste artwork. But where did his inspiration come from?

IF ONE PERSON can sensibly be credited with single-handedly influencing punk's look then it is artist Jamie Reid, Sex Pistols record sleeve designer and Malcolm McLaren's co-conspirator. However, Reid's trajectory towards this leading role was unplanned and almost accidental.

"I loved football and I could have played profession-ally," he explains. However, a waning interest coupled with academic failure pushed Reid towards art school.

"I really blew it at school by the time I was 16," he recalls. "I was feeling very dissipated. I was always one of those kids who was drawing all day, so I went to art school. Back then you could get in without any qualifi-cations and get a grant."

Attending Croydon Art School from 1964, Reid, like many of his fellow students at the time, soon found the student riots in Paris in 1968 a profound influence, galvanising his already strong political beliefs. Spurred on by their French counterparts, the Croydon students staged their own sit-in, occupying college buildings for almost a month and allowing one of Reid's fellow students the opportunity to flex the organisational skills that would come in handy in 1976.

"Malcolm McLaren was sound," says Reid. "He was quite a catalyst." The pair then collaborated on a film project chronicling the history of London's Oxford Street, from the hangings of Tyburn to its role at the heart of commerce and consumerism.

With the influence of the Paris riots and Situationist slogans strong in his mind, Reid left art school in 1970 and established Suburban Press. This was an anarchist printing press in south London producing material that would form the foundation of the Sex Pistols' imagery.

"We were printing for all sorts of local groups – the women's movement, the black movement, squatting groups," explains Reid. "I was messing about with design, but because we had no money I was cutting up newspapers and doing collage. It was from there that the look for punk came."

REID'S IDEAS AND convictions were behind many of the images Suburban Press produced, revealing an unlikely inspiration for punk's strongest images. "My family has always been very involved in Druidism," explains Reid. "It was definitely an influence that's always been there."

Suburban Press was clearly creating ripples – a fact not lost on McLaren, who, when establishing the Sex Pistols in 1975, contacted his former classmate.

"I'd actually gone to live on the Isle Of Lewis *[in the Outer Hebrides]* for a year, and while I was up there McLaren got in touch. He said to come and work with him in London on this project that he'd got. This turned out to be the Sex Pistols. They were just the perfect mar-riage between the images I was creating and music. I was blown away the first time I heard them. I thought it was very real at a time when music had become unreal."

Reid has gone on to work with other artists, includ-ing Tenpole Tudor, Boy George and, most recently, Afro Celt Sound System, as well as continuing his painting. Today, he acknowledges that his work with the Sex Pistols was truly pioneering. "It was great," he says. "It meant you could get stuff directly into the street and all over towns. It was very immediate and direct. With God Save The Queen we got on the front page of the Daily Mirror within two weeks of it coming out."

Jamie Reid, the collage kid who redefined graphic art.

WORDS: PAUL STOKES

Anarchy In The UK poster

"Ray Stevenson [renowned punk photographer] did the contacts and I took it from there. It was an attempt to make the point about the declining empire. It's horrific, stamping on people's cultures wholesale – which is what America is doing now."

Pretty Vacant poster

"This actually came directly from when I was working on Suburban Press. The image was created in collaboration with a group of people in San Francisco called Point Blank. They'd made this unofficial timetable that was a complete replica of the San Francisco bus timetable but sent the buses in different directions, they never connect."

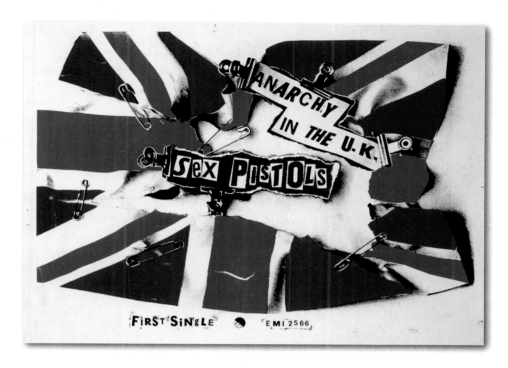

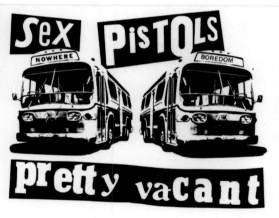

"We had no money, so I was cutting up papers and doing collage. That's where the look for punk came from." JAMIE REID

Sex Pistols sleeves

"I passed a travel shop and saw a holiday brochure. I took that, cut it up and put the song's lyrics in the bubbles. Pure plagiarism. With The Great Rock'n'Roll Swindle, it's almost like you can see the film within the sleeve."

SOMETHING'S GONE WRONG AGAIN

Pop-punk turned the Buzzcocks into stars. Yet while one half of their songwriting partnership loved fame, the other found it profoundly disturbing. Soon the party would come crashing to a halt.

ON THE NIGHT of Wednesday 26 April 1978, Pete Shelley went back to his hotel room, alone, and washed his socks in the sink. Earlier that day, his band, the Buzzcocks, had made their debut on Top Of The Pops. As for all groups forged in the anti-establishment crucible of punk, the show was a bone of contention.

The Clash's implacable opposition to playing TOTP had given their peers cause for thought: for some, an appearance on the show was tantamount to collaboration with the enemy. Others regarded the seditious potential of corrupting a nation's youth worth the indignity of miming before an audience of adolescents.

Having previously espoused the DIY ethic via organising the Sex Pistols' first Manchester gig and then their self-released debut record Spiral Scratch, before taking their place on May 1977's White Riot tour, the Buzzcocks were core punk players. Since signing with United Artists in 1977 they had released two singles, Orgasm Addict and What Do I Get?, which had effectively redefined the love song, and then an auspicious debut album, Another Music In A Different Kitchen, serving notice of the band's pop sensibility.

For a frustrated generation, punk offered fulfilment without conforming to mainstream society's conservative ethics. The Buzzcocks were at the vanguard of this cultural revolution. And, despite its cheese factor, TOTP was a means to spread the word.

Because Musicians' Union restrictions forbade the band miming to the actual record, that morning they went to Wessex Studios in north London to cut a BBC-friendly version of I Don't Mind. Then it was off to the show. Punks they may have been, but the Buzzcocks were born between 1955 and '58, and had lived their musical adolescence through TOTP. They were excited, not least because this was a new domain.

"It felt a bit phoney," guitarist Steve Diggle recalls. "You're looking at the audience and thinking, 'This probably means nothing to them, 'cos after us it's Dean Friedman.' But, at the same time, my rationale was remembering watching Top Of The Pops as a kid, and there'd always be one or two people on that were good and the rest was crap. So I imagined some kid at home thinking, we had Boney M and some other shit... but at least the Buzzcocks were on."

In fact, the Buzzcocks were television naturals. Shelley ignored the instructions to pretend the cameras weren't there and stared out the viewers at home.

Diggle was gauchely energetic, a street urchin throwing classic rock shapes. Drummer John Maher was assured bordering on bored. And bassist Steve Garvey was a geometrically cheekboned beauty. Unlike the opportunists infiltrating punk's body politic, the Buzzcocks never pandered to an audience – they didn't have to.

But afterwards, rinsing his socks, Shelley felt the euphoria ebbing away. In its place seeped doubts and unsustainable longings.

"It was phenomenal," he says. "Everything you'd hoped for. And I'm washing my socks, going, 'Isn't there supposed to be somebody who does this for you?' There was that whole disillusionment. You understand that it doesn't get any better. That once you become famous, certain things may change – people are interested in you, which is always nice. We all crave attention. But it doesn't get away from who you are and what you are. In fact, it'll only make things worse."

LESS THAN TWELVE months later, the Buzzcocks were again on TOTP with Everybody's Happy Nowadays. The intervening period had witnessed five more appearances on the show, including three in support of Ever Fallen In Love (With Someone You Shouldn't've), which had taken up an 11-week chart residency. The Buzzcocks had transcended their punk roots. Shelley's confused, anti-macho love songs showed they were crazy for romance. Which happened to be very punk indeed.

"Punk was about expressing things in songs that wouldn't be talked about," says Shelley. "There was a language of songs – Oooh, baby, baby – and then there was a language of what it was like to be living your life. Punk was about taking away all that pretence and saying it like it was and being honest. It was liberating."

The music business, however, has no use for sensitive souls. True to the spirit of the times, the Buzzcocks worked as if terrified that by stopping they would never again be able to restart. There was a tour to coincide with every single released – in 1978, this meant every two months. Their second album, Love Bites, was released just seven months after the first.

(Right) The Buzzcocks outside TJ Davidson Rehearsal Studios, Manchester.

(Previous page, from left) Steve Diggle, John Maher, Pete Shelley and Steve Garvey, Manchester, 1978.

WORDS: KEITH CAMERON. PHOTOS: (PREVIOUS PAGE) FIN COSTELLO/REDFERNS, (THIS PAGE) ADRIAN BOOT/URBANIMAGE.TV

"A tour meant 30 dates, and if you had a day off you'd be in the studio," says Diggle. "We never stopped. The nature of the group was: here's a new song – and it'd be done in 10 minutes."

Inasmuch as it emerged from one of their demo sessions, Everybody's Happy Nowadays represented Buzzcocks business as usual. But both the song's sardonic content – based around a mantra, "Life's an illusion, love is a dream", inspired by Aldous Huxley's Brave New World – and its chaotic playing on TOTP betrayed a malaise at the band's heart. The punishing schedule was taking a toll on Shelley. As the band's star rose, his heart sank. Buzzcocks gigs became witness to extremes of fan behaviour, be it invading National Front gangs provoking violence or teenage girls tearing off Steve Garvey's shirt.

PETE SHELLEY SOON discovered that life as a pop commodity wasn't conducive to resolving the existential dilemmas that coursed through his songs. During the October 1978 tour to promote Love Bites, Buzzcocks manager Richard Boon frequently had to persuade Shelley not to quit the band. "All the generated froth around you becomes claustrophobic," Shelley says. "Neil Diamond said fame is the price you pay for being good at what you do. It wasn't meant to be me the star and you down there. But I'm talking to people and they're metaphorically on their knees, saying, 'Oh, you're so wonderful.' And you feel like shit. Touring fucks you up anyway – if it's not the booze, it's the drugs. I wasn't geared up to being adored. I dealt with it by getting out of it."

For his Everybody's Happy Nowadays TOTP appearance on 8 March 1979, Shelley wore a lurid jacket, a gift from his parents. From his top pocket protruded a buttonhole fashioned from the sum total of money in his wallet: a fiver and three ones. Diggle had previously suggested setting fire to a wheelbarrow full of cash in Trafalgar Square. Shelley's consumerist critique, although subtler, still jammed the BBC switchboard with complaints about his "flaunting of wealth".

"It wasn't as much as you got for a week on the dole!" Shelley laughs looking back. "By now I was taking lots of acid. On Top Of The Pops I was off my trolley. Everybody's Happy Nowadays was me going, 'Fuck off!' I'd ceased to care. Of course, once you do that, it all goes to hell in a handcart!"

Two years separated the Buzzcocks' signing to United Artists and their first US tour, which opened in Boston on 30 August 1979. But in that time the band had profoundly changed. Within weeks of signing, bassist Garth Davies was gone, sacked for increasingly unreliable drunken behaviour. At least Steve Garvey's subsequent arrival meant the band became a more potent musical unit. However, it was the departure of one Andrew Lauder, United Artists' A&R man, that proved more significant in the long-term. Although CBS were offering more money, the Buzzcocks signed to UA because they liked Lauder, who believed in giving artists creative control. He didn't demur when the band told him their first single would be Orgasm

EVERYBODY'S HAPPY NOWADAYS BUZZCOCKS

"Punk was about expressing things in songs that wouldn't be talked about... being honest. It was very liberating." PETE SHELLEY

Pete Shelley on Top Of The Pops, 6 July 1978. (Inset) Buzzcocks in the real world, Manchester, 1978.

Addict, an arch commentary on the compulsion of sex, featuring use of the F-word and bon mots like "beating your meat to pulp".

"Not a chance of being played on the radio," agrees Shelley. "It took a lot of bottle. Andrew Lauder was a visionary. It was good to be with people who weren't baulking at having to deal with a band called Buzzcocks. It brought about an opening up of what people could express. It wasn't just what would sell. That was no longer the driving force."

Lauder left in 1978 to set up his own label. This deprived the Buzzcocks of a powerful ally in the record company boardroom, and Shelley missed his reassuring

presence. His expressions of alienation were very real. By the time the band left for America, they had finished their third album, A Different Kind Of Tension. Its last track, I Believe, contained one of Shelley's existential refrains: "There is no love in this world anymore."

America cemented his embattled sense of self. The second night at New York's Club 57 ended in disarray after a dispute with the gig's sponsor, radio station WPIX FM, during which Maher tore down an onstage ID banner and band photographer Ian Rogers headbutted a WPIX FM representative. The Buzzcocks were smuggled out of the venue and, accompanied by various Ramones, fled down St Mark's Place.

BY THE TIME the tour reached the West Coast, the enthusiastic patronage of their US label boss, Miles Copeland of IRS, had generated massive anticipation. The same night as the Buzzcocks sold out the 5000-capacity Santa Monica Civic Center, Elvis Costello was at the Whisky A-Go-Go in Hollywood – capacity 500. Diggle thought: "Fucking hell, Elvis is playing there?"

"It got mad," he says. "Drink, drugs. Wild stuff. Proper American rock'n'roll scenes. It affects you. I mean, we embraced it, we loved it. But it was like a Saturday night with no Sunday morning – you couldn't read the papers and chill out. No matter how wrecked you were, the next day you're like, 'Fucking hell, it's 8.30am and we're on a plane!' It took its toll. I got a bit lost, but I think Pete was more lost than me."

"It did my head in," agrees Shelley. "Americans have no sense of irony. Nobody was listening to a fucking word I was saying. Everyone's bouncing around us, going, 'Yay! This is fantastic!' And it was a nightmare. I was in a meltdown situation. Steve was in his element. His whole dream has been to be put on that pedestal. His reason for doing things is different to mine. Mine has always been, you've got the opportunity to communicate with people. It's what the punk ideology always was. But Steve was not an instrumental part of the methodology or the ideology of Buzzcocks."

Twenty-five years on, the differing perspectives of the two main Buzzcocks suggest the only real harmony between Steve Diggle and Pete Shelley prevails onstage. Interviewed separately, each likens their relationship to that of brothers, bonded by shared experience but with little in common. These "ideological differences", as Shelley puts it, kicked in as the band finally began to unravel in 1980. That March, United Artists was taken over by EMI, leaving the Buzzcocks defenceless to the commercially driven priorities of a corporate company. They responded by making their least commercial records. Envisioned as a series of singles to subsequently form an album, Parts 1-3 were taped over two months in four different studios; the kinetic momentum of 1977-'78 was gone. "We'd done three albums in two years," says Shelley. "Everybody was wrecked."

With regular producer Martin Rushent unavailable, the band turned to Martin Hannett, renowned for his work with Joy Division and who had produced Spiral Scratch back in '76. The sessions were chaotic and drug-drenched – Hannett the shaman, the band his (mostly) willing disciples. "You couldn't start without having 10 joints," says Diggle. "There was coke all over the desk and the speakers. We were used to it on the road, but I wouldn't recommend making a record like that."

HALFWAY THROUGH MIXING at West London's Townhouse studio, the drug-abstinent Garvey walked out. Some days nothing would get done until 2am as everyone awaited the arrival of heroin and cocaine for Hannett to make speedballs. Shelley confronted his inner demons by method recording. Because Strange Thing was about depression, Shelley recorded it on antidepressants. For Are Everything, an LSD-fuelled riddle on the meaning of life, he gave up writing straightforward narrative. Instead, the song's psychedelic murk laid bare a young man on the verge of a mental precipice, his journey assisted by the decision to only work on the track when he was on acid.

"It was about being honest," says Shelley. "Are Everything tried to express what the drug experience revealed to me. Martin would be playing it and I would be under the desk, quaking with fear. There was no way I could carry on. I was going to that place you don't want to go to. Admitting to the utter desolation of any dream I'd had of how things would turn out, when I was naive and just being a punk."

The end was nigh. Increasingly estranged from each other and cut adrift by EMI after none of the Parts 1-3 singles made the Top 60, the Buzzcocks half-heartedly regrouped at the start of 1981 to make their fourth album, to discover that years of living beyond their means had left them destitute. Garvey couldn't even afford a bass amp.

Instead of attempting to make an album under such circumstances, Rushent took Shelley to his home studio to work on some demos. Using synthesizers and computer programs, they recorded a version of Homosapien, a song Shelley had written back in 1974. Rather than impose the Buzzcocks' group structure on to this new musical direction, on 6 March 1981, Shelley had a solicitor send letters to Diggle, Garvey and Maher "dissolving the partnership – because that's all it was".

Pete Shelley on the road and getting lost in the USA, 1979.

"You couldn't start a session without 10 joints. There was coke all over the desk." STEVE DIGGLE

Diggle: "I thought he was a fucking coward. He could have phoned me. By that time I was thinking we should give this up because it's become a nightmare. We'd done everything we could."

Shelley: "It was cowardly, but it would have been more cowardly to continue. There's no point having a band if you're going to make them compromise their own individuality. I was trapped – so I got out before the endgame kicked in."

In September 1981, Homosapien was released as Pete Shelley's debut solo single. Almost exactly eight years later, the classic Buzzcocks line-up began a US tour, heralding the start of an ongoing reunion that sees Diggle and Shelley still recording and gigging together today, alongside bassist Tony Barber and drummer Phil Barker. It's testimony to their core romantic ideals that the Buzzcocks are the only band of the punk era to survive as a credible artistic force. "The energy and vitality is still there," says Diggle. "Plus, we sing those songs with more experience now. The music's there forever."

"It's still the same kid who started back then who's sat here now," says Shelley. "The same passion, the same vigour – and it still matters." The singer's eyes are suddenly brimming with tears. "In fact, it matters even more."

(From left)
Sid Vicious,
Johnny Rotten
and Steve
Jones play
Stockholm,
Sweden,
July 1977.

NORTHERN EXPOSURE

Banned from playing live in England, in July 1977 the Sex Pistols invaded punk-hungry Sweden to play to gangsters, runaways and Vietnam deserters. Giovanni Dadomo witnessed the carnage.

THE SEX PISTOLS are at large in Stockholm, capital of Sweden. It is a tedious place, fit only for exiles and the living dead. Last week our heroes gave a strained performance before an audience of over-23s. Meanwhile, the sleeping city streets are in the grip of the Rags, a singularly unpleasant form of local delinquent.

That first night of their Scandinavian mini-tour ground itself into nothingness with an impromptu party in a hotel room. Much beer was quaffed and many a word

spoken, each as unmemorable as the other. One or two people laughed occasionally and one far from unattractive blonde stumbled drunkenly around, finally collapsing in a heap at Johnny Rotten's feet. Some 20 people were involved, with the genders split evenly. Every person there looked as if they'd just got off a plane from London – despite the fact that less than half the company was British.

One young Swede offered John Rotten a highly sophisticated tape recorder for £100 – less than half its actual cost.

172

BLÅGUL

The boy would, he promised, steal the same from his place of work. Later, he confessed that his father owned the company. "But I hate my father," concluded the son, whose clothes were ragged and hair short and spiky, according to the demands of contemporary fashion.

Rotten sat in the corner with a beer and said very little. Young girls took turns to sit close and attempt conversation. His replies were polite, yet curt and disinterested. Meanwhile, the babble continued all around him. And the young girls giggled. One was in plastic with the face of a doll, a second was still a child, and a third was dressed in red. Steve Jones and Paul Cook, the guitarist and drummer, gave up early. An hour or more of inconsequential chatter followed their exits. Finally, Rotten got up. "I'm bored," he said. "I'm going to bed." And then he left the room.

It was like a cinema when all the fuses blow. Suddenly everyone wanted out.

NEXT DAY, THURSDAY, starts at 2pm. John Rotten strides purposefully down the corridor. He has on a long peaked cap and a vast, blotchy denim jerkin over a leather jacket. He looks like a fugitive from Rommel's Afrika Corps.

The Sex Pistols gather in the hotel lounge, next stop: Suicide. This turns out to be a pokey little shop in the old town, all narrow cobbled alleys and no cars. The shop itself is full of familiar jumble: T-shirts with stencils, transparent ties and studded leather bracelets. All very 'SEX' and yet much shabbier than the originals.

Cans of beer and popping flashbulbs. Steve sips and chats: "I've never been so bored in my life." John wanders around, manages to find plenty of bits and pieces. A shirt covered in stencils, a particularly garish tie. At 10.15pm the band are back in the dressing room of the Happy House. There are huge crowds in the streets outside and plenty of Polis [Swedish police]. Seems the Rags are out in force tonight. The Polis block off the street outside to keep the troublemakers at bay.

This time most of the young fans from yesterday have been let into the hall. Still,

there are two or three hundred left outside. "Can you get me a ticket? I'll give you money… lots of money…"

Rotten's curled up in the corner once more as the others turn up. An antique hippy arrives, hobbling on a walking stick. Seems he's a former Vietnam deserter with no passport. Can't go home… Mentions Little Feat's Lowell George somewhere in his ramble.

"Oo?" says Paul Cook. "Oh, got little feet has he? Poor sod."

The second show picks up where the first left off. Starts great and stays that way. Sex Pistols at magnum force. Great rock'n'roll – warts and all.

"WAAAHH!" go the Swedes as the curtain opens.

"Owww yer doin'?" says Rotten.

"WAAAHH!" go the Swedes.

"It's awwwllrrrright!!" says John triumphantly leaping head-first into Anarchy. And then, "Number two!" And straight into I Wanna Be Me.

And "WAAAHH!" go the Swedes as the number tilts into its false finish. Then they bounce furiously once more through the last verse.

"'Avin' fun?"

"YEAH!"

"Good!"

More rock'n'roll: I'm A Lazy Sod, Outta My Head [Did You No Wrong] with howling feedback from Steve, and more: Submission, featuring Rotten's astonishing cackle solo in the middle and fading on the crazy dolphin sounds only he knows how to make. By No Feelings, Sid's engaged in

Young Swedes feel the Pistols' live heat.

BY NO FEELINGS, SID'S IN A SPITTING CONTEST WITH THE FRONT ROW.

a non-stop spitting contest with a bunch of kids at the front. With Problems, John's voice has already hoarsened to something like the sound of a rusty power tool. And the Swedes cheer themselves silly for God Save The Queen.

"If you want more you'll have to ask for it," says Rotten; a far cry from the "Don't waste my time" of the early days.

"We want more," chant the obliging Swedes. One Pretty Vacant comin' up, fresh from the furnace. Whammer-lama!

PHOTO: © DENNIS MORRIS

"Wannauvverwon?"

"WE WANT MORE! WE WANT MORE!"

Paul Cook starts up No Fun. Suddenly everyone's Sydney Greenstreet, sweat pouring from all the ducts and never enough handkerchief to soak it away. And someone who remembers says it was just like the Stones 10 years before. Amazing what a foul-mouthed pop group can do, given the right time and place.

Twenty minutes later the band are relaxed in a closed-off first-floor bar. Steve and Paul are listening to a cassette of the gig. "Phaw! Listen to that guitar," says Paul. And, yeah, maybe Steve did play a couple of crazy bits but nobody noticed when it was *then*, back when it really mattered. Sid's chatting to various odds and sods, and John's trying to avoid the same. The radio man from this afternoon still wants to know if the interview was OK, and everyone else wants to know something too. "They never say what you want them to say anyway," says John to no one in particular before finding sanctuary under a table.

Not for long. A minute later there are screams, shouts, car-horns wailing and the sound of running feet from the street below. Seconds later, everyone's at the windows. We see Polis running off down a side street, shortly followed by the arrival of an ambulance. Ten minutes later the nasty stories get through.

Seems one girl had four safety pins pulled right through the ear lobe, others had them torn from their cheeks. Lots of fighting; arrests, 40 or 50 people taken to hospital. Eventually the band and the rest of the party are told it's time to leave. Down the back stairs and into the waiting limos, and out of the hotel with a full

escort of Polis, including a couple of vans and motorcycles.

After an hour or so stuck in one of the hotel rooms, Paul, Steve and Sid decide they want to go out. John isn't interested. Probably doesn't feel none too splendid anyway, having recently emptied the contents of his stomach – "Guinness and bits of tatter," says Rotten – into a toilet. Only outside the locked doors of the hotel there's a bunch of geezers combing their hair and pulling 'Marlon Brando in The Wild One' poses and none of them look like autograph hunters. Road manager John 'Boogie' Tiberi tries vainly to keep everyone out of sight, but the Rags split back to their motors when two Polis cars draw up.

Considering the number, it's probably best to stay put, then. "Nah. They ain't got no bottle," says John. "If you charged 'em they'd run away." But the hotel staff insist we return to our rooms. Seems there's a chance that somebody's broken in already. Accordingly, a couple of burly

Johnny Rotten, Daddy's Dance Hall, Copenhagen, 13 July 1977.

cops search the building from the bottom up, each with a mean-looking Alsatian straining at the leash.

ROTTEN'S ROOM IS so tidy it's almost as if it's uninhabited. One of the double beds is folded away, making the room look even bigger. The other bed's freshly made. John hasn't used it, prefers the long yellow sofa. With disarming courtesy he offers a choice of beers or Cokes from the fridge. There's a book on the dressing table, a large hardback with a Swedish text. But words aren't needed – the large coloured pictures which cover most of the pages tell all: a step-by-step record of the development of the human foetus, from egg to birth.

"Someone give it to me last week," says John. He points to various pictures with a mixture of awe and discomfort. The same way most people react when they're exposed to something so familiar yet so alien. Somewhere among mostly disposable chit-chat there's the odd bit that sticks in the brain. Like, remember how Sid was in a band called The Flowers Of Romance?

"I given 'em that name," John says. "It was the name of a song we used to start with in the early days. Just noise, no music – just to confuse the people who said we couldn't play."

And no, certainly not, comes the reply as to whether Sid's settled down a lot since he's been in the band: "He's always been like that."

But bugger the psychology, eh, John? Just tell us about your

'wardrobe'. Rotten leans across to the beaten suitcase by his feet and begins a detailed inventory, seemingly amused by the question. And so, pausing only to inform his audience that he's recently had an attack of the scabies, John Rotten flips open his suitcase and begins to itemise, thus: "One waiter's jacket which I nicked. One soap bag which contains no soap, nothing except a toothbrush and face towel which I haven't used. A mohair jumper that's fallen to bits and I don't want any more. A jacket which I couldn't consider any more 'cos I'm bored with that kind of thing. A towel which I nicked from a hotel… A shirt what someone give me which is apparently what the Swedes wore when they were peasants working in a field – 90 years old, this geezer assured me. One white tuxedo which Sid give me. One pair of biker gloves which…" he chuckles. "I don't know why I bought them. A tie. Two seals."

Two seals?

"Exactly. Little toy ones, one about six inches high with silver fur, and a muddier little brother some two or three inches smaller. Real tourist bait. Aren't they cute? I thought that was really horrible because they kill a live one to make them. I had to have one to prove that, yeah, that is vile. I thought it was horrible. Poor little things. Innit sad?

"A rubber T-shirt, which I bought. That's part of those stupid bondage pants,

"Sure you've got it, Sid?" Cook, Jones and Vicious backstage in Stockholm.

PHOTOS: © DENNIS MORRIS, JÜRGEN ANGEL

ROTTEN PAUSES ONLY TO iNFORM US THAT HE'S RECENTLY HAD SCABiES.

which I can't remember where I put. Think I might've lost them. What a pity," he all but sneers.

And more yet…

"A hat. A shirt which was given to me by Boogie," Rotten goes on. "A T-shirt, which was given to me by a club. A long pair of

socks. And a pair of Levi's which was given to me.

"So all that I brought," he concludes, scanning the jumble around his feet, "was a belt, two pairs of socks, two pairs of underpants, a shirt, a tie, a pair of denims, a pair of bondage pants, a denim

top and a white coat. And that's it, that's all I had. It's all I own.

"It's ridiculous but I hate clothes and I can't stand owning them. Anybody want this?" says Rotten, holding up the ragged blue mohair jumper. "Look at it! It's a classic. My God! You can chase the moths out with it. Anybody wannit?"

Along with a dose of scabies?

"Oh no," John laughs. "I only said that to be fashionable. Don't be silly."

Suddenly his face falls. "All I've got," he says, pointing down at the ragged pile. "Don't you feel sorry for me?"

THE MEN IN BLACK

At first, The Stranglers laughed off their reputation as women-hating, leather-clad thugs. But as they became embroiled in UFO conspiracy theories and Viking mythology, the darkness became very real.

WORDS: IAN HARRISON. PHOTO: REDFERNS

AS 1977 MOVED into 1978, the unravelling of punk was alarming those closest to the scene. With method punk bands appearing all the time and new mutant strains emerging from the provinces, the Sex Pistols' final disintegration at San Francisco's Winterland on 14 January 1978 seemed like the last gasp.

"It was a strange time," says The Stranglers' guitarist and co-frontman Hugh Cornwell. "The writing was on the wall for punk, and everyone was nervous about what would happen next. We weren't even sure if we had a career any more. But it did leave us with a blank canvas."

For the next three years The Stranglers would focus their efforts on filling this canvas with a single colour: black. In time, their brushstrokes would get wilder and darker. Deeds of dreadful note would be done in their name as hard drugs, thuggery, imprisonment, UFOs and luck seemingly too bad to be coincidental gathered around them.

How much of this bad reputation was their own doing has become central to this most divisive of groups' mythology. The media played their part, reporting on every transgression with relish. The Stranglers would develop many ways to defend their turf, often by getting their retaliation in first.

"They always had a jug of water onstage," recalls Ian Grant, The Stranglers' co-manager between 1976 and 1980. "Except it wasn't – they'd pissed in it. If anyone started gobbing they'd throw it over the front row. Then they'd say, 'Now you're Stranglers piss-heads.'"

A BAND COULDN'T ask for a better year than The Stranglers' 1977. Active since 1974, they'd re-thought their malevolent showband origins and ridden the punk wave to two UK Top 10 albums and three Top 10 singles. Though cast as cartoon degenerates in the tabloids, their musical sophistication set them apart from other punk bands. But their destructive tendencies were becoming a problem. "Things were polarised in 1978," recalls bassist and co-frontman Jean-Jacques Burnel. "It was a case of, 'If you're not with us, you're against us.' But the spirit of the group was very strong. We were veterans of violence being directed at us, because being in The Stranglers *was* violent, from the start."

Lately followed by the Hell's Angels, and still accompanied by their private militia, the Finchley Boys, the Stranglers were also infamous for the short-fused, martial arts expert Burnel's appetite for fisticuffs. In punk's first year alone he attacked The Clash's Paul Simonon and rock journalist Jon Savage. Meanwhile, various ambiguities on matters of sexual politics had the group pegged as misogynists as well as thugs. Nevertheless, being too vile even for punk had a certain cachet. "That reputation was justified," admits Cornwell. "Anyone who knew us knew we had a good sense of humour, but anyone reading about us would believe that we were the most evil, humourless people on earth. We had a top-flight publicity man, Alan Edwards, who made the most of anything that happened. We were just happy for the recognition."

The group was strange and singular enough to begin with, satisfying few, if any, of the prerequisites of the punk ethos. Keyboardist Dave Greenfield, a science-minded occultist, actually had a moustache. Drummer Jet Black, noticeably mature for a pop star, had played in '50s jazz combos. Burnel, of French parentage, was a classically trained guitarist who ran with bikers. Then there was Cornwell, a songwriter and guitarist of uncommon flair, but with a tendency to follow his demons.

"Hugh was an ageing hippy," says Grant. "Jet used to go looking for UFOs and would say things like, 'Jesus was a man in black from another planet.' Dave never spoke, he just came out with one-line quips. He said to me once, 'I'll show you the meaning of life', which we took to mean a tab of acid. JJ could lose it because he was so fit and strong through karate, but then he'd have guys coming onstage to take him on."

In December 1977, punk's most maladjusted group went into Bear Shank Lodge studio, Northamptonshire, to record Black And White, their third LP. The songs were more mysterious and perplexing than

"We were veterans of violence, because being in the band was violent from the start." JEAN-JACQUES BURNEL

PHOTO: RAY STEVENSON

anything the band had created before. Conceived as a split between 'black' and 'white' sides, it showed a group going deeper into a new milieu; this was music of greater finesse, with songs of apocalyptic negativity. Curfew is about the rise of fascism; Death And Night And Blood (Yukio) was Burnel's song to Yukio Mishima, the homosexual samurai novelist who committed ritual suicide in 1970; Enough Time dealt with nuclear fallout. Released in 1978, the album reached Number 2 in the UK.

Significantly, Black And White was the first, fateful, meeting of the group and the concept of the Men In Black. These were black-suited aliens said to intimidate those who've had encounters with UFOs into silence, and part of a wider cosmic conspiracy that alleges extra-terrestrials rule the world. Cornwell was so intrigued he suggested they write an entire LP about the subject.

If their thoughts were turning to the cosmos, there was also an earthier side. On their first US tour in April, they responded flippantly to the feminist Housewives' Movement who were protesting outside a date in Michigan. "I wrote a very inflammatory statement: 'The Stranglers have always loved women for their movements and will continue to do so,'" says Cornwell. "That was us having a laugh at someone's hysteria. But you do things for a laugh sometimes and then think, 'God, that backfired.'"

The band's image as overgrown kids sniggering with obscene delight at thoughts of sex received final clarifi-cation – to their detractors at least – in September.

"I was living in Acton with three girls: my girlfriend, her 16-year-old sister and a stripper called Lynn," recalls Burnel. "We were getting accused of being sexist, so Lynn said, 'This is bollocks, I'll show them who's in control.' So she recruited a few of her colleagues to help out, and my girlfriend's sister asked if she could take part too. They came onstage with us during Nice 'N' Sleazy when we played Battersea Park. Afterwards the press said we were exploiting them and being sexist, but the point was the girls showing how easily they could control the guys. I mean, one of the Finchley Boys came on and took his trousers off! It was very tongue-in-cheek."

WHETHER OR NOT they were really joking is what gave The Stranglers their peculiar edge. While so much of their work was mordant and dour, the toilet humour showed a group laudably blunt in their baseness. On the cover of a June '78 Melody Maker, Burnel provocatively declared: "Everyone knows Americans have smaller brains." Death threats from Ramones fans followed. In December, disgusted that their US label A&M wanted to release a Best Of as their first American album, they went to their management's UK office and asked how to send a telex.

"They sent a telex saying, 'Dear A&M, Get fucked. Love, The Stranglers,'" says Grant, still mildly incredulous 27 years on. "So A&M put all their money and energy into The Police and Joe Jackson instead, and made them very successful in America. I went into the American offices about three years later, and The Stranglers' telex had been blown up into a big poster in the reception."

Things fared little better in Germany. Burnel, allegedly, refused to fly Lufthansa. Was he not over-fond of Germans? "None of them were," snorts Grant. "At the first gig in Germany, we were having a party in my room with some fans – me, JJ and Hugh. Jet walks in and goes, 'If our parents had done a better job you wouldn't be here right now.' Fucking hell, Jet!"

By this time their sole manager, Grant was ideally placed to view the wreckage as The Stranglers' wacky race went on. On their second visit to Japan in 1979 they went home with a bad cheque from a crooked promoter and lost £18,000. A tour of Australia was distinguished by old-fashioned outrage: during an interview on a current affairs show, they told the fans watching at home how great drugs were, while in Adelaide they were again picketed by women's groups.

"They were the true punks because they didn't give a hoot who they offended," says Grant. "JJ and Hugh were always obnoxious because they thought they should be. It was mischief, but it wasn't malice. JJ was a soft guy at heart – he came from a sheltered background. When his mother was around he wouldn't wear his leather jacket, he'd put a blazer on."

Away from his mother, though, the waggish Burnel ensured there was no shortage of hi-jinks throughout 1979. With a particular hatred of journalists, he made it his mission to make them pay for their poor opinion of his beloved group. Record Mirror's Ronnie Gurr was kidnapped in a van and terrorised by the bassist and some loyal Finchley Boys. Deanne Pearson was abandoned in the Portuguese countryside where she was covering the video shoot for Nuclear Device. French writer Phillipe Manoeuvre was singled out for the most elaborate punishment. "We were recording The Raven in Paris to save tax," recalls Burnel. "This young reporter kept hassling us, so I agreed if he came along I would 'accord' him an interview. So I took him to the first floor of the Eiffel Tower, 300 feet up, de-bagged him and tied him with gaffer tape to one of the girders. And left him there."

Suitably, The Raven was distinguished by strange measures of all kinds. Recorded in June 1979, the back cover showed the band on a Viking longship, while the title referred to one of the Norse god Odin's birds that acted as his eyes on creation. This time, subjects included Iran's Islamic revolution and genetic engineering. Cornwell admits the atmosphere was becoming claustrophobic in The Stranglers' bunker.

"We were intensely involved with the idea of the Men In Black – probably not to our good. It made us terribly depressed. We were reading Nostradamus's predictions about the Shah of Iran, and wondered if the world was going to end, every day. When you're taking a lot of mind-expanding substances and you're high most of the time, it affects the way your mind works. We were having drug-fuelled paranoid visions."

At first, it didn't slow their progress. In August 1979 the Stranglers supported The Who at Wembley, scoring a Number 14 hit with Duchess the same month. Released in September, The Raven would reach Number 4. That November, though, the group's luck turned. Cornwell, on the way back to London from a show in Cardiff, was busted for heroin possession. It wasn't all he was carrying. In his bag was a party pack of drugs, including cocaine, marijuana and magic mushrooms. He was sentenced to eight weeks' jail and a £300 fine. An appeal on 21 March 1980 was unsuccessful. "My thinking was, 'You can't arrest me,'" he says today. "Going inside was, for me, the beginning of the dark ages. It was alright until we did The Raven. After that it was very difficult, very dark."

THE STRANGLERS COULDN'T afford to show any weakness. On 3 and 4 April they played two benefit gigs at the Rainbow, Finsbury Park with The Cure's Robert Smith and Peter Hammill among those deputising for Cornwell. Cornwell was represented by a cardboard cutout, hanging from a noose.

His incarceration cost the band around £250,000. A series of concerts in India was cancelled, and The Stranglers' karmic opposites – The Police – ended up getting there first. When the band finally visited their singer in Pentonville, they didn't have enough money on them to buy him a cup of tea. As Cornwell quips, it wasn't the only time that year when The Stranglers would all be together in jail.

After his release on 25 April, Cornwell declared that his drugs career was over. It wasn't: he simply became more careful. When the group resumed recording their next album at Pathé Marconi in Paris, and embarked on a European tour, they became embroiled in their worst episode yet of futile destruction.

The Stranglers put it in black and white: (clockwise from front) Jean-Jacques Burnel, Jet Black, Dave Greenfield and Hugh Cornwell, 1978.

"They were doing heroin, which effectively made them unmanageable," says Grant, who had decided to end his association with the group. "All this stuff about bad luck and the Men In Black – the bad luck was just foolishness. They were a band that was going to take over the world and the reason they didn't is because they fucked it up. I was constantly thwarted and frustrated."

THERE WAS MORE bad luck to come. Today, Grant insists that he went to see Jet Black at his home in Tewkesbury, where he told the group they were paying their insurance on a monthly basis. When a van containing their equipment was stolen that October, no one had paid the premium. The group lost £46,000 and almost split. January 1981 finally brought a reason to be cheerful when The Stranglers received suspended sentences over the Nice riot. But reviews of the Top 10 album The Gospel According To The Meninblack were unfavourable, and its release marked a new phase. "People said, 'They've disappeared up their own arses,'" recalls Burnel of the techno-sounding concept LP about how God was an astronaut and religion a sinister control system. "But after we purged ourselves of our Men In Black obsession we moved on... If you think negatively, negative things will happen. And we stopped doing that."

Effectively bankrupt and without a Top 10 single since September 1977, the group emerged with a secret weapon. A waltz-time harpsichord piece by Dave Greenfield, later to be called Golden Brown, had been saved for their next album, La Folie. Telling of the pleasures of opiates and a woman of Cornwell's acquaintance, it would become the band's most famous single and reach Number 2 in February 1982.

The Stranglers would last for another eight years of slowly diminishing returns. The violent side to Burnel would eventually cause a terminal rift with Cornwell. Tiring of his former friend's temper, having been kicked through a papier-mâché wall by him in Rome in 1985, Cornwell left in 1990 to go solo. Burnel still plays in a reconstituted Stranglers alongside Greenfield, Black and singer Paul Roberts.

"I don't regret having done what I did," says Burnel of his infamously explosive temper. "It was fun at the time, it was a release. I find provocation amusing, and when the blood is up... But it would be a strange person who doesn't learn. I've been doing karate for over 30 years now and I can't fly off the handle any more. But then, it was a time of explosion and red mist, a chemically altered time..."

"Going inside was the beginning of the dark ages. It was alright until we did The Raven." HUGH CORNWELL

Released in 1986, the Nice In Nice single was a humorous dig at their imprisonment in Nice in 1980. The reality was anything but comical, except to the likes of Ronnie Gurr, Deanne Pearson, etc.

En route to Italy and Greece, the band organised an impromptu show at the University of Nice. Abandoning their set because of electrical problems, The Stranglers made some ambivalent statements from the stage and the student body set about destroying the university's glass amphitheatre, causing £50,000 of damage. The band was arrested for inciting a riot. Imprisoned, Burnel threatened suicide while the unsinkable Jet Black thought in column inches. Grant was dispatched to bail them out.

"After I got out of jail I ended up straight back there in France, which really bummed me out," says Cornwell. "It was awful – cockroaches coming out of the floor, real squalor. And we were falsely imprisoned. We'd got on a real roll of bad luck. Rather then controlling events, we let events control us. We were too naive."

Through My Eyes

Ian Dickson was working as a graphic designer for a mobile crane company when one lunchtime he bought a second-hand Russian Zenith B 35mm camera. Within a couple of years he was photographing bands at Newcastle City Hall, leading to a job with Sounds – the first music paper to champion punk.

Read this

Young punks, July 1977

Fans hanging around outside the Marquee on Wardour Street in London. They're there to see The Damned and are touting issue two of New Pose fanzine, featuring The Stranglers.

Hurry up, Ari

The Slits' Ari Up, 11 March 1977

The Slits were punk's first all-female band, here seen supporting The Clash at the Harlesden Coliseum. Also appearing that night were the Buzzcocks and Subway Sect.

This way up

**Debbie Harry and
Chris Stein, May 1977**

The following month, Ian Dickson
photographed another punk
twosome – from New York new
wavers Blondie – while they
shopped for shoes in Oxford
Street. The group were in the UK
for a 10-date tour with Television.

Going
underground

**Subway Sect,
11 March 1977**

The four teenagers from Mortlake
in south-west London support
The Clash in Harlesden, six months
after the Sect's debut at the
legendary 100 Club Punk Festival.

One-chord
wonders

The Adverts, April 1977

Taken outside Dingwalls, Camden
Lock before that night's gig. The
band formed around the nucleus
of punk couple TV Smith and
Gaye Advert (centre).

Wanna riot

The Clash, 11 March 1977

The group headlining at the
Harlesden Coliseum, a fleapit
cinema specialising in martial arts
movies. Note the 19-year-old
Shane MacGowan dancing in
front of Mick Jones (right).

My way

**Sid Vicious and
Vivienne Westwood,
15 November 1976**

Vicious, who three months later
would join the Sex Pistols, attends
their show at the Notre Dame Hall,
off London's Leicester Square. He
and Vivienne had been friends
since the previous summer, when
Vicious and Rotten had begun
hanging out at 430 King's Road.

Up in smoke

**Dave Greenfield,
September 1977**

The Stranglers keyboardist – who
maintained his moustache and
long hair throughout punk –
pictured during the autumn tour
to promote their second album
that year, No More Heroes.

Floored

**Shane MacGowan,
11 March 1977**

Later that year the young Irishman
would form The Nipple Erectors,
and in 1982, The Pogues. Here at
The Clash's Harlesden Coliseum
gig, he ended up as he would
many more times: horizontal.

If it ain't Stiff…

The Damned, 1977

Formed in July 1976, indie label
Stiff Records were quick off the
mark with their new signings,
allowing The Damned to claim
both first UK punk single (New
Rose) and album (Damned
Damned Damned). Here (from
left), Dave Vanian, Captain
Sensible, Rat Scabies and Brian
James celebrate in inimitable
fashion outside the Stiff offices
on Alexander Street near London's
Westbourne Grove.

Ice queen

**Siouxsie Sioux,
11 July 1977**

Although the Banshees' pounding,
glam-inflected version of punk was
a big attraction in London during
the scene's second summer, they
remained unsigned. Here they play
the opening night at The Vortex,
on a bill that included Adam And
The Ants, The Slits and Sham 69.

Home truth

**X-Ray Spex,
June 1977**

The group's singer, Poly Styrene,
claimed she was making a point
with this shoot in Hastings:
"No smart lad wants to be an
industry-doll," she deadpanned.

The Last Days Of Sid

After the Sex Pistols crashed and burned, Sid Vicious moved to New York with girlfriend Nancy Spungen. A relentlessly ghoulish story of love, smack, prison and murder was about to unfold.

Crawling from the wreckage of the Sex Pistols, the seriously smacked-out Sid Vicious and his girlfriend Nancy Spungen decided to move to New York. To raise cash for the trip, he pulled together The Vicious White Kids, a one-night-only punk supergroup featuring Sid on vocals, original Pistols bassist Glen Matlock, The Damned's drummer Rat Scabies and Rich Kids guitarist Steve New.

22 August 1978

The "Vicious White Kids" play at the Electric Ballroom, London. The audience includes Elvis Costello, Blondie, Joan Jett and Captain Sensible of The Damned.

Rat Scabies (drummer, Vicious White Kids) The group was originally to have been called Sid Sods Off – but Vicious White Kids was an amalgamation of The Rich Kids, The White Cats (Scabies' then current band) and Sid Vicious.

Shane MacGowan (vocalist, The Nipple Erectors and later The Pogues) The place was packed out with a really hip audience. There were a lot of transactions going down – people joining groups, buying drugs, fucking each other in the toilets, you know, the usual stuff.

Rat Scabies Sid walked onstage and some punter gobbed at him – so he smacked him with the mic stand.

Frank Murray (manager, Electric Ballroom) Sid took up the role of lead singer without an instrument, and loved it. He kept throwing Elvis shapes and grabbing his crotch – he was doing it years before Michael Jackson. He obviously hated being a bass player, and this was his band. It was as though he was living out his fantasy of being the singer and getting all the attention.

> ## "Sid walked on stage and some punter gobbed at him – so he smacked him with the mic stand."
> RAT SCABIES, DRUMMER, VICIOUS WHITE KIDS

Rat Scabies We only had a 20-minute set, so we had to play it twice! Nancy joined us onstage for the second set.

Frank Murray Nancy just squealed into the mic like a bad dose of feedback.

Late August 1978

Sid and Nancy fly to New York and move into the Chelsea Hotel.

Steve Dior (musician/friend of Sid) The first thing we did was enrol them at the methadone clinic. They had acquired sizeable heroin habits in London.

7 September 1978

Sid plays the first of several gigs at Max's Kansas City, New York. His band includes former New York Dolls Jerry Nolan and Arthur Kane, plus Mick Jones of The Clash.

Terry Ork (booker, Max's Kansas City) Nancy became Sid's manager. They'd come by Max's and Sid wanted to do a gig. They needed money, because they were on heroin.

Bob Gruen (photographer) Sid was stoned and pathetic. Arthur Kane was on bass, so all Sid had to do was just sing. They would start a song, but they hadn't rehearsed, so they'd stop because Sid had forgotten the words.

New York state: Sid at Max's Kansas City with Mick Jones and Jerry Nolan (both obscured), bassist Arthur Kane and guitarist Steve Dior, September 1978.

Sid at the Electric Ballroom, London, 22 August 1978.

Mick Jones (guitarist, The Clash) We just about managed five songs. Five songs for five bucks. It was a nightmare between shows, it was full on. Sid was sort of semi-there. It was a serious drug thing. Me and Joe [Strummer] kept looking at each other, because we couldn't believe it. The people there were as out of it as you can be without actually being dead.

Bob Gruen (photographer) Mick looked a bit lost – the band were so lame.

28 September 1978

Sid plays another gig at Max's Kansas City.

Chris Spedding (rock guitarist) I went backstage afterwards and when I shook Sid's hand I felt wetness. I saw blood in my hand. I thought he was cutting my hand with broken glass, because he was well known for self-mutilation, but then I saw that it was his blood, and ice, not broken glass.

Unholy alliance: The Vicious White Kids, aka Matlock, Vicious, New and Scabies, plus Spungen.

A mortuary van collects Nancy Spungen's body at the Chelsea Hotel, 12 October 1978.

Sid returns to court with his mother, Anne Beverley, November 1978.

8 October 1978

Nancy phones her mother, Deborah.

Deborah Spungen She said he'd been hitting her. I spent the following days worrying. And then she didn't call. And never called again.

12 October 1978

At 9.30am, a phone call alerts hotel staff that someone is injured in Sid's room. When emergency personnel arrive, Nancy is dead from a stab wound to the stomach.

Sid Vicious There was blood everywhere. On the sheets, on the pillowcase, all over the mattress and the floor leading into the bathroom. My first thought was that she had been killed.

13 October 1978

In court, Sid is charged with murdering Nancy Spungen. With bail set at $50,000, he is admitted to the Detox Unit at Rikers Island prison.

16 October 1978

Virgin Records wires $50,000 to Pistols manager Malcolm McLaren to bail Sid from jail.

Malcolm McLaren One of the reasons I want Sid out is to make a new album in New York. With a bit of luck the money from the record might pay for the trial.

23 October 1978

Sid slits his wrists in the room he is sharing with his mother, Anne Beverley, at the Hotel Seville, Madison Avenue.

Malcolm McLaren He had been suffering rapid methadone withdrawal over the weekend, and by that evening he panicked. They patched up his arms and gave him 50 milligrams of methadone, which stabilised him.

28 October 1978

Sid attempts suicide again in the Hotel Seville, by slashing his wrists with a razorblade and a broken lightbulb, before trying to jump out of the window. He is admitted to the psychiatric ward of Bellevue Hospital.

30 October 1978

Sid phones Deborah Spungen and begs her to visit him. Soon afterwards, she receives a final letter from him.

Sid Vicious (to Mrs Spungen) We always knew that we would go to the same place when we died. We so much wanted to die together in each other's arms. I cry every time I think about that. I promised my baby that I would kill myself if anything ever happened to her, and she promised me the same. This is my final commitment to my love.

5 December 1978

Sid is involved in a fight at the Hurrah club, New York. He is arrested the following day.

Rockets Redglare (comedian, drug dealer) Patti Smith's brother and his girlfriend were in front of us. And Sid was dancing around, playin', playing around, and… he fucked up. I think he did something to Patti Smith's brother's girlfriend, and they got into words. Sid hit him with a beer mug.

1 February 1979

Having been sent back to prison, Sid is released on bail again. Sid celebrates at the Greenwich Village apartment of a new girlfriend, actress Michelle Robinson. At the party he takes a hit of heroin supplied by his mother.

Anne Beverley He knew the smack was pure and strong, and so he took a lot less than usual.

2 February 1979

Sid dies of a heroin overdose in Michelle Robinson's bed.

Anne Beverley He was lying there quite peacefully. I shook him until I realised he was very cold and very dead.

Sid Vicious (suicide note) We had a death pact. I have to keep my half of the bargain. Please bury me next to my baby. Bury me in my leather jacket, jeans and motorcycle boots. Goodbye.

> "He was lying there quite peacefully. I shook him until I realised he was very cold and very dead." SID'S MOTHER, ANNE BEVERLEY

Johnny Rotten I heard it on the news. Nobody bothered to tell me. I felt nothing at the time. It's like the information of anyone's death. It doesn't hit you at first. In a curious way, I felt almost relieved.

In the course of their first US tour, The Clash arrive in California.

Joe Strummer (frontman, The Clash) I woke up to be told that Sid Vicious had died. I couldn't eat my breakfast.

The Pretenders play their first London gig at the Moonlight Club, West Hampstead.

Chrissie Hynde (The Pretenders) Someone came up to me and said, "Wow, what about Sid?" I looked at him and said, "What about Sid?" Then I realised no one had told me about Sid because they were afraid it would bum me out before the gig. Instead, I found out right before I went on.

Sources: Please Kill Me (The Uncensored Oral History Of Punk) by Legs McNeil and Gillian McCain (Little, Brown & Co, 1996); David Dalton's Sid Vicious feature in MOJO magazine, February 2005; England's Dreaming by Jon Savage (Faber & Faber, 1991); And I Don't Want To Live This Life by Deborah Spungen (Corgi Books, 1984)

THE NUTTERS' CLUB

When The Damned were resurrected in 1978, guitarist Captain Sensible seized control. Roll on five years of hits, hammer fights, jet-set drugs and broken hearts.

WORDS: ANDREW PERRY.
PHOTO: ACE RECORDS

THE DAMNED, AS we had first known them, died one night in France in October 1977. Not many dates into a badly planned, under-funded European tour, drummer Rat Scabies finally wigged out. Delirious from booze, drugs and malnutrition, he got into a fight in a French hotel lobby, trashed it single-handedly, then got beaten up by security men while, he claims, his bandmates looked on laughing.

Rat repaired to his room to lick his wounds. He drank two bottles of brandy, set up a campfire in the middle of the floor and climbed outside on to his window-ledge in an apparent bid to commit suicide. It was his 21st birthday.

The Damned had once been part of punk's inner circle. They had been billed to co-headline the Anarchy tour but, after falling foul of the Pistols/Clash politico elite, were shunned and treated as outsiders. Now they were in terminal decline, accelerated by internal disagreements. The band's autocratic leader and songwriter, guitarist Brian James, had brought in a second guitarist, Lu Edmonds, to try to make them sound like the MC5.

"We didn't need another fucking guitarist," says Scabies, né Chris Millar. "We'd got Brian James. I worshipped his playing. The idea was, Lu might be a catalyst for us to do something new. He wasn't. It just meant Brian did less."

The second Damned album, Music For Pleasure, packed a shadow of its eponymous predecessor's punch. It flopped. Scabies quit. The Damned's label, Stiff, dropped them. Regardless, they limped onwards with various stand-in drummers until early '78, when Brian, fed up with the tension and failure, called time. On 8 April, with Scabies back on drums, they played a final show at London's Rainbow Theatre.

"Jim Capaldi, from Traffic, came into the dressing room," recalls Brian. "None of us had ever met him – he just turned up, carrying all these old Traffic albums that looked like he'd found them in a skip. He pointed at them and went, 'This was me, you know...'"

The Damned looked destined for the same tragic fate – but survived. After making some of the most furious rock music of all time, urinating and vomiting on their audience, being repeatedly banned for crimes real and imagined, setting fire to hotels, administering and receiving countless thumpings, and being the first to do almost everything that a punk rocker might ever dream of doing (first single, album, US tour, split, etc) – after all this, what Captain Sensible refers to as "the Chaos Years" still lay ahead.

Beyond all expectation, they went on to make an album that would rival Damned Damned Damned in raw excellence. It spawned chart hits and helped to reshape and re-energise punk into the '80s. Perhaps most remarkable of all, they did it without their mentor, gang leader and "bloke who did everything" – Brian James.

TWENTY-FIVE YEARS on from that miraculous turnaround, Rat Scabies would balefully admit that if the original Damned was a band with four front men, he was the only one that never got his turn. Initially, Brian ruled the roost. In the mid-'80s, singer Dave Vanian led from the front, hence the nocturnal leanings of Grimly Fiendish, Eloise and the Phantasmagoria album.

In between, The Damned underwent a remarkable transformation thanks to the wayward whims of their bassist Ray Burns, aka Captain Sensible. So far, Sensible had cut a ludicrous dash through punk. He was the nutter who would appear onstage drunk, wearing his trademark red beret and cricket whites, throw up, splatter the front rows with a fire extinguisher, make a racket for 10 minutes, fall over and pass out. He was punk's lunatic fringe incarnate.

According to those who knew him, though, this volatile persona masked a fragile disposition. "Ray had been thrown out by his parents when he was 12," says Nick Kent, who'd gigged with him in a fleeting pre-Damned group. "He was sleeping on Brighton Beach. He was a bit of a mess."

Scabies, who shared blue-collar employment with him at Croydon's Fairfield Halls, says Burns ended up as

(Right) Forever Damned: Captain Sensible in California, February 1982.

(Previous page) The re-formed Damned in New York, spring 1979: (from left) Captain Sensible, Rat Scabies, Alasdair 'Algy' Ward and Dave Vanian.

PHOTO: ALISON S BRAUN/CORBIS

the toilet cleaner there because he was the least popular among the other staff. Through The Damned's first phase, when everyone else on the punk scene was squatting, getting off with each other and doing drugs, the Captain did all that while living back at home in Selhurst with his mum, herself engaged in a struggle with mental illness.

Vanian: "His bedroom – it was an absolute mess. It was all done out like a railway station waiting room. Before they pulled down Selhurst station, he'd broken in and stolen all the signs. He loves his railways. The bed was the only giveaway that someone lived there."

Sensible was destroyed when James announced that he was splitting. The guitarist was five years older than him, and his drive had effectively rescued young Ray from oblivion. However, Burns had always been a guitarist. He'd only played bass out of deference to Brian.

"Those two were never going to get on," says Scabies today, "not while Captain was hanging out at Crass's commune and reading his Socialist Worker, and Brian wanted to be a rock star in a limo."

None too confident of his own abilities, and in awe of James's, Sensible manned the bass until the issue of a second guitarist was floated. If anyone was going to play guitar, thought the Captain, it should be him.

Vanian: "He had racks of tapes in his room – years of him writing songs, weird things that he'd done on his own. All very eccentric, but some of it was brilliant."

Despite these grievances and private ambitions, James's quitting pole-axed Sensible. "I didn't see it coming," he says today. "I would've been happy to continue. I'd always wanted to be in a band and fart-arse about onstage, but it looked like it was back to the toilet-cleaning for me."

Suddenly deprived of the structure of life in The Damned (however impoverished and unhealthy), Sensible went off the rails. He decamped to Amsterdam, where he slept on the floor of a houseboat. That summer, in a haze of booze and drugs, he recorded Jet Boy Jet Girl, his opportunist "cover of a cover of Ça Plane Pour Moi by Plastic Bertrand".

Eventually he returned home. Just as in the winter of 1975-'76, no one in London seemed to be in a solid band; everyone was just flitting about between rehearsal groups. The Captain formed one called King. They played a couple of gigs in France and recorded a John Peel session, but it wasn't going anywhere.

Punk was always going to be a quick burnout thing. None of its key players – art school failures, suburban freaks and single-parented losers to a (wo)man – really believed their blazing-eyed revolution would lead to anything long-term, let alone a career. By 1978, the music industry had succeeded in reinstating a culture of compliant rock stars in it for the money. New wave groups such as Squeeze, Dire Straits and The Pretenders supplied the new sound without all the grief.

BUT THE DAMNED notched up another punk first: they were first to re-form. It began when Sensible phoned Scabies, and Rat confirmed that his combo, The White Cats, was as directionless as King. Rat put together a gig at the Electric Ballroom under the name Les Punks, with himself on drums, Vanian singing, Sensible on guitar and their old partner-in-amphetamine, Lemmy, on bass.

Sensible: "You'd always end up on Lemmy's sofa, and he'd be playing you his World War II videos. He'd be nudging you to keep you awake, because Lemmy didn't sleep a lot. To get my own back, I got him onstage doing SOS, the ABBA song. I won a tenner for that!"

"Sensible's bedroom was done out like a railway station waiting room... an absolute mess." DAVE VANIAN

That was a one-off, but the three Damned folk hung together and were soon gigging as The Doomed with King's singer, Henry Badowski, on bass. After clearing it with Brian, they started 1979 as The Damned again, with a new bassist – Alasdair 'Algy' Ward, previously with The Saints.

Sensible: "Algy was pretty raunchy, a big boozer. He used a metal plectrum to get that fuck-off bass sound. He had a brusque exterior, but that crumbled after half-a-dozen drinks – he had an extremely soft centre. But he carried a hammer around in his pocket, just in case. His battle cry was, 'Where's me 'ammer?'"

Temporarily Damned: at the invitation of Brian James (second right), Lu Edmonds (centre) joins the band for the recording of their second album, 1977.

(Left) Trainspotter Sensible introduces Algy and a friend to some of his bedroom compositions.

Vanian: "We found that we still had a strong following. We had no label but the shows had queues round the block. In London, 100 people climbed three floors up scaffolding and broke in through the roof, but there wasn't a mention of us in the papers. At the NME, they were told not to review The Damned – ever."

The band met with a similar brick wall label-wise. The only offer came from Chiswick, the pioneering indie that had funded The Damned's first-ever demos. Tentative sessions began at RMS Studios in Croydon. One of the first tracks they came up with was Love Song, a dose of irrepressible punk that the Captain had been tinkering with in his bedroom. Despite taking The Damned's high-speed audio chaos to new levels of disorder, Love Song became a hit. Released in April 1979, it charted at Number 20. The band mimed it twice on Top Of The Pops. It was a big moment for the Captain.

"I knew we could do it," he says. "We'd been champing at the bit. That's the thing about The Damned: despite the lunacy, the chaos, all the stupid mistakes, this band survives because through some stroke of luck a bunch of people came together who all have the potential to write cracking tunes."

Chiswick booked them in to record an album. His confidence buoyed, Sensible began to unload the contents of those secret bedroom tapes, and plenty of other strange ideas, into The Damned's new repertoire.

THREE TURBULENT YEARS on from the summer of '76, UK punk's aftershocks could be felt everywhere. Some of the original players, such as John Lydon with PiL, had scarpered from the epicentre and taken flight in experimentalism. Other, newer faces loitered around the three-chord aesthetic, forming a staunch, inflexible neo-punk movement. There were caricaturists, weirdoes, idiots, imitators, meatheads, fashion ponces, arty types, born-again mods, but it was hard to trace a pure form of punk rock that was moving forward.

By a bizarre coincidence, the two records that would do so were in production at the same time and the same studio. When The Damned vacated Studio One at Wessex and moved to the smaller room to finish mixing, The Clash came in to record London Calling.

The Damned camp had been wary of The Clash after getting frozen out on the Anarchy tour, but generally

Howzat!
The Damned
play Hemel
Hempstead
Pavilion, 1981.

realised this had been orchestrated by the band's managers. Happy Damned/Clash co-existence can be seen on the DVD accompanying The Clash's London Calling: Deluxe Edition, where, during a jam, a beaming Sensible knocks out a bone-headed drumbeat. Yet there was one moment of friction.

Vanian: "Captain blew up a condom, drew a face on it – 'The Clash Stink' or something – and floated it up to the ceiling in their studio. It wasn't meant badly, but Mick Jones wouldn't work until it was taken down."

London Calling was serious, full of soulful commitment, all about opening up punk to a rich musical heritage. What The Damned were up to next door was chalk and cheese, mood-wise, but was equally about defying the command that punk should exclude everything that had gone before.

"Sadly, punk had evolved," Sensible says, "into a uniformed affair where everyone looked like The Exploited, and we weren't that way inclined. We wanted to follow our own agenda. We always thought that punk was an experiment and the whole idea was there are no rules."

The Damned began to let their more outré preferences seep into what they recorded, looking beyond the accepted confines of punk instrumentation. "It was such a joy to be in a studio and be able to do whatever you

wanted," says the Captain. "'See that old Vox Continental organ sitting over there? Let's chuck it through a guitar fuzzbox and see what happens!' That became I Just Can't Be Happy Today."

Sensible's approach to lyric-writing was equally experimental: "I had a Ferguson reel-to-reel quarter-inch tape machine, and I'd put the microphone up against the TV speaker and tape the adverts – like, *[sings]* 'Get into Orbit, Orbit sugar-free gum, with the coolest taste, and it's kind to your teeth, and that ain't bad!'

"They were dead catchy tunes, written by the best tunesmiths in the business. So I taped the ads, turned the tapes backwards, and the melodies that came out became the basis of my contribution to the LP. I just sped them up three times, and played them really loud on guitar."

ALTHOUGH THE CAPTAIN was mostly piloting the ship, a chaotic collective atmosphere prevailed. Scabies wrote the feral Machine Gun Etiquette. Vanian served up the waltzy These Hands and Plan 9, Channel 7. The unhinged spirit of the Machine Gun Etiquette album was encapsulated by Smash It Up, a childishly destructive pop-punk anthem that was banned by the BBC after a tabloid reported that punks had been chanting it at a party that erupted into violence.

On the LP, though, it was prefaced by an instrumental overture that Sensible had written for Marc Bolan, with whom the band had toured just before he died.

Punk and prog, hard and soft, virtuoso and arse-about-face, inspired and idiotic, sinister and silly, The Damned Mk II were too muddled for punk's more earnest followers. In October '79, Machine Gun Etiquette peaked at Number 31. The band itself was too messy and contradictory to survive.

"The worst night was probably in Le Havre," remembers Sensible. "I knew the coppers were going to arrive at the hotel soon because there were petrol bombs in the street. Rat was in the room above me, there was all this smashing going on. These curtains flew past my window, in flames. Then I heard dogs in the corridors. We went to the cop shop the next morning, and we couldn't see Rat, but we could hear him shouting, 'Sell the drumkit, do anything…!'"

And Algy's sparky temperament meant that the line-up wouldn't last long: until January 1980, to be exact. Sensible: "Rat's got a sharp tongue on him, and Algy didn't care for it. They had a good old bottle fight. It wasn't really about anything – 'I'm drunker than you!' 'No, you're not!' 'Where's me 'ammer?'"

"People would come up and slip you little packets of powders so that you'd entertain them." CAPTAIN SENSIBLE

Paul Gray from Eddie & The Hot Rods replaced Algy, but the craziness rolled on. On tour later that year, Gray legendarily called his girlfriend and asked her to get a pen and write down his will.

Through it all, though, The Damned as a rule-breaking musical entity continued to flourish. As its title signified, The Black Album saw Vanian's partnership with Sensible prosper. Sides One and Two constituted perhaps the band's most coherent material to date. Side Four featured some ropey live tracks from a fan-club gig.

Side Three, however, was on another planet entirely, comprising an ominous, 16-minute odyssey masterminded by Vanian, which incorporated found sounds such as rainfall and violins snatched from Scheherazade, a 19th-century orchestral piece by Russian composer Rimsky-Korsakov.

Chiswick dropped the band. Much legal wrangling ensued, but The Damned landed at NEMS, who, for the inaugural Friday The 13th EP, put them in touch with producer Tony Mansfield. Through his association with Mansfield, Sensible secured a solo deal at A&M, which allowed him to offload his poppier songs. At the end of his album sessions, to make up the numbers, he dashed off a perfunctory version of Happy Talk, from the musical South Pacific, which became an unlikely chart hit in summer 1982.

"There was friction with Rat, but I couldn't help that," recalls Sensible. "I mean, I was a toilet cleaner and suddenly someone's offering me the opportunity to make a stack of cash. I grabbed it, even if it meant doing a pile of steaming turds like Happy Talk. But then you'd turn up to do a gig in Glasgow, and there'd be posters saying, 'Captain Sensible And The Damned'. Which didn't go down terribly well."

With tension rife, The Damned signed to Bronze, home to Lemmy's Motörhead, and made the '60s pop-influenced Strawberries. Then Bronze went bust. "We were touring America," Scabies recounts, "and Captain picked up some old slapper, who's driving him around in a limo. They're renting the bridal suite and drinking champagne. Captain's doing a thousand grams of coke a day, and the rest of the band are still at the poxy Holiday Inn, sharing a Wendy burger. Nobody would sign The Damned because Captain was more dominant than Dave. That was why we parted company with Captain."

Sensible: "I started gigging with my own band. I had a limo at my disposal, pretty girls. And by the end of the '80s I was penniless. I was robbed blind. I never did anything that evil – no needles, but anything else that was available. People would come up and slip you little packets of powders, so that you would entertain them. None of that's good for your health, so I did seek professional help. But I did have a bloody good time."

SENSIBLE REJOINED THE Damned's original line-up for a late '80s reunion tour that subsequently fell apart after a row between James and Scabies. It's also likely James found it hard to accept that the second half of the show – devoted to material written since his departure – was more enthusiastically received.

These days, Vanian and Sensible have a slick, five-piece line-up of The Damned, signed to The Offspring's Nitro label. Just before Christmas 2004, they toured a Machine Gun Etiquette silver anniversary show. "Touring now is a much nicer experience," says Sensible. "You can get up in the morning and check out the local public transport system. Instead of the manager kicking the door in at one o'clock in the afternoon, they have to wait for me to come back from trainspotting."

To his delight, a tram system has been introduced in his native Croydon. And his famous red beret is on display in the local museum.

noise annoys

From '60s-era garage rock to 21st-century upstarts – here are The 77 Greatest Punk Albums Ever...

Here Are The Sonics

The Sonics

ETIQUETTE, 1965

 Initially intended as a simple dance number to rival The Twist, The Sonics' debut single The Witch was anything but. Instead, it introduced lead singer Gerry Roslie's manic vocals and became the biggest-selling single in America's Northwest. The following album was equally volatile, comprising a frenetic take on Little Richard's Good Golly Miss Molly, plus originals including the fearsome Strychnine, in which The Sonics espoused the virtues of necking poison.

The Seeds/ A Web Of Sound

The Seeds

GNP CRESCENDO, 1966

 The 1966 debut album from Sky Saxon's Seeds embodied the menacing attitude, born-loser mentality and rudimentary rhythms of punk rock a decade earlier than its supposed year zero. Saxon's sneering delivery rivals Johnny Rotten for snotty defiance. A Web Of Sound followed the same year, later counting Johnny Thunders, The Ramones and Mark E Smith among its fans.

Peel Slowly And See

The Velvet Underground

POLYDOR, 1995

 Commercially ignored during their lifetime, The Velvet Underground broke ground in both Lou Reed's songwriting – detailing the seamier side of sex, drugs and romance – and the group's innovative blend of dissonant guitars and electronic distortion. This 5CD box is the place to hear the most music by the most important punk godfathers/mothers in one place. The four principal VU studio albums are here, with an abundance of demos and outtakes to tempt the enthusiastic collector.

The Big Bang!

Best Of... MC5

RHINO, 2000

 They were probably the toughest group to come out of an area infamous for its lame-brained garage bands, but Detroit's MC5 self-destructed after just three albums, all of which are represented on this compilation. For many, the heavy-riffing live debut album, Kick Out The Jams, was the highpoint. After manager John Sinclair was jailed for marijuana possession, the band recorded Back In The USA, an amped-up take on Chuck Berry. Swansong album High Time was patchier, but featured the magnificent Sister Ann, which boasts one of the most aggressive guitar intros in the whole of rock history.

The Stooges

The Stooges

ELEKTRA, 1969

 The Stooges came together after James 'Iggy' Osterberg abandoned his career as a blues drummer to make music that was just as primal but expressed his own distinctly white, Midwestern frustrations. Aided by guitarist Ron Asheton, he achieved his aim with the band's magnificent debut album, filled with raw guitar riffs accompanying the perennial adolescent complaints of boredom and inarticulate lust. Seven years later a generation of UK punks would start learning the riffs to No Fun and I Wanna Be Your Dog and clutch Iggy's self-destructive nihilism to their safety-pinned bosom. Tellingly, the Pistols played No Fun as part of their set.

trousers, wrong drugs. Still, great rock'n'roll songs…

The Essential Radio Birdman: 1974-1978
Radio Birdman
SUB POP, 2001

Taking their name from The Stooges' 1970, and their high-velocity ramalama from the MC5, Radio Birdman's righteous yell and heavy powerchords were Australia's answer to the scenes revolving round CBGB and the 100 Club, and kick-started an Antipodean movement that would also include The Saints and The Scientists. Opening with a tribute to TV's Hawaii 5-0, Aloha Steve And Danno, this album compiles the highlights of Birdman's brief, brilliant career. Much of their catalogue was unavailable on CD until Sub Pop acknowledged grunge's debt to the band and compiled this release.

The Modern Lovers
The Modern Lovers
HOME OF THE HITS, 1976

As good as it was, at the time The Modern Lovers' first album was something of

Raw Power
Iggy & The Stooges
CBS, 1973

Raw Power represented an astonishing comeback for The Stooges, who'd disappeared into junkie oblivion after being dropped by Elektra Records in 1971. This time they'd gained hotshot Detroit guitarist James Williamson, who contributed magnificently tough riffs to Iggy's depictions of decadence and death trips. More conventional than its predecessors, Raw Power was also bursting with classic anthems, including the apocalyptic Search And Destory.

Horses
Patti Smith
ARISTA, 1975

"Jesus died for somebody's sins, but not mine." Could that be the greatest album-opening lyric of all time? If not, it's close, and if it's not as shocking now as it was in 1975, the Horses album certainly helped push the door open for punk and new wave. A rough'n'ready fusion of visionary poetry with scabrous rock'n'roll.

Teenage Depression
Eddie & The Hot Rods
ISLAND, 1976

When Joe Strummer first heard about punk, he was reading about the Hot Rods, who'd signed to Island in 1975. Until the real stuff appeared on vinyl, the thrills offered here were the closest anybody could get to the new sound: if Anarchy In The UK hadn't happened, The Hot Rods' Do Anything You Wanna Do could have been the manifesto, and On The Run and Get Across To You still exude the sweaty scent of summer 1976. But by the time Teenage Depression was released, anybody with an interest in self-realisation had spotted the flaws: wrong hair, wrong

New York Dolls
New York Dolls
MERCURY, 1973

This brash, thrift-store ragbag of androgynous males encapsulated punk's ineptitude, attitude and 'anything goes' diktat five years ahead of their time. Formed in Manhattan in 1971, but landing a record deal two years later, they delivered two great, but flop, albums – their eponymous debut, followed by Too Much Too Soon. Both were delicious reflections of their chaotic stage show and guitarist Johnny Thunders' louche majesty, but it's the first that really shocked, with trashy classics Personality Crisis, Lonely Planet Boy and Looking For A Kiss.

an anti-climax. The line-up that recorded these songs had disbanded, and the material was taken from demos cut four years prior to its release. Yet it's still the scintillating link between The Velvet Underground and the actual dawn of punk, with special kudos going to future Talking Head Jerry Harrison's buzzing keyboards. Jonathan Richman never again wrote songs as disturbingly provocative as Hospital and She Cracked, or anthems as celebratory as Roadrunner and Modern World.

All Times Through Paradise

The Saints

EMI, 2004

In August 1976 came the raw blitzkrieg of The Saints' (I'm) Stranded, a single from the cultural backwaters of Brisbane, Australia every bit as revolutionary as debuts by The Ramones and Sex Pistols that same year. Ignored at home, a deal with EMI followed, leading to the ferocious howl of debut album (I'm) Stranded. Alienating the punk cognoscenti by refusing to conform to the King's Road stereotype, they added R&B horns to politically motivated follow-up Eternally Yours, railing against punk scenesters, record companies and, on the raucous Know Your Product, consumerism, while their third, Prehistoric Sounds, added a jazz influence. This excellent 4CD box compiles the Aussie pioneers both live and in the studio.

Marquee Moon
Television
ELEKTRA, 1977

Formed in 1974, Television had plenty of time to get their chops together before releasing one of the greatest debut albums ever in 1977. An aloof, self-contained unit, Marquee Moon was full of confidence, riding on edgy drums and solid basslines. Meanwhile, Tom Verlaine and Richard Lloyd's harsh rhythms and fluid solos dropped one of the great dual guitar teams fully formed into the punk milieu. Still crackling with tension and tremendous energy, no one who played on it has ever done anything to match it since.

Damned, Damned, Damned
The Damned
STIFF, 1977

Purveyors of Brit punk's first single, 1976's thumping New Rose, The Damned were also smartly off the blocks with this, the scene's debut album. Cut with producer Nick Lowe in just 10 days, it captures the band in their visceral pomp, and its 12 short, sharp blasts add up to barely 30 minutes. Neat, Neat, Neat and See Her Tonight, to name just two, remain thrilling amphetamine blurs.

IV/Rattus Norvegicus
The Stranglers
UA, 1977

Even the sleeve of this album out-punked the punks: if it weren't enough for JJ Burnel and Dave Greenfield to be

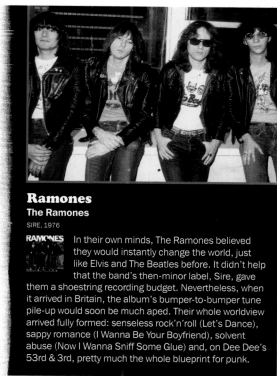

Ramones
The Ramones
SIRE, 1976

In their own minds, The Ramones believed they would instantly change the world, just like Elvis and The Beatles before. It didn't help that the band's then-minor label, Sire, gave them a shoestring recording budget. Nevertheless, when it arrived in Britain, the album's bumper-to-bumper tune pile-up would soon be much aped. Their whole worldview arrived fully formed: senseless rock'n'roll (Let's Dance), sappy romance (I Wanna Be Your Boyfriend), solvent abuse (Now I Wanna Sniff Some Glue) and, on Dee Dee's 53rd & 3rd, pretty much the whole blueprint for punk.

looking powerfully weird in make-up, Greenfield also wore a moustache. This unnerving state continued when you put the record on: musically miles ahead of the Grade-Three-CSE-mentality punk bands, Peaches and (Get A) Grip (On Yourself) are catchy, melodic pop-punk shot through with cartoon menace. Slagged in the '80s for its allegedly misogyny, you can justify it today on the grounds that no one was wallowing in Rattus Norvegicus's ordure more than the group themselves.

The Stranglers

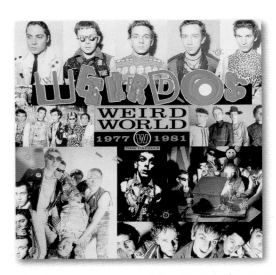

punk outsiders with their exuberant tribute to the capital, In The City, to biggest group in England by December 1982, when the soul-pop of their swansong, Beat Surrender, topped the charts. Frontman Paul Weller married the energy and attack of the new wave to the classic songwriting tradition of The Kinks' Ray Davies, unsentimentally portraying the British way of life and creating a body of work of such enduring popularity that this box set made the UK Top 10 on its release 15 years after The Jam's split. Includes a disc of demos and rarities.

1234 Punk And New Wave 1976-1979

Various Artists

UNIVERSAL, 1999

Though biased towards UK artists, this 5CD, 100-song box set is still a comprehensive punk overview. The familiar treasure trove – Sex Pistols, Clash, Ramones, Buzzcocks – is still strewn with less-celebrated nuggets, including The Saints' (I'm) Stranded and Swell Maps' Read About Seymour, while worthy yeomen, including the Yachts and Patrik Fitzgerald, also get their due.

Weird World Vol 1 1977-1981

Weirdos

FRONTIER, 2002

Los Angeles' Weirdos were a day-glo response to the challenge thrown down by UK punk. They established their presence in 1977 and were granted the honour of supporting The Damned in LA that May. Although their legacy was limited to two singles and two EPs (they split in 1981), they're now recognised as pioneers, welding Ramones-style powerchords to a jagged sensibility. Their second 45, the crunching We Got The Neutron Bomb, is their definitive moment.

Direction Reaction Creation

The Jam

POLYDOR, 1997

This 5CD set soundtracks The Jam's progress from small-town

The Clash

The Clash

CBS, 1977

It was the angriest record ever, like Bob Dylan meets The Stooges. Almost 30 years after the fact, The Clash remains a profoundly disturbing experience. The album's frantic tension derives partly from the battle-line situation between The Clash and their record label. Every song, though, has its own terrifying sense of purpose, whether it's about hating America's amoebic culture, white youth's lack of insurrectionary oomph or London's employment vacuum. When Joe Strummer's voice rips into London's Burning, Cheat or White Riot, it's impossible to remain unmoved. Modern rock arguably began here.

Rock'n'Roll Cleopatra

Wayne County & The Electric Chairs

RPM, 1993

Even with hindsight, it's hard to call whether Wayne/Jayne County's public progress towards a sex-change operation was challenging life-in-art, a canny exploitation of our worst voyeuristic tendencies, or just plain tragic. Maybe it was all three combined. County's Electric Chairs were not among punk's greatest practitioners, but the genre pastiche of Eddie & Sheena and the sweary daftness of Fuck Off would prove oddly influential.

PHOTO: KATE SIMON; BOB GRUEN/STAR FILE

The best way to sample the band is through this 20-track collection, culled mostly from the late-'70s albums, The Electric Chairs and Storm The Gates Of Heaven.

Blank Generation
Richard Hell & The Voidoids
SIRE, 1977

Formerly with Television and The Heartbreakers, Richard Hell (né Myers) was a pioneering CBGB scenester from whom Malcolm McLaren borrowed his ripped T-shirt aesthetic. Sex Pistols duly rewrote Hell's anthem Blank Generation as Pretty Vacant. This relatively late addition to punk's canon features some more considered songwriting. Love Comes In Spurts is still puerile garage rock, but The Plan deals carefully with incest, while Betrayal Takes Two finds Hell's herky-jerky delivery jousting with abstract, expressionist guitar.

L.A.M.F. The Lost '77 Mixes
Johnny Thunders & The Heartbreakers
JUNGLE, 1995

After the New York Dolls collapsed, Johnny Thunders and Jerry Nolan turned up in London with their new band the day the Sex Pistols exploded into notoriety on the Bill Grundy show. After dragging themselves around Britain on the Anarchy tour, they recorded this speedy, Stonesy homage to junk (Chinese Rocks), failure (Born To Loose) and crap relationships (every track).

The Boys
The Boys
NEMS, 1977

The Boys dealt in vigorous, harmony-laden anthems that hymned teen romance and adolescent angst. With a Norwegian keyboardist (Casino Steel)

Never Mind The Bollocks Here's The Sex Pistols
Sex Pistols
VIRGIN, 1977

Without this, nothing: 38 minutes of pure disgust. Almost all of its dozen tracks – including the singles God Save The Queen, Anarchy In The UK, Pretty Vacant and Holidays In The Sun – have entered the lexicon of youth/rock/anomie. Even now, Johnny Rotten's rage erupts like nothing heard before or since: the defiant scream of Problems; the way Bodies spews on its targets with a furious passion; the situationist satire of Holidays In The Sun… What is he on about? Does he mean any of it? Does he believe any of it? We'll never know. Instead just wonder why you haven't become desensitised to his awful, overwhelming rants. Three decades of shock and awe, now that *is* art.

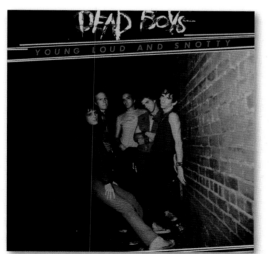

and a diminutive teenage frontman (Duncan 'Kid' Reid), they were always oddities, and while their debut included such punk knock-offs as Sick On You, their forte was guitar pop with plenty of opulent melody.

Young, Loud And Snotty
Dead Boys
SIRE, 1977

The Dead Boys rose from Rocket From The Tombs, a pre-punk band from Ohio that also gave birth to Pere Ubu. They landed at CBGB comparatively late, and with their Nazi gear and singer Stiv Bators' Iggy-style self-laceration were viewed as dumb out-of-towners by the established scene. Their debut album supplied just the kind of songs that its title

suggested, featuring stand-outs Down In Flames and the immortal Sonic Reducer.

Pink Flag
Wire
HARVEST/EMI, 1977

If brevity is the soul of wit, then Wire's debut is punk at its most perspicacious, delivering 21 tracks in 35 pin-sharp minutes. Pink Flag's detached, compressed atmospheres, with singer Colin Newman's surreal lyrics, represent a cerebral response to punk's year zero. Not for them nihilist sloganeering or old Johnny Thunders riffs. Instead, Wire proffered arcing, oblique rock songs – Feeling Called Love and Strange sounded like hits from a world ruled by Brian Eno. Post-punk starts here…

Rocket To Russia

The Ramones

SIRE, 1977

For their third album, The Ramones were under pressure to make some changes after Leave Home had virtually replicated their debut, albeit with inferior tunes. This was just the ticket, as producers Tommy Ramone and Tony Bongiovi (founder of New York's Power Station studio) separated Joey Ramone's voice from the homogeneous scuzz. Songwise, it's the Ramones' finest hour, with Rockaway Beach, Cretin Hop, Surfin' Bird and Sheena Is A Punk Rocker – all teen frustration and gooey romance – among their very best.

Suicide

Suicide

BRONZE, 1977

Martin Rev and Alan Vega played their first gig – entitled Punk Rock Mass – in 1971 but remained unsigned until '77. Their debut album is built on the most primitive rock'n'roll chord sequences. The only instrumentation is Rev's tinny rhythm machine and distorted keyboards, over which Vega declaims in short, edgy bursts like a disturbed Elvis impersonator. Ghost Rider is relentless, Cheree a sweet ballad, but the lengthy psychodrama of Frankie Teardrop hints at their crowd-baiting live shows, which at least once sparked a riot.

Another Music In A Different Kitchen

Buzzcocks

UA, 1978

 The Buzzcocks were always a band of much greater finesse than the gobbing punk national average. Their songs were tuneful vignettes of love, confusion and ambivalent sexuality balanced by frontman Pete Shelley's increasingly experimental arrangements. Here, the rollicking pop of I Don't Mind rubs up to the driving, metronomic Moving Away From The Pulsebeat, yet the whole record hangs together as a cohesive album. Anyone who found a special Buzzcocks balloon, released into the wild to promote the album, could swap it for a copy. The LP was, incidentally, nearly called A Housewife Choosing Her Own Juices In A Different Kitchen.

Crossing The Red Sea With The Adverts

The Adverts

BRIGHT, 1978

The Adverts took every possible punk cliche – rudimentary chords, sneering vocals, the politics of boredom – and twisted the lot into something that both encapsulates and transcends its era. Much of that has to do with TV Smith's magnificent melodies, infused with nuances that ripen wonderfully with age. Four of the songs, including Gary Gilmore's Eyes, were singles. But everything here, from One Chord Wonders to the desperate finale of Great British Mistake, is perfectly formed, '77-era punk rock.

Anthology

Generation X

EMI, 2003

 Not for Generation X a two-fingered salute to the Establishment. Instead, they employed glam-rock producers (Nicky Chinn and Mike Chapman) and wrote songs about love and the 1960s. Pinning naive lyrical sloganeering to a pop sensibility, they scored hits with their first singles – Your Generation, Wild Youth and Ready Steady Go. This 3CD set gathers these and other highlights from their two-LP output, while also adding their unreleased third album from 1979 and an entire live performance from Japan.

Manchester scene, punting a portfolio of Lou Reed and Bowie glam covers before thrilling London's Roxy and Vortex and landing a bit part in Don Letts' documentary, The Punk Rock Movie. Cranked Up Really High, from 1977, set their bruising manifesto. An ode to amphetamine, it was delivered at punishing speed. As was this, their 1978 album, which includes the kick-in-the-head terrace chant Where Have All The Boot Boys Gone? plus a ferocious rendition of Quick Joey Small.

Bops, Babes, Booze And Bovver
Nips'n'Nipple Erectors
BIG BEAT, 1987

Years before The Pogues, Shane MacGowan gave the world The Nipple Erectors (later The Nips). Their 1978 debut gave us punk-rockabilly hybrid King Of The Bop. Top moment, though, was Gabrielle, on which the brakes were applied to magnificent effect.

Singles Anthology
Vic Godard & The Subway Sect
MOTION, 2003

Halfway between the Pistols and PiL, Subway Sect grasped punk's parameters and possibilities from the moment Vic Godard and Rob Simmons first saw Rotten at the Marquee. With Britain in the grip of strife and decay, their grey clothes, suburban Bowie vocals and diversity were positively East Berlin in outlook. Shame, then, that their records were so infrequent – a 1978 LP was scrapped, their 1980 debut came too late and the A- and B-sides on this 24-track compilation span 20 years of singles.

The Modern Dance
Pere Ubu
MERCURY, 1978

Harsh, poetic, absurd and shockingly original, Pere Ubu's debut LP sounded as if it came from some weird parallel world. Formed in Cleveland in 1975, Pere Ubu allied tremendous rock energy with vocalist David Thomas's turkey squawk and Allen Ravenstine's garbled sax and synthesizer blasts. The band rehearsed and played in The Flats, home of Cleveland's blast furnaces and chemical plants, and a song such as Street Waves still remains the ultimate ride through the windswept city at night.

Do It Dog Style
Slaughter And The Dogs
DECCA, 1978

This Wythenshawe quartet honed their craft on the local

Parallel Lines
Blondie
CHRYSALIS, 1978

And in an instant, punk was dead. Producer Mike Chapman (The Sweet, Mud) was charged with turning the most promising of New York's bands into a hit machine. Hanging On The Telephone had as much energy as anything from the new wave, while Picture This and Pretty Baby added girl-group melodies and angst. You couldn't pogo to Sunday Girl, but if you'd already come this far from bin-liner chic with Debbie and her five blokes in their too-tight mod suits and skinny ties then synthesizers and metronomic rhythms were the obvious next step. The success, however, tore Blondie apart. But with Parallel Lines the dancefloor and the indie kid had been introduced: the '80s started here.

The Punk Singles 1977-80
999
CAPTAIN OI!, 2003

Beginning life as 48 Hours and becoming 999 in June 1977, this lot looked suspiciously old. Despite this, 999 cut a swagger with powerful blasts of jagged pop topped with frontman Nick Cash's mewling vocals. Debut single I'm Alive was so fast it almost tripped over itself – a trait recognised by the 78rpm promo pressing of follow-up single Nasty Nasty. But it'll be for June 1978's brooding Emergency that 999 will be remembered. Inconsistent on album, they're best sampled on this collection.

The Image Has Cracked
Alternative TV
DEPTFORD FUN CITY, 1978

While the media preferred to reduce punk to a Sidney Vicious cliche, the reality was always more complex. Mark Perry's Alternative TV was a good case in point. Disheartened by Pistols copycat bands, the Sniffin' Glue fanzine founder and punk's most respected cheerleader formed one of the movement's more maverick outfits. Drawing on everything from early Frank Zappa to anthemic mod, this debut reinvented art rock for the untrained, unwashed generation, while giving an early outing to the young Jools Holland.

Fulham Fallout
The Lurkers
BEGGARS BANQUET, 1978

The Lurkers attracted attention in early 1977 footing bills at The Roxy with a sub-Ramones wall of scree that was so simple-minded it was at first impossible to work out whether they were serious or not. Their first album, Fulham Fallout, demonstrated that they were, actually, a serious proposition. Opening track Ain't Got A Clue was brutally kinetic, while the disturbing Gerald showcased The Lurkers' reflective side – something hardly to the fore on their demolition of Then I Kissed Her, recast as Then I Kicked Her.

Why Don't You Kill Yourself
The Only Ones
EDSEL, 2004

The Only Ones were barracked at an early London show for wearing flared trousers. With one member over 30, they didn't fit the punk template. But frontman Peter Perrett, with his leopard-print shirts and eyeliner, proved one of the premier songwriters of the late '70s. He mixed up Lou Reed's

The Undertones
The Undertones
SIRE, 1979

Belfast's independent Good Vibrations label loosed the Teenage Kicks EP in September 1978. Within a month, the Londonderry band signed to New York's Sire Records, home of the Ramones. It was unprecedented: scruffy garage bands from Northern Ireland just didn't make international waves in the mid-'70s. Such speed of recognition was ironic considering The Undertones had formed in 1975. Teenage Kicks wasn't a fluke, and follow-up singles Get Over You and Jimmy Jimmy were just as irresistible. Their debut album was a pop rush that showed a sparkling talent for seamlessly fusing humour with a winning melody.

Machine Gun Etiquette
The Damned
CHISWICK, 1979

When The Damned split in April 1978 and re-formed a year later, minus guitarist-songwriter Brian James, nobody held out much hope. However, while The Clash hatched London Calling in the studio next door, the new Damned sculpted their own vision of punk's future. It was one that stayed true to the original louder-faster ethos – witness Noise Noise Noise, the title track and Melody Lee – but in Anti-Pope also featured a 96-bar improvised interlude. On I Just Can't Be Happy Today, Dave Vanian also began to find his own voice as the doomy godfather of goth. The singles Love Song and Smash It Up were chart hits, and the album continues to be celebrated by fans of punk at its most free-thinking.

street suss with an English matter-of-factness and a hint of glam. This potent combination yielded one of the era's most irresistible adrenalin rushes in Another Girl Another Planet, included on this 42-song compilation that wraps up all their CBS recordings.

Greatest Stiffs
Wreckless Eric
STIFF, 2001

If punk was cheap-speed thrills, flashy violence and kinky glamour, Eric Goulden was a lukewarm coffee under strip lights, followed by a fumble in the back row of the cinema. The punk credentials of his songs are tenuous but his voice, rudimentary guitar and finger-up-to-the-industry attitude marked him as a reliable

travelling companion, in the company of fellow Stiff Records songsmiths Nick Lowe, Ian Dury and Elvis Costello. From Whole Wide World to It'll Soon Be The Weekend to Hit And Miss Judy, everything here suggests that he deserves to rank with them to this day.

Q: Are We Not Men? A: We Are Devo!
Devo
VIRGIN, 1978

This first album-length broadcast from Planet Devo was every bit as out-there as the group's flowerpots-and-jumpsuits image. Closer to what would become new wave, these Akron, Ohio oddballs wrote songs with titles such as

Mongoloid, Space Junk and Jocko Homo, featuring epileptic time signatures, sci-fi electronics and surreal lyrics. They even showed their irreverence towards all that had come before with a unique deconstruction of The Rolling Stones' (I Can't Get No) Satisfaction – one of this record's many highlights.

The Scream
Siouxsie & The Banshees
POLYDOR, 1978

A triumph of mystique and imagination, The Scream was austere and artful, distinctive and idiosyncratic. Infused with the band's legendary contrariness and cool intelligence, it was a long time coming but worth the wait. Siouxsie whooped like a squaw, then bellowed like Nico, often in the same breath, while bassist Steven Severin, drummer Kenny Morris and guitarist John McKay virtually redefined the sonic possibilities of their respective instruments.

Part Time Punks: The Very Best Of
Television Personalities
CHERRY RED, 1999

Riveted by The Jam's 1977 gig at the Hammersmith Odeon, fans Dan Treacy and Ed Ball formed their own take on mod-inspired punk, releasing their 1978 single, 14th Floor, a musically inept, delightfully humorous slice of social commentary about life in a towerblock. The same year's EP, Where's Bill Grundy Now? included Part Time Punks, a goading swipe at the scene's commercial homo-genisation. Ball soon left to form The Times, leaving Treacy to carry on. The music still resonates warmly today.

The Clash
LONDON CALLING

Mark E Smith, opened up by telling the audience, "The difference between you and us is that we have brains!" The Fall proceeded to use their grey matter to create one of the most enduringly mysterious punk documents. Informed by crime and horror fiction, the post-industrial north-west and The Velvet Underground, it's as much fun as demonic paranoia can be.

Inflammable Material
Stiff Little Fingers
ROUGH TRADE, 1979

 Named after a lyric in a Vibrators song, Belfast's Stiff Little Fingers started life peddling punk covers. Persuaded to pen songs about their troubled homeland, singer Jake Burns'

London Calling
The Clash
CBS, 1979

Working title: The Last Testament. As the 25th Anniversary Edition's bonus DVD explains, The Clash conceived their third album as rock'n'roll's last stand, an idea encapsulated by the cover image of Paul Simonon splintering his bass. The Clash hooked up with inspired but barking-mad producer Guy Stevens, though London Calling, as it was ultimately called, was anything but final. Gathering together threads of reggae, jazz, blues, New Orleans funk and more in a spontaneous, modern sound, it was the past reshaped into a brilliant future.

First Issue
Public Image
VIRGIN, 1978

 John Lydon's first post-Pistols offering alienated many punks.

Sounds described it as an "arrogantly thin attempt at breaking free of Rotten's past". Even drummer Jim Walker now rates it as a rip-off. But with old pals Jah Wobble (fat, dubwise bass) and Keith Levene (jagged, flanged guitar) in tow, Rotten made music that suited his complicated persona. The songs were long and, in the case of the opening Theme (key refrain: "I wish I could die"), gleefully tortuous.

Live At The Witch Trials
The Fall
STEP FORWARD, 1979

When The Fall released the live album Totale's Turns in 1979, the band's leader,

Germ Free Adolescents
X-Ray Spex
EMI INTERNATIONAL, 1978

 Years before the term existed, the teenage Poly Styrene (née Marion Elliot) was pushing the pop boundaries as the first 'riot grrrl'. Her lyrics riffed on consumerism, the environment and artifice with a caustic wit that has aged better than much of the era's worthy proselytising. Her vocals were backed by spiky, sax-fuelled grooves and ripping guitars. This, the band's sole LP, remains influential: just listen to Identity and Oh Bondage, Up Yours! to hear the blueprint for modern punks such as The Yeah Yeah Yeahs.

PHOTOS: IAN DICKSON, CHRIS WALTER/RETNA

218

Sham 69 — The Complete Collection

throat-shredding bark was soon delivering polemical punk essays, leaning heavily on The Clash's blueprint. Rita Marley's Johnny Was became their de rigueur reggae cover – and the only track to throttle down from Ramones speed – while Suspect Device and Alternative Ulster remain stirring anthems to grimly real disenfranchisement.

Unknown Pleasures
Joy Division
FACTORY, 1979

The sleeve shows radio waves emitted by a pulsar, which is apt as there is something of deep interstellar space in Unknown Pleasures. Here Ian Curtis fronted a spectral rock band and stopped time to better contemplate doubt, fear and the inevitable annihilation of the self. Sham 69 it was not. While Martin Hannett's steely, static production made it one of the most momentous of all punk artefacts, Curtis's early death would cement a myth that still pulses.

The Complete Collection
Sham 69
SANCTUARY, 2004

December 1976 saw the NME's Julie Burchill calling Sham 69 "potentially great". And they were great, despite being undermined by everything pulled along in their wake. It didn't matter how many Rock Against Racism benefits they played, Sham 69 were always going to be seen as making bootboy music for bootboys. Yet Borstal Breakout's visceral rush and the joyful zip of Hurry Up Harry are testaments to Sham's innate greatness. And they had ambition: second album That's Life dramatised a day in the life of a directionless kid. Sham's catalogue contains enough gems to satisfy even the most po-faced naysayer.

Cut
The Slits
ISLAND, 1979

The Last Of The Great Unsigned Punk Groups surprised everyone with this sophisticated debut that bubbled with post-punk invention. New drummer Budgie steadied the beat while dub producer Dennis Bovell opened up the sound, leaving Viv, Ari and Tessa free to experiment. The results were revolutionary and as far from the band's early ultra-punk work as one could imagine. Songs such as So Tough, Love Und Romance

and Instant Hit were brilliantly recast for new, positive times, creating a sense of liberation that was reinforced by the group's semi-naked warrior pose on the cover.

Gang Of Four
Entertainment!
EMI, 1979

In its day, Gang Of Four's debut was punk's most savage/extreme record, stealing the march from The Clash for sheer political and musical muscle. Entertainment! implemented the movement's anarchist rhetoric (destroy to create, etc), deconstructing rock's accepted flow and putting the pieces in service of fierce anti-monetarist ideas. Backed by an awesomely taut, funky rhythm section, Andy Gill made harsher noises than any guitarist ever had before.

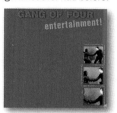

Fresh Fruit For Rotting Vegetables
Dead Kennedys
CHERRY RED, 1980

San Francisco's Dead Kennedys blended warp-speed rhythms with toxic surf riffs, rockabilly and horror-flick drama to create a sound that was musical as well as energising. Frontman Jello Biafra's lyrics conveyed political outrage using savage humour (in 1979 he ran for mayor of San Francisco and came fourth out of 10 candidates). The quartet's debut was a tuneful torrent of hyper-articulate bile that caricatured right-wing tyrants (Kill The Poor), liberal poseurs (Holiday In Cambodia) and yuppie fascists (California Über Alles). The entire US indie scene – from Black Flag to Nirvana – can be traced back to here.

struck a chord with punk fans looking for something more than basic rage.

Singles: Going Steady
Buzzcocks
UNITED ARTISTS, 1979

Like a punk Kinks, Buzzcocks minted a succession of irresistible pop singles. Which makes the Going Steady compilation – the band's first eight United Artist singles and B-sides – the definitive Buzzcocks LP. Singer Pete Shelley's mellifluous hymns to onanism (Orgasm Addict), disappointment (What Do I Get?) and romantic disappointment (Ever Fallen In Love), gush breathlessly past, while Autonomy and Something's Gone Wrong Again reveal the group's darker side.

The Crack
The Ruts
VIRGIN, 1979

When The Clash started getting arty, The Ruts stepped into their shoes. For a while Malcolm Owen's band had the chops to make the leather jackets forget The Clash altogether. Examine the evidence: In A Rut, Babylon's Burning (a Top 10 single), Staring At The Rude Boys and Jah War. By mid-1980, though, Owen's life was falling apart: he'd lost his wife and band; in July he was found dead of an overdose.

Germicide
The Germs
SLASH, 1979

One of the only US punk bands to really give Rotten & co a run for their money in terms of controversy and attitude, The Germs imploded soon after the release of their sole full-length album, singer Darby Crash dying of a heroin overdose not long after. Formed in 1977, within two years they'd somehow managed to nail an irresistibly primal garage-punk sound that, at least in the studio, stayed just the right side of chaos. This feral Stooges-on-PCP noise would inspire countless others following in its wake.

The Raincoats
The Raincoats
ROUGH TRADE, 1979

While The Raincoats' debut album had plenty of primitive energy, it also contained hints of a new post-punk dawn with its flexible arrangements and song structures. The reggae and funk rhythms bounced against each other, tag-team vocal harmonies chimed, scratchy violin occasionally replaced the strident guitar, and the impressionistic lyrics were declaimed with a liberating homespun matter-of-factness. The end result

The First Four Years
Black Flag
SST, 1984

Before Henry Rollins joined them for the Damaged album, between 1978 and 1982 Black Flag had set the bar high with a string of self-released singles and compilation cuts. Helping define the nascent sound of hardcore punk, this bunch of Hermosa Beach misfits, potheads and surfers hammered out high-velocity metal-punk with an intensity few could match. With Keith Morris, Dez Cadena, Chuck Dukowski and Chavo Pederast taking turns to bark themselves hoarse above the riotous racket, these jams are still considered by many, even Rollins himself, to be among Black Flag's finest.

We Are All Prostitutes
The Pop Group
RADAR, 1998

Although the musical wake-up call may have sounded throughout 1976 and '77, many misfits, visionaries and radicals only came to prominence during '78 and '79. None of the new vanguard was more thrilling and infuriating than The Pop Group, a disparate crew of jazz, James Brown, dub and Captain Beefheart buffs from Bristol whose music blithely defied everything their name stood for. This compilation is worth hearing for the title track alone, where Mark Stewart delivers a ferocious

anti-capitalist rant over a funk backing. Heroic!

Los Angeles
X
SLASH, 1980

Singer Exene Cervenka and bassist/vocalist John Doe formed X in 1977 after meeting at a Los Angeles poetry circle. Following a long gestation, they cut their debut with The Doors' Ray Manzarek producing. The latter's Hammond organ flourishes occasionally intrude on the band's garage-punk signature. X would later amplify their psychedelic and country influences but Los Angeles mainly comprises Blitzkrieg fare, most acutely Sex And Dying In High Society.

...And Out Come The Wolves
Rancid
EPITAPH, 1995

 Their influences tattooed proudly on their forearms, Rancid absorbed the iconic sensibility of The Clash and lifted The Specials' uptight skank for their crossover hit, Time Bomb. That song's homage to 2-Tone's sartorial splendour and the band's MTV-friendly look (mohawks, tattoos, chains) all combined to produce a strong image. But frontmen Lars Frederiksen and Tim Armstrong's troubled pasts, including heavy drug abuse, confirmed they'd paid their punk-rock 'dues'. The romantic sense of rebellion saw Rancid easily dominate the mid-'90s punk landscape.

Songs The Lord Taught Us
The Cramps
ILLEGAL, 1980

The Cramps began life in 1972 when Erick Purkhiser picked up hitchhiker Kristy Wallace. Eight years later, the pair – now renamed Lux Interior, a demented, shrieking frontman, and Poison Ivy Rorshach, a guitarist dominatrix – commandeered Sun Studios for their debut album. With drummer Nick Knox, guitarist Bryan Gregory plus producer Alex Chilton, they ripped through The Johnny Burnette Rock'n'Roll Trio's Tear It Up, The Sonics' Strychnine and self-penned numbers such as TV Set and Zombie Dance, adding demonic howls and growling feedback in equal measure.

Playing With A Different Sex
The Au Pairs
HUMAN, 1981

 Somehow The Au Pairs never drew the plaudits of those two other bands that fused punk and new wave with bass-heavy funk, Talking Heads and Gang Of Four. Although compared by critics to the latter, their scratchy, edgy thump was less angst-ridden. This 1981 debut album didn't avoid politics altogether, taking on the abuse of imprisoned Northern Irish women on the track Armagh. But, mostly, The Au Pairs dealt in sexual relationships from a feminist perspective, mirroring the redefinition of gender roles that punk helped instigate.

Nevermind
Nirvana
GEFFEN, 1991

Though the tumult of his private life would ultimately do for him, for Nevermind, Kurt Cobain was able to make a lucrative sense of his inner turbulence. A growing confidence led Cobain to fuse his love of The Beatles' melodies with his group's metallic punk. Producer Butch Vig finessed Cobain's demos, while mixer Matt Wallace polished it all to a radio-friendly sheen. Cobain rewrote Boston's More Than A Feeling for the epochal Smells Like Teen Spirit and saluted Killing Joke on the enigmatic Come As You Are, punk's serrated edge gilded by Cobain's near-infallible pop sensibility – a formula that, bassist Krist Novoselic acknowledged, bands such as Hüsker Dü had perfected before them. Crucially, though, Hüsker Dü never enjoyed the heavy rotation on MTV, which catapulted Nirvana and the fragile Cobain into the mainstream.

Milo Goes To College
The Descendents
SST, 1982

Initially a non-descript LA surf-pop group, under the influence of hormones and square-peg alienation, The Descendents soon evolved into a pop-punk force. Recorded before singer Milo Aukerman really *did* leave the band to study biochemistry, the group's debut clocks in at barely more than 20 minutes of Ramones-meets-Beach Boys buzzsaw angst and spite, a barrage of perfect pop songs hurtling past in a coffee-wired blur. If you've ever wondered to whom the likes of Green Day owe their baggy pants and wallet chains, look no further.

Complete Discography
Minor Threat
DISCHORD, 1988

Hardcore titans Minor Threat may not have known it in 1981, but they were about to launch a wave of punk abstemiousness. "I've got better things to do than sit around and smoke dope," they proclaimed on mission statement Straight Edge. Formed in Washington DC in 1980, Minor Threat had split by '83, later mutating into Fugazi. Their legacy – both musical and ideological – is out of all proportion to the number of records they released.

Zen Arcade
Hüsker Dü
SST, 1984

Recorded in a hurricane 85 hours, Zen Arcade is still breathtaking today. Locked in competition, songwriters Bob Mould and Grant Hart pieced together a fable of an abused kid running away to the big city, into the clutches of drug dealers, prostitutes and Buddhists, via blasts of corrosive nosebleed hardcore (Pride), power pop (Pink Turns To Blue), fragile piano segues and lengthy jazz excursions. Defying the preconceptions then hampering hardcore punk, it anticipated the blossoming of American underground rock in the '80s.

Hate Your Friends
Lemonheads
TAANG!, 1987

Arriving on the Boston scene after Dinosaur Jr but before the Pixies, for their first three albums Lemonheads featured two frontmen: future pin-up Evan Dando and the under-valued Ben Deily. Hate Your Friends was filled with buzzsaw pop-punk, which owed a debt to Hüsker Dü and the early Replacements but was no less exhilarating for that. Highlights include the anthemic Second Chance, a hardcore take on Amazing Grace and (on the reissue) surging, bittersweet love song Ever – a long-lost gem by the long-forgotten Deily.

PHOTO: REX

Superfuzz Bigmuff
Mudhoney
SUB POP, 1988

Having gorged themselves on The Stooges and Black Flag, Sub Pop's then-hottest band delivered this mini-album, named after their favourite FX pedals and providing a raw alternative to late-'80s hair-metal. The booze-fuelled quartet swung between febrile garage-punk (In'N'Out Of Grace) and sludgey heavy metal (Mudride). The CD version adds six tracks from their early singles – including signature anthem Touch Me I'm Sick – making this an essential document of the Seattle sound, three whole years before Nirvana's Nevermind.

Repeater
Fugazi
DISCHORD, 1990

The bluntness of Fugazi's song titles – Greed, Blueprint – belied the complexity of Ian MacKaye's music and lyrics. Having learnt from hardcore's artistic dead end in his previous band Minor Threat, MacKaye and his bandmates cooked up a new sound, subtly informed by dub's sense of space and rhythm. The lyrics eschewed punk's playground polemic for an involved protest against rampant capitalism. Selling their CDs at $10 and gig tickets at $5, Fugazi walked it like they talked it.

Up The Bracket
The Libertines
ROUGH TRADE, 2002

Already on the brink of collapse while making this debut album, The Libertines reignited punk's explosive energy for the new millennium, however momentarily. Produced by The Clash's Mick Jones, these are songs of wilful self-definition, druggy self-destruction, doomed romance and spitting disregard for anyone who disagrees. However shortlived, The Libertines' sound was about miracles rising from chaos. Thanks to the sparky chemistry between Carl Barät and Pete Doherty, some amazing, swooping things happened here.

Your New Favourite Band
The Hives
POPTONES, 2001

The experience of playing on Sweden's tediously worthy hardcore scene turned these students of all things garage-punk into self-referencing antagonists. They dressed up to offend, and the song, which broke them worldwide, Hate To Say I Told You So, was intended as a wind-up. The Hives made two albums of puzzlingly sensible punk-pop, cherry-picked to create this brilliant, breathless compilation of catchy tunes.

A Long Way To Nowhere
The Parkinsons
FIERCE PANDA, 2002

They landed their first gig in London without a demo tape, but The Parkinsons didn't disappoint. Live, frontman Alphonso Zheimer prowled, growled and paced the stage, lifting moves from Rotten and Iggy Pop, wrapping his frame around microphones and speaker stacks while the rest of the band bashed out noisy sub-three-minute guitar-driven rock. Their first album made good on their live reputation, with producers The Jesus And Mary Chain's Jim Reid and Ben Lurie capturing their energy.

WHAT HAPPENED

OOK and Steve Jones offer a hand of greeting to new boy

Sham

super

Y of Sham 69
of the Sex
join forces in
is year.
I the pair
ogether
the group
and
ass,
ven
mp, not
e also

NEXT

After punk's brief,
brilliant explosion,
The Clash went dub,
the Pistols came back
for the cash and three
young Californian
kids hatched a plan...

NO FUTURE?

The Clash began the 1980s by making Sandinista!, a triple album full of free-wheeling dub and political rhetoric. But for many it would be seen as punk's greatest folly.

WORDS: IAN HARRISON. PHOTO: PENNIE SMITH

The Clash pose for the Sandinista! cover shoot, King's Cross, London, November 1980.

THE CLASH WERE playing for high stakes when they entered London's Wessex Studios in August 1980. If they got their fourth album right, and delivered the knockout blow the American success of London Calling was crying out for, the payback could be beyond their wildest dreams.

So when CBS executives called mixer Bill Price in to a meeting at their London headquarters, they wanted a reassurance that the as-yet-incomplete Sandinista! album was not taking any unnecessary risks.

"I was explaining how we were halfway through the mixing," recalls Price. "And one of the executives said, 'I hope it's not going to be a double album, is it, Bill?' I said, 'I can guarantee you it's not going to be a double album.' He said, 'Phew! Thank Christ for that.' So I said, 'It's going to be a triple.' They said, 'Ha! Ha! Good one.' I don't think they believed it until the six sides of Sandinista! were delivered to the mastering room."

Six sides, 36 tracks and 144 minutes that threw funk, punk, rap, rock'n'roll, soul, jazz, soca, gospel, *musique concrète* and acres of dub reggae into the experimental blender, all while scoring left-wing political points on the state of the world and never once singing a straight pop song with hit potential. The band even named it for the US-overthrown Marxist government of Nicaragua, and, when promoting it, spoke of wanting to play gigs in the USSR and Cuba.

Had the comrades gone insane? They were certainly bullish about these possibly career-wrecking moves. "Some bands say we'll do it for fun, yay, pop-beats-surf-whacko-daddio, five-and-six-and-a-hamburger!'" declared Strummer. "We're a bit more serious than that." Sandinista! *serious*?

SANDINISTA! IS EITHER the finest expression of everything The Clash stood for, or a voluminous folly wearing the biggest flares in the shop. In truth, as the grandest, most unwieldy, most incoherent, most bloody-minded statement of their career, it's a bit of both. "The problem was," says drummer Topper Headon, "that by the time we got to Sandinista!, we were touring all the time, we weren't writing. We'd begun to fragment.

"Mick wanted it to be a triple album, whether we had the songs or not." TOPPER HEADON

I'd started doing too many drugs, Mick wanted to record it all in New York so he could be near his girlfriend... we were four very selfish people really. But we still knew that there was this spark there, where we could turn up to the studio with no material and come away with a triple album, and all these different types of music."

Early signposts to the chaos to come were not hard to find. The four sides of London Calling had shown The Clash's intention to dispense with punk rock orthodoxy, as did the remarkable nine-minute dub mix of Armagideon Time prepared for the 12-inch single of that album's title track. Another indicator was the band's declaration, in January 1980, that the coming year would see them release a new 45 as soon as the previous one dropped off the charts.

These two stances – uncompromising musical experimentation allied with the urge to go into production overdrive – met on 2 February 1980, when the band went into Manchester's Pluto Studios with Mikey Dread, the Jamaican deejay who was appearing with them on their 16 Tons UK tour. The Clash and Dread produced Bankrobber, the opening salvo in the year-long singles blitz. The bass-heavy skank was initially rejected by CBS (it would eventually reach number 12), but was, in spirit at least, the first single from Sandinista!.

"I never heard of punk rock before I met The Clash," says Dread. "When I met them, Jesus, I felt sorry for them! They were unwashed, wore old clothes full of holes... but I wanted to push reggae, to make it international, and so did they. I knew I had to help them."

After the 16 Tons tour's short US leg, mid-March saw the group plus Dread decamp to Jamaica to record at Kingston's Channel One studio. They cut a version of the 'Trad Arr' tune Junco Partner, first sung by Strummer in The 101'ers in 1975, but had to get out when

Simonon, Strummer and Jones on the European 16 Tons tour, May 1980.

ghetto dwellers began to turn up seeking a little of these uninvited British rock stars' wealth. At this point Simonon went to Vancouver on a six-week leave of absence, playing a punk bass player alongside Ray Winstone and ex-Sex Pistols Steve Jones and Paul Cook in the dubious film now known as Ladies And Gentlemen, The Fabulous Stains. Still intent on recording, the remainder of the group headed for New York – a decision Bill Price regards as highly significant. "I distinctly remember the record company being very much against it! Expense, I guess, and I think the element of control came into it. In fact, when we were in the States there wasn't any management or agent, nobody in authority present at all – just us. There was no control."

AS WELL AS removing potential obstacles to free expression, it was serendipitous that The Clash hit New York just as hip hop was breaking big. On the radio, WBLS and KISS FM were pumping out such rap hits as Kurtis Blow's The Breaks and Spoonie Gee's Spoonin' Rap. Human drum machine Topper's ability to play beats to order was also crucial in realising these new sounds; galvanised and emancipated, the band set to work at the Power Station on 53rd Street.

Though they were able to cut a version of Eddy Grant's Police On My Back with Jones on bass, the studio soon revealed its limitations. The Clash were obliged to work the 10am to 10pm slot and, an array of solid backing tracks apart, nothing else of note was recorded. Price suggested that they move operations to Electric Lady studios. The venue for Jimi Hendrix's 1968 album, Electric Ladyland, it still featured cosmic murals on the walls. With The Rolling Stones recording their Emotional Rescue album upstairs, Price manned the desk from noon until 6am daily, making a far looser regimen possible. Having secured a three-week booking, The Clash called home for reinforcements.

In early April help came in the form of keyboardist Mick Gallagher and bassist Norman Watt-Roy from Ian Dury's band the Blockheads. "We flew over with Topper, and when we got to the hotel the band went to a meeting with Martin Scorsese, who was thinking of doing Gangs Of New York," remembers Gallagher. "It was a big reunion – Topper came back wearing Joe's trilby!"

When on the first of eight days of work the two Blockheads got to the studio Gallagher remembers that at that juncture the group had no songs for them to work on. Neither were any of them present. Still, they started jamming, and when Topper turned up and joined in, the funky, driving rhythm track Price recorded became the basis for The Magnificent Seven. The foundations for the similarly rap-influenced Lightning Strikes (Not Once But Twice) were worked up in the same way, and the next week would see him and Watt-Roy develop versions of Hitsville UK, Something About England and Charlie Don't Surf.

A pattern had been set. Songs were begun spontaneously, rarely with all the members of the band in attendance. Fragments of music would be saved until those other members decided to contribute; otherwise, Strummer described the process as "songs actually being written as they're going down". After unexpectedly bumping into Jones in Greenwich Village, Strummer's old busking buddy Tymon Dogg contributed and sang Lose This Skin, while The Voidoids' Ivan Julian jammed along to The Call Up. The fact that Julian recalled playing along to the song's rhythm track for an hour and a half gives some insight into just how free-range the sessions at Electric Lady were. When things were rolling, Strummer would declare, "I can see Hendrix's ghost around the corner!"

IN MAY THE group returned to the UK for their final studio stop, Wessex in Highbury, north London. Finished vocals were to be recorded, mixes completed and, inevitably, more tracks laid down. Indeed, engineer Jerry Green has said that the recording rate went up in September, with longer and longer nights spent in the studio. Mikey Dread beefed up the album even further with such cavernous, psychedelic dubs as the Washington Bullets remix Silicone On Sapphire and Living In Fame, a version of If Music Could Talk that gave the finger to the 2-Tone bands and their pretensions to mixing rock and reggae. It was at this late stage that it became clear that all the music recorded was to be used.

Even members of The Clash have questioned this sheer volume of material, and charges of intentional absurdity have been levelled at the inclusions of Clash classics sung by Mick Gallagher's kids. Maria Gallagher was just four when she recorded her version of Guns Of Brixton. Gallagher and Strummer would then suggest that Mick's young sons, Luke and Ben, record a new, polite-sounding version of Career Opportunities (they received a ghetto-blaster each for their trouble). Even more reviled was Mensforth Hill. A backwards mutation of Something About England, the track references Menwith Hill, the top-secret US military listening station in Yorkshire known for its sinister 'golf-ball' radomes.

"I remember walking into the studio, and I said, 'What are you doing?'" recalls Topper. "They said, 'We're recording this track backwards!' I said, 'Why?' The answer was: because we haven't got enough fucking material. Mick was like, 'I want it to be a triple album, so it's gonna be a triple whether we've got some songs or not.' And there's that one where we turned those little boxes upside down and you got cow and sheep noises

[Shepherd's Delight]... I listen to that nowadays, and think, 'God, and they sacked me for taking drugs!'"

With Jones in the control room, Strummer's place was in his Spliff Bunker. A weed-smoker's retreat built out of flight cases, it was also his favoured spot to write lyrics. Mikey Dread remembers him poring over the apocalyptic prophecies of Nostradamus; San Francisco radical Mo Armstrong provided other more political reading matter. It's tempting to imagine the narrative world of Sandinista! – of geopolitics, fear and hope – taking shape amid the Spliff Bunker's plumes of ganja smoke. But other interpretations can be read into Strummer's need for his own space. The creative tension

PHOTO: PENNIE SMITH

"Mick was very creative, but when he took his guitar off he was like a 12-year-old." BLOCKHEADS GUITARIST MICK GALLAGHER

between him and Jones is well documented, and it seems unlikely that it would have lessened in such a pressurised atmosphere.

Yet Gallagher's impression of the relationship between the two emphasises how essential their differences were. "Joe was the one with the bigger vision, beyond The Clash. Mick was very creative in the studio, but when he took his guitar off he was like a 12-year-old. He would like to think he was more important than Joe, and Joe would like to think he was more important than Mick! But it worked. That was the energy that was The Clash."

There was one last gag to be played before recording drew to a close. On 10 September the Blockheads had

dressed as policemen to play their single I Want To Be Straight on Top Of The Pops. The Clash had asked their sax player, Davy Payne, to go over to Wessex afterwards, so he, Gallagher and fellow Blockheads John Turnbull and Wilko Johnson drove over in their police gear and mounted a pretend drugs bust. "I was on the top of these stairs looking down into the big room," says Gallagher. "I could see Mick sauntering towards the bunker with this huge spliff in his hand, and I went, 'YOU! Stay there!' And he turned round and all these sparks came off his trousers as he tried to put it out. So I walked up to about two foot away, and then he saw it was me and gave a very nervous laugh."

No one thought of Strummer in the Spliff Bunker. Twenty minutes later, when the session restarted, he peered out to see a studio full of policemen, one of whom was playing the saxophone.

BEARING A SERIAL number – FSLN 1 – that referenced the acronym for the Nicaraguan political movement Frente Sandinista de Liberacion Nacional, Sandinista! was released on 12 December. Reaching Number 19 after London Calling's 9, it seemed to leave nothing less than sour tastes all round. In order to sell a triple LP for £5.99, the band had agreed to CBS's term that they would have to sell 200,000 copies in the UK to qualify for any royalties. Four months after the LP's release, Simonon was telling Rolling Stone that the band's situation was "debt, debt, debt". They were also stuck in a contract seemingly without end, and would score no significant hit singles from the album.

The fact that Clash manager Bernie Rhodes was again making his presence felt also augured another, ultimately disastrous shift in the band's internal power structure. Just as terminal, Topper had managed to turn his heroin use into a full-blown habit, meaning the sentiments contained within Junkie Slip cannot have been lost on him. To cap it all, with few exceptions, the music press canned Sandinista! ruthlessly.

But if many of these complaints have faded gently into history, Sandinista! has endured. The Clash would never be as free again. Tune in today to this album that exists on no one's terms but its own, and what once seemed like too much now seems like not enough. The cost, however, was heavy.

"Sandinista! was the end of The Clash as we know them," says Price. "I guess they lost control afterwards. I don't know what the politics were, but I think it got out of the band's hands. Events were controlling them. They were still coming up with the music, but... but you've got to move on, haven't you?"

Strummer gets stuck into another political tract, Pluto Studios, Manchester, February 1980.

THANKS TO ANDREW PERRY FOR THE TOPPER QUOTES

The original polemical punks, Black Flag emerged into soft-rock-fixated California to face media condemnation, fan violence and sustained police harassment.

Black Flag's Henry Rollins cuts loose at the 20 Grand Club, Ormond Beach, Florida, May 1982.

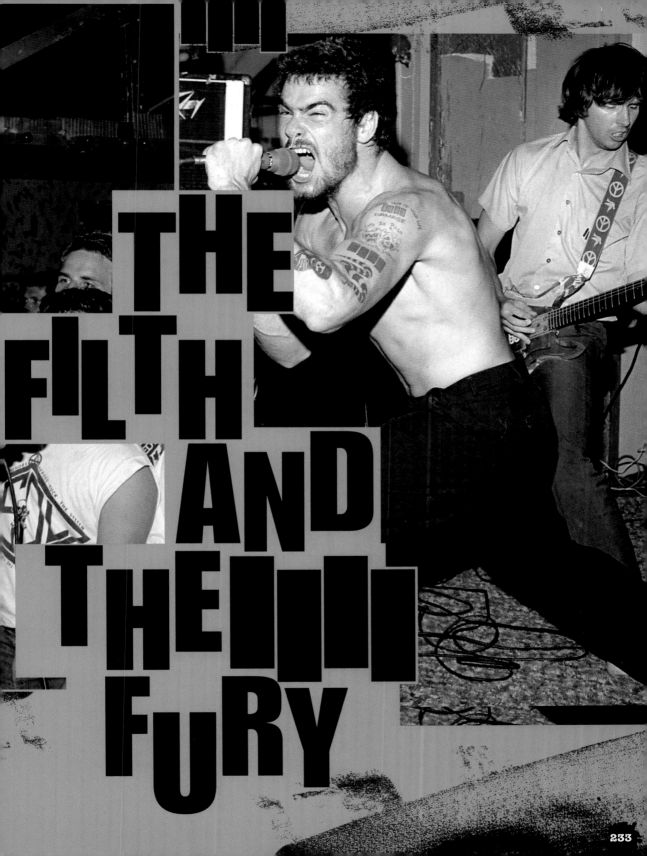

THE FILTH AND THE FURY

ON 8 OCTOBER 1980, Black Flag played the Whisky A Go-Go in their home city of Los Angeles. A decade or so earlier, the Whisky had been the crucible of the West Coast counterculture, hosting legendary performances by The Doors, Love and Buffalo Springfield. Black Flag's presence on Sunset Strip seemed a perversion of the hippy ideal that the venue represented – indeed, the promoters had been reluctant to book them at all.

Flyers for the evening's two shows depicted a sinister drawing of a blonde girl warning Charles Manson: "Charlie, you better be good. It wasn't easy getting in here, you know."

The night was a fiasco. Two weeks before, Black Flag's gig at the Hewitt Street Hideaway had ended with hundreds of LAPD cops chasing the crowd out of the venue. At the Whisky, a mini-riot occurred when LA County sheriffs ordered ticket-holding fans to leave before the band's second performance. "Suddenly Sunset Strip was closed off," says photographer Glen Friedman. "Cops were beating the fuck out of kids. It was nuts."

With Black Flag's second sold-out show of the night subsequently cancelled, Los Angeles DJ and scenester Rodney Bingenheimer put the band's fans on air, and they complained about the police; the Whisky's manager told the LA Times that "it wasn't a riot until the police showed up" – and was fired.

The Whisky cancelled its other upcoming punk-rock shows. Flag guitarist Greg Ginn and bassist Chuck Dukowski ran cop-baiting radio commercials ("Attention all units! Chief Gates is in an uproar!"), while the LA Weekly cautioned: "Fans of bands with 'reputations' like Fear, China White, Black Flag, the Circle Jerks, etc: if you want to continue seeing these bands then you have to shape up. The violence is going too far when every gig turns into a riot."

Three years into their career, Black Flag were seen as a genuine threat to social order. But the resistance they would meet – and the music they would make – was only to get tougher. "When I first joined Black Flag, I thought I was ready," says Henry Rollins, enlisted as vocalist in 1981. "Greg Ginn taught me otherwise."

Almost all the songs on the band's landmark debut LP – Damaged, released in October 1981 – were written by Flag founder/guitarist Greg Ginn and/or bassist Chuck Dukowski before Rollins joined. It's a remarkable album,

but arguably Everything Went Black and The First Four Years, compilations of the band's earlier recordings, are even better. "The finest Black Flag record is The First Four Years," wrote Rollins in his 1994 Black Flag memoir, Get In The Van. "There wasn't anything like it anywhere else," he says today, "and I didn't think that I measured up. I did the best I could."

This is the story behind Black Flag's first four years: how a group of self-described "geeky, nerdy beach rats" from California reshaped punk rock into an intense and darkly satirical music divorced from fashion moves and art-school pretences. Music that almost no one was ready for.

GREG GINN'S INTEREST in music began late. Born in 1954, he spent his teenage years in Hermosa Beach, California developing a one-kid radio equipment business. A serious teenager, he wanted nothing to do with the local brain-dead surfer culture. It wasn't until Ginn got to UCLA that he became interested in music. Aged 19, he picked up his younger brother's guitar and "just started banging on it. When I first started there wasn't any punk rock, but my playing was very aggressive. I liked to play music that was more physical release than mental exercise. It was an antidote to studying."

By the time Ginn finished studying at UCLA in 1974 he was visiting Rodney Bingenheimer's English Disco glam spot and getting into hard-rock bands, especially The Stooges. Hanging out at the local record store, he made friends with the shop's most out-there employee, fellow Hermosa Beach resident Keith Morris.

"The record store was all laid-back, sip wine, sniff coke, feathered-hair stuff – The Eagles, Jackson Browne, Stevie Nicks – which I was not into," remembers Morris. "Greg and I shared the same musical interests: Black Sabbath, Grand Funk Railroad, Black Oak

Heads down: (from left) drummer Robo's hand, Greg Ginn, Chuck Dukowski and Dez Cadena at the Vex in East LA, 1980.

(Inset) Bassist Dukowski, sans mohawk, May 1982.

WORDS: JAY BABCOCK. PHOTOS: (PREVIOUS PAGE) WIREIMAGE.COM (THIS PAGE) GLEN E FRIEDMAN

> ## "One time while Greg was talking to some record company guy, I unzipped my pants and urinated on the guy's legs." KEITH MORRIS

Arkansas… We drove up to the Santa Monica Civic to see Thin Lizzy and Journey. I'd developed some really bad habits – drinking, drugs, partying…"

Morris went to work for Ginn at his electronics business, SST. While Morris followed the British punk scene, Ginn's interests lay elsewhere: "I picked up on punk from New York clubs like CBGB. The music scene here was so run by the industry that bands didn't play – they showcased. The Ramones played at the Roxy in December '76. That may have been the turning point."

With a set of fast, brutal songs that Ginn had penned – including the four tunes that would form Black Flag's debut Nervous Breakdown EP – he and Morris spent 1977 trying to find a rhythm section for their band, Panic. Short of a bass-player, they borrowed the services of Gary McDaniel, aka Chuck Dukowski, of local acid

metallers Wurm. "The songs were cool and Keith was great," remembers Dukowski. "He was a very emotive little guy. As far-out as Iggy, and not self-conscious. By 1977, there was some major suckitude! Kiss were sucking, Aerosmith were sucking. That's why punk rock could walk in. It was wide open."

Panic recorded eight songs in December 1977 at a Hermosa Beach studio. Dukowski became a permanent fixture, and after the departure of first drummer Brian Migdol an ad for a replacement attracted Roberto Julio Valverde, a Colombian national. Says Morris: "[When] we auditioned him he set up his drumkit all level, and he had this stiff robotic drum style – all arms. You put robot and Roberto together and you get… Robo! Plus he had amazing cocaine. We were fortunate."

"There was a lot of mystery about Robo," says Dez Cadena, a fan who later became their vocalist. "He was

supposedly a Colombian general. He would never tell us exactly how he got into the country." Robo, who today claims he was there on a student visa, was overjoyed: "It was fast rock, hard, and I didn't care about the lyrics."

THE NAME PANIC was being used by a couple of other outfits, so Ginn's younger brother Raymond, aka Raymond Pettibon, suggested Black Flag. Dukowski thought it particularly cool ("it's got the political kind of anarchist, fuck-all-y'all thing"); it was also the name of a popular bug spray.

The local punk/garage label that supported them – Bomp! – had cashflow problems, so Ginn pressed up 2,000 copies of the four-song, five-minute Nervous Breakdown EP for $1,000 and released it on his own SST label. The garish cover was by Pettibon, whose artwork would feature on almost all of Black Flag's releases, plus those of other SST artists such as the Minutemen.

Unable to get a gig anywhere, Black Flag booked a January '79 afternoon show at Moose Lodge, a small recreational hall for military veterans in Redondo Beach. The show drew barely 100 people but was a harbinger of the troubles to come. "I was out of my mind," says Morris. "Two or three nights prior, we'd partied with the Ramones, The Dickies and *[legendary Germs singer]* Darby Crash. I'd given myself a skinhead. Towards the end of our first set, I started swinging like Tarzan from the American flag on the side of the stage. These vets didn't take kindly to that; there were 40 senior citizens chasing me around Moose Lodge. I slipped out to the parking lot, put this black wig on, walked back in and did a second set. They didn't even know who I was. And there stood Rodney Bingenheimer and *[Dead Boys singer]* Stiv Bators."

Bingenheimer: "It was wild. I thought they were the American Sex Pistols – they had the same sound, same energy."

Morris gave Bingenheimer the band's new record and he began playing it on his Sunday-night radio show on KROQ. A June performance at a folk speakeasy in the San Fernando Valley resulted in a riot and a glowing review in local punk-rock monthly Slash: "For the 15-song set nothing stood in Black Flag's way… A truly impressive debut: volatile, angry. See them before they get banned."

Black Flag began to infiltrate Hollywood. They played a string of shows in LA that summer, but it was a Sunday-afternoon concert in Manhattan Beach's Polliwog Park that sealed their notoriety. "The US Air Force Orchestra was scheduled to play and couldn't make it," explains Morris. "They needed a band to fill in. Greg persuaded the guy from Manhattan Beach Parks and Recreation that we had Fleetwood Mac songs

in our set. There's 20-dozen picnicking families there and then a line of leather-clad, torn-Levi's, spiky-hair guys come in – surf rats, skaters, druggie friends. We launch into our set, and for 10 minutes it rains orange peels, cantaloupes, Kentucky Fried Chicken."

The Manhattan Beach Recreation Department's special events supervisor later apologised in a press release: "We plan to screen and audition every act from now on… nothing like this will ever happen again."

By late summer '79, things were happening. Slash magazine made Nervous Breakdown Number 1 on the staff favourites chart. Pettibon designed a logo: an unfurled flag broken in three places so it appeared as four solid black bars: a symbol perfect for tattoos and graffiti. "We had

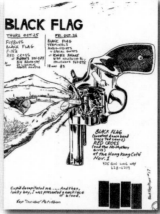

"Cops were beating the fuck out of kids. It was nuts." PHOTOGRAPHER GLEN FRIEDMAN

Original singer Keith Morris, who left to join Circle Jerks. "I was freaking out on cocaine and speed," he explains.

(Above right) Black Flag gig posters, designed, like almost all of their artwork, by Raymond Pettibon, Ginn's brother.

graffiti everywhere – freeway overhangs, underpasses," says Morris. "We were the original LA taggers."

The band were getting regular LA gigs and attracting youths from Orange County, which was developing a violent surf-punk scene around hardcore bands such as TSOL and Agent Orange. Black Flag began to receive a different kind of attention.

Dukowski: "I had this old Ford Econoline van with Black Flag and a million other band names all over it. Cops would pull me over. I wanted out of Hermosa."

Morris: "Hermosa Beach was a conservative community. They tried to run people out of town: hippies, radicals, drug dealers. They considered us anarchists and terrorists – like we were building a nuclear device in our rehearsal space."

In a sense, they were. Songs recorded in October '79 included Revenge, Depression, Clocked In and Police Story: "Understand/We're fighting a war/We can't win/They hate us/We hate them." After the two-day sessions, Morris was gone. Says Ginn: "Keith wanted out because it was impinging on his party scene."

Morris: "I'd become like a monkey let loose, soaked in alcohol, freaking out on cocaine and speed. One time, while Greg was talking to some record company guy, I unzipped my pants and urinated on the guy's legs. I'd run my course."

Black Flag found a new singer: Ron Reyes, a Kiss-loving street kid of Puerto Rican heritage who'd followed the band since before the Moose Lodge show.

He knew all the songs, and could leave immediately for a tour up the West Coast. Then, in March 1980, Reyes quit the band mid-show at the Fleetwood in Redondo Beach. Recalls Robo: "The Orange County surfers cut off their hair and turned into punks. They were fucking maniacs! At the show, they'd start going in circles, punching each other. Ron had met a girl and at this show she got into the middle of that shit and Ron didn't like it! He took off with her during the set and went back to Vancouver."

Dukowski: "Ron was living too hard – drinking a lot – and trying to be a vegetarian too. He freaked out."

IT TOOK BLACK Flag another five months before they found a replacement: 19-year-old Dez Cadena, an old friend of Reyes. Robo: "Dez fitted right in – he really kicked it out. We lined up shows: Hollywood, Orange County, South Bay, East LA. Punk rock was spreading like wildfire."

And Slash magazine's prophecy was coming true: Black Flag were getting banned. In the Los Angeles Times on 29 June 1980, a feature titled 'Violence Sneaks Into Punk Scene' argued that bands like Black Flag were to blame for their audience's unruly behaviour.

Ginn: "It tied Black Flag and violence together. I thought, 'You have more problems at some heavy metal show with a bunch of drunks.'"

Dukowski: "We were pouring our aggression into the music – we were *not* acting. But what can you do when violence breaks out? Stop the show every second? The old rock culture people were trying to beat up the kids.

Eventually the more aggressive elements of the punk rock crowd fought back and took those people down."

Ginn: "People thought that it was great publicity, but any time you're misrepresented it's gonna hurt you. Every interview was: 'What about the violence?'"

The band journeyed up the West Coast again. Arriving in Vancouver, they were greeted by Ron Reyes. "People warned me to stay away from Ron because he was 'a little angry'," says Cadena. "I was passing out flyers at a gig and Ron came running out of nowhere and hit me on the head with a brick. I figured he was mad at me for not going to see him while he was in Black Flag. I just preferred Keith."

The aftermath of October 1980's Whisky A Go-Go fiasco left Black Flag disillusioned. Sixteen days later, arriving for a soundcheck at Baces Hall in East Hollywood, they found cops already there.

Dukowski: "They had a command post in the parking lot across the street, helicopters circling. The gig starts and… boom! They copied their strategies from the Romans and busted with the phalanx."

Ginn: "That was when the cops got really aggressive. They were beating women."

Camera crews from the late-night NBC talk show Tomorrow captured the band's performance – as well as LAPD cops in riot gear charging across Sunset Boulevard at Flag fans who were sarcastically Sieg Heiling at the officers. A mohawked Chuck Dukowski appeared on the show, explaining that Black Flag were not white supremacists and it was the LAPD who were the Nazis. After a January '81 show in Crenshaw ended in $4,000 worth of damage, a melée between bottle-throwing fans and baton-wielding cops, and one LAPD officer being slightly injured, Dukowski complained: "The cops call up every club we play and try to discourage them from booking us. They even told a TV documentary team that if they showed up at one of the gigs, they'd all be killed."

Black Flag toured the US three times from 1980 to '81. It was not easy. Ginn says the band were under constant police surveillance. Playing questionable venues on hearsay information passed to them by other punk bands, they were making very little money – $5 per diem each, if that.

Former Nirvana bassist Krist Novoselic recalls the impact of those shows: "It was pre-internet. How do you reach these remote places? You had to go out there and do it. Black Flag coming to your town was like an affront to popular culture: 'We're gonna get your children! In your own backyard, with Xs between our eyebrows!'"

"I thought they were the American Sex Pistols." SCENESTER RODNEY BINGENHEIMER

IN 1981, BLACK Flag released the Reyes-fronted Jealous Again EP, and, with Cadena as singer, the Six Pack EP and the Louie Louie/Machine single. Jealous Again also featured You Bet We've Got Something Personal Against You!, a Dukowski invective against former vocalists Morris and Reyes. Reyes' name was changed to Chavo Pederast on the sleeve.

"We didn't want to give him credit 'cos he wanted to tear us down," says Dukowski. "Fuck that schmuck."

That summer, Black Flag played to their largest crowds ever, including headlining the 3,500-capacity Santa Monica Civic. The mainstream was repulsed. Rolling Stone dismissed Black Flag and other LA punk bands as "fast, hard-driving bands whining that the air is bad, America is materialistic, love sucks…"

The constant touring was taking a physical toll. Robo was losing so much weight that he returned to eating meat after eight years, and Cadena's distinctively

Rollins and Ginn sweat it out at the Milestone, Charlotte, North Carolina, June 1985.

(Inset) A fleeting incarnation of the group in winter 1983, featuring (from left) Dukowski, Cadena, Ginn, Rollins and drummer Bill Stevenson.

cigarette-hoarse voice was regularly giving out. He happily stepped across to second guitar and made way for a new vocalist: a 20-year-old former skateboarder and singer for minor DC hardcore band S.O.A.. His name was Henry Rollins.

"Black Flag were my favourite non-DC band," says Rollins today. "I'd never heard anyone play guitar like Greg Ginn. I saw them in New York City in spring 1980. Chuck came out before the rest of the band, making fucked sounds on his bass and yelling. It made me want to kill people."

Rollins quit his job scooping ice cream and travelled with the band for the rest of the tour, appearing onstage during the encores.

The morning after Black Flag had left to begin the tour, the police descended on the SST headquarters, which doubled as their living space. Mike Watt, Minuteman bassist and SST Electronics employee, was there. "I guess they thought 'the tour' was code for a big drug shipment," he says. "They tore the place apart but there was nothing to find. They said I was the 'brains' of the operation. I was summoned to court four times – even got assigned a public defender. Finally, Greg and his pop came in and the judge settled it in his office. There was a zoning violation 'cos one of us slept in the attic. Fifty dollars in court charges."

Rollins was learning what it meant to be in Black Flag: "It was a wake-up call. The police in California wanted to intimidate you and make you feel powerless. Whenever there was a sheriff at the door, it was Greg who had to deal with it. He had balls of steel."

Black Flag moved in to a practice space in West Hollywood, next to a recording studio. With a huge backlog of songs, they decided to make a complete album with Rollins on vocals and scrap the previous recordings of the same songs. (They would later surface on Everything Went Black.) Working with an $8,500 budget, the band recorded Damaged in less than three weeks.

"Henry was easy," says Dukowski. "When you told him to reach down deeper and give you more, he did it. He was really good."

Damaged's blunt lyrics summarise a four-year history of police conflict (Police Story), disdain for the media (Rise Above), dissatisfaction with a mainstream society (Spray Paint, No More, Six Pack and TV Party) and growing paranoia (everything else). But it's the sound of Damaged – fast, heavy, raw and disciplined – that conveys the fury and frustration quicker than the lyrics.

A plan to distribute Damaged via an MCA subsidiary fell apart as soon as MCA chief Al Bergamo heard it. Speaking to the LA Times in 1981, Bergamo described it as "immoral", saying: "This record bothered me. I found it an anti-parent record… it certainly wasn't like Bob Dylan or Simon & Garfunkel."

A rival distributor released the album. Because the cover featured a photo of a skinhead (Rollins), Black Flag began to attract a racist skinhead audience, who were disappointed to find that not only were the Flag not racists, they had grown their hair long and started playing Sabbathesque dirges.

BY THE TIME the band's next studio albums appeared in 1984 – the uneven My War and frightening Slip It In – Robo, Dez and Dukowski were gone. The music became more exploratory, the anarchic fun and black satire replaced by Rollins' brooding disgust. Ginn pulled the plug in 1986.

What had the whole trip been like for the 'new guy'?

"It was getting to sing the best songs you'd ever heard," says Rollins. "There was a very heavy mindset. Greg and Chuck had a commitment to the band and SST that made everyone else struggle to keep up."

"It was all [for] the music," concludes Greg Ginn. "A lot of times we didn't have a place to live, but we always paid for a place to practise. That was the beginning and end – the music."

Blank Generation

Brought up in Washington DC, Kate Simon inherited her love of photography from her father, a keen amateur lensman. After meeting Bob Marley during his legendary show at London's Lyceum in 1975, she worked with the reggae superstar and other Jamaican artists before embracing the punk scenes on both sides of the Atlantic.

England needs us

The Clash, London, December 1976

The group – minus on-off drummer Terry Chimes – pose on the trolley ramp of the warehouse opposite their Camden Town rehearsal space. This image became famous as the front cover of The Clash's first album.

I wanna be your boyfriend

Dee Dee Ramone, CBGB, New York, 1977

The Ramones bass-player gives NYC singer/songwriter Helen Wheels a hug outside the no-frills club where the band first appeared on 16 August 1974.

In the flesh

**Debbie Harry,
New York, 1977**

Iconic images of Blondie's singer, shot on a rooftop on West 58th Street. Harry was adopting a more glamorous image, reflecting the group's move towards a poppier, more mainstream sound.

A different kitchen

Buzzcocks, New York, 1979

The band hang out in Chinatown, on their first major US promotional visit. Within a year the Buzzcocks would split, following the release of their third album, the 'existentialist' A Different Kind Of Tension.

Take that

Johnny Rotten, London, 9 May 1977

Johnny larking around in the dressing room after The Clash's performance at the Rainbow on the White Riot tour. Rotten rarely missed an opportunity to knock the Pistols' chief rivals in print.

Rockin' Horses

Patti Smith, 1977

Patti photographed at the Boston home of sometime Patti Smith Group member Andy Paley, who played keyboards on the band's early tours. Note the ironic visual reference to her debut album.

Lift-off

The Ramones, CBGB, 1977

Joey and Dee Dee at the club
that rapidly became their spiritual
home. When the two first
rehearsed together with Johnny,
Joey drummed while Dee Dee
sang and bashed out basic
E-shape barre-chords on guitar,
although he couldn't do both at
the same time. When Joey turned
up with a couple of self-penned
songs, it was decided that he
should take over on vocals and
Dee Dee should switch to bass.
Three years later, the latter's
playing technique had hardly
become more delicate – hence
the two spare Fender basses
visible here.

D-U-M-B

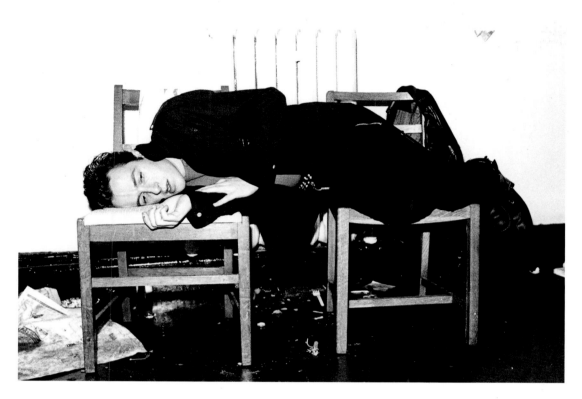

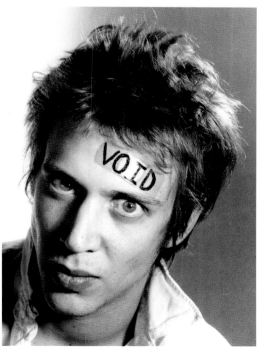

Chairman Mellor

**Bristol Locarno,
21 November 1978**

Joe Strummer takes five on the Sort It Out tour. The motorcycle boots were a memento of The Clash's September 1978 visit to New York, where they had mixed their second album, Give 'Em Enough Rope.

No logo

Richard Hell, 1977

The former Television bassist and Heartbreaker promotes his new group, The Voidoids. In autumn 1977 the band flew to the UK to support The Clash on their Get Out Of Control tour.

Board youth

**Joey Ramone,
New York, 1977**

The Ramones frontman calling the shots at his home in the Bowery near CBGB. The D-U-M-B placard was to become a famous Ramones stage prop.

accountancy IN THE UK

When the Sex Pistols sensationally decided to stage a comeback in 1996, they made no bones about their motivation for re-forming. Let's hear it for the Filthy Lucre tour.

251

IN THE LAST minutes of a March 1996 Monday lunchtime, three Sex Pistols are inching down London's Oxford Street in a small white Fiat. Steve Jones is at the wheel. The car in front, which Jones is following, leads a three-car convoy out past Holborn and east towards Shoreditch. Nobody pays any attention to the Fiat or its once notorious occupants.

In the back is Glen Matlock, once more the Sex Pistols' bass guitarist after 19 years. He is two feet away from a driver who, legend has it, once ejaculated in a French bread roll and fed it to him as elevenses. If the mood is therefore a little tense, there is always Paul Cook – sharing the back seat with Matlock – to mediate, as he did all those years ago.

They could be any trio of 40-year-olds out for a spin… if not for the disbelieving laughter of the journalists filing out of the press conference back at the nearby 100 Club.

"Fergie is the Clash of the Royal Family."

"We've found a common cause and it's your money."

"Finsbury Park is not a stadium. It's a field."

Never mind the Sex Pistols, here's the Filthy Lucre tour. In his blue velvet Vivienne Westwood suit, Steve Jones indicates a right turn into Eagle Wharf Road.

A YEAR AGO, Paul Cook wasn't thinking about a Sex Pistols reunion. The "semi-permanent" drummer in the Edwyn Collins band weighs up all this Pistols-are-reborn business and, like Walter Matthau in The Odd Couple, sees the irony of it all. "This has all come about when we're quite busy," he laughs. "There's been times over the last 15 years when we were all sitting on our arses doing nothing for a year or so."

Glen Matlock has also been occupied. After a bout of invisibility starting in 1984 and lasting 12 years, he has recorded a solo album called Who's He Think He Is When He's At Home? On a visit to LA before Christmas 1994, Matlock met with Jones and John Lydon casually, and returned home thinking things had gone well.

Jones is underachievement personified; he has lived in Los Angeles for 13 years without forming a successful band, the latest being the Neurotic Boy Outsiders with John Taylor and Duff McKagan. Finally, Lydon has been finishing a solo LP in America and intends to reactivate PiL (current line-up: John Lydon) one day.

So these four are hardly bored. Nor are they particularly impoverished. But when somebody offers you about £1 million each to re-form the most dangerous English rock group there has ever been, you'd be foolish

not to hear them out. And you could decide that… "We have unfinished business." (Cook) "We're going to go out on a high note." (Matlock) "I'm sick of opening for some cunt who is doing well." (Jones)

And what about Lydon, the former Johnny Rotten, always painted as the curdled refusenik in any Pistols-to-re-form rumours? His rationale was uniquely irrational. "A hundred thousand perverse things ran through my head," he says, "and I thought: Why. The. Hell. Not?"

The arrangements were made by telephone – not difficult, since the Pistols had kept in touch over the years in various permutations of two and three. Once everyone agreed, European promoters were swift to move in (one London venue phoned Matlock offering the band "anything… *anything*" to play there. They're not going to). But there is one small point. The four original members of the Sex Pistols had not been in the same room since 1977.

The Peninsula in Beverly Hills is one of LA's oldest and grandest hotels. It has a roof-garden dining terrace, a complimentary Rolls-Royce chauffeur service, and guests are furnished with business cards with 'In Residence' written under their name in gold leaf. The guest can play his copy of Never Mind The Bollocks….on the CD player in his voluminous suite. Very soon, John Lydon and Steve Jones will arrive in this very room.

On the night that followed the last Sex Pistols gig – at Winterland in San Francisco on 14 January 1978 – Lydon didn't have a hotel to sleep in. He attempted to get into the after-show party but found himself banned

WORDS: DAVID CAVANAGH. PHOTOS: (PREVIOUS PAGE) BRIAN RASIC/REX. (THIS PAGE) RICHARD YOUNG/REX

"We've found a common cause and it's your money."

JOHN LYDON

by the group's manager, Malcolm McLaren. The Pistols had just played to their largest ever audience (roughly 5,000). Lydon returned to England, ending up in a flat in Chelsea five minutes' walk from the Roebuck pub in King's Road, where the Sex Pistols had first met only two-and-a-half years earlier.

Lydon's concluding comment at the Winterland went: "Ever get the feeling you've been cheated?" In his uproarious autobiography, Rotten: No Irish, No Blacks, No Dogs, he explained that those words were addressed not to the crowd, but to the Pistols – and to himself. "I felt that my life had been stolen from me by lesser beings. Our inabilities ruined something truly excellent."

A loud coughing is heard outside the room and the bell rings. Steve Jones enters warily while Lydon walks over to the wastepaper bin, bends over and deposits a mouthful of phlegm into it. He drags the bin over to an armchair. "Spitoon," he explains.

When Diana Rigg was in The Avengers, certain episodes would begin with her creeping up on Patrick Macnee's blind side and saying coyly, "We're needed." This is the initial thrust of John Lydon's angry opening statement; how punk has become, in American hands, a Grammy-endorsed travesty; how Rancid, Green Day and other bands have "got it wrong"; how the '90s have yet to witness a group possessing a fibre of the ferocity of the Sex Pistols.

Lydon is warming up with a coffee. Jones, who has been sober for 12 years, is drinking mineral water. Jones is the first to confess that, as regards the Filthy Lucre joyride, "the price was right".

"*Absolutely* the price was right," agrees Lydon in the emphatically sardonic fashion that for him constitutes conversation. "Money obviously plays a *great* part in all of this and there ain't nothing wrong with that because for once in our poxy lives we're going to get paid for doing something. There are too many people who have been living off our backs and reputations for too long."

What, then, is the price?

Lydon: "It's none of your business. I mind mine; you mind yours."

Nobody tabled what the Sex Pistols considered a serious offer until this year. In the interim, Lydon admits, the process of compiling his book had "purged" him of long-festering antipathy towards his former band. "I looked back and I thought, 'There were some bloody good moments being in that band, and it's nothing to be shy about.' I'm quite proud of my Pistols inheritance and I've come home to collect." He pauses. "*Uncle's died.*"

Tempted by the idea of a highly lucrative tour, he had then applied that most Lydonian of logics: what is the thing people expect least from John Lydon? Exactly. A Pistols reunion. Let's do one. "It's such contradictory behaviour," he notes gleefully.

"No, the real reason we're doing it," says Jones, "is 'cos we love music."

He may laugh. Not one note of music has yet been played by the re-formed Pistols. They have still to meet all together, let alone rehearse. Neither Lydon nor Jones care to speculate what the music will sound like after all these years.

Jones: "I'm not going to play any twiddly guitar, if that's what you mean. I can play the same three chords better than 19 years ago."

Lydon is more interested in the potential clash of personalities when they all meet up again. "This will be a family at war," he says, laughing (and Lydon actually says hee-hee-hee whenever he laughs). "The audiences don't need to be violent or full of animosity. Just watch the people onstage."

"We don't really like Glen very much," adds Jones.

"At all," says Lydon. "Hee-hee-hee."

Nevertheless, Matlock's consent to the Filthy Lucre tour was "a prerequisite" for Lydon: "I mean, the guy wrote the songs with us. You have to give it up for that."

"Those were the best times," adds Jones. "That's where we was creative. When Sid fucking joined the band, the music went out the window. 'Put your finger there, Sid. Up a bit more…'"

Lydon: "Sid was alright at the beginning 'cos he was good at miming. Then he had a lot of people around him telling him he was marvellous."

Jones: "You should go solo, Sid! You don't need them guys! Ah, God bless him anyway."

Would he approve of this tour?

Jones: "Who fucking cares?"

Lydon: "Irrelevant."

THE SEX PISTOLS have absolute control over every aspect of the Filthy Lucre tour, the first time they've been afforded such a luxury. Malcolm McLaren, who once assumed those powers, has given this project his fullest damning. Anne Beverley, mother of the late Sid, says her boy would be "spinning in his grave" at the Pistols re-formation.

"But then again we always felt we *were* in control," says Lydon. "I mean, we did have a manager. *[To Jones]* What was his name?"

Jones: "Ernie Leadbetter."

Lydon: "Who we'd hardly see. We'd read about him in the press, bragging about how he'd do this, that and the other."

Jones: "It's definitely going to be a lot different than getting 15 quid a week."

Lydon: "And the 20 quid gigs. *[To Jones]* Remember? Driving up in a fucking van all the way to the Lake District to get beaten up in Bolton by a bunch of Teds?"

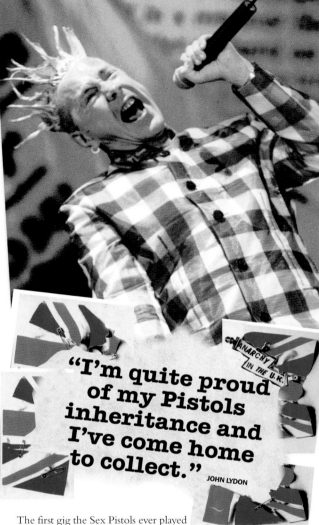

"I'm quite proud of my Pistols inheritance and I've come home to collect."
JOHN LYDON

The first gig the Sex Pistols ever played was in November 1975 at St Martin's College of Art. Matlock, who was a student there, arranged it. The gig has gone down in legend. "A performance lasting 10 minutes," says the Guinness Book Of Rock Stars. "Twenty minutes," says Cook, "total chaos." Lydon: "There was not one single hand-clap."

"We were pretty aggressive for the time," chips in Cook. "Confrontational. I don't think people liked that for some reason. We was all terrified at our early gigs."

Matlock: "Malcolm used to say, 'Would you like a drink?' And he'd buy everybody a quarter-bottle of something, which you'd have just before you went on. John used to go for the whisky and I'd have vodka."

Cook: "I think it'll be a lot more enjoyable now. Pete Townshend was saying how he hated every moment of The Who when he was in them. I can totally understand that, 'cos the Pistols weren't really a happy experience. It was so tense, everyone was uptight around that time, the aura of violence around… It just weren't all that nice."

"The early audiences," says Lydon, "were not the cliches that The Sun and Daily Mirror would have you believe. You'd get John Travolta types there. You'd get the Roxy Music, overly dressed type. You'd get some little teenyboppers. You'd get bootboys mixing it up with bikers. Girls: very much so. You'd get a total mish-mash of everyone and everything."

All that's certain about the Sex Pistols gigs is this: the audiences will be large. Whether they break down into pockets of approval and coteries of cynical opprobrium will only become apparent on the day. It is hard to imagine people paying £22.50 to go to Finsbury Park just to boo. But Lydon and Jones expect a mixed reaction – and have no idea which songs, if any, they will play.

"Obviously, there's going to be a good amount of people who hate us," says Jones. "But I'd rather that. Who wants to be mediocre?"

"We never played to an audience that completely liked us anyway," says an animated Lydon. "I don't care, they can hate us all they like. Get your money's worth either way. Make your own enjoyment… We're getting paid anyway, so fuck you."

There are 12 songs on Never Mind the Bollocks…, the album they released on Virgin in 1977 and which entered the charts at Number 1. With the addition of B-sides (eg, Satellite, Did You No Wrong, The Stooges' No Fun), "live favourites" (eg, Stepping Stone) and… er… they need to write some new songs, surely?

They are all very non-committal on the subject. Matlock doesn't see that writing new songs would be a problem. Cook would love to have "one or two" new tunes in the set. Lydon can't guarantee they'll enjoy playing the old ones. Jones says that they might hate each other on sight and blow the entire tour.

"That could happen," giggles Lydon. "There's shit-loads of money being bandied about, but if it comes down to it and we really can't get on, then that's it. Bye-bye. Fuck off. Hope you all go bankrupt. *It's just life.*"

(Left) Lydon forgets to rinse out the conditioner at Finsbury Park, June 1996.

(Below) Sidney couldn't play guitar… but his mother said he would have been "spinning in his grave" at the reunion.

It wouldn't be the first time any of us had taken a walk. I've done it several times."

The last song the Pistols wrote while Lydon was in the band was Belsen Was A Gas. A horrid display of poorly judged shock tactics, this was credited to Vicious on the soundtrack of Julien Temple's movie The Great Rock 'N' Roll Swindle, but was actually written by Lydon. He doesn't want to sing that one any more, does he?

"No, not at all. It was a very nasty, silly little thing that was never really meant to go anywhere. It was supposed to be left on the cutting room floor."

Jones, who was in the bathroom, returns. Lydon asks him if he can remember what was the last Lydon/Pistols song to be written.

"Oh… was it that Belsen bollocks?"

THE ROEBUCK PUB no longer occupies 354 King's Road, Chelsea. It is now the Dome Café Bar. In 1975, the Roebuck was the boozer of choice for those who hung out at Malcolm McLaren and Vivienne Westwood's clothes shop, SEX. The Roebuck is where green-haired, 19-year-old Finsbury Park waster John Lydon first clapped eyes on 18-year-old Glen Matlock (a sales assistant at SEX) and light-fingered Shepherd's Bush schoolmates Steve Jones (19) and Paul Cook (18). Lydon hated them all on sight.

"Arrogance of youth," says Lydon now. "Showing off. I wanted to come across as the greatest thing since sliced bread, but I really impressed on the others that I was nothing more than a git."

Needing a singer – Jones had tried fronting the bands as "QT Jones & His Sex Pistols" – they auditioned him at McLaren's shop (he sang along to Alice Cooper on the jukebox) and booked him for a rehearsal, miles away in Rotherhithe, to which he alone turned up. Why on earth did Lydon persevere with these people?

"Because I thought it was a way out," he says testily. "What else did I have going for me? I could clearly see that the alternatives would be crime, or crime."

What about joining another band instead?

"I never thought about another band. I wouldn't have done it with anybody else. That first meeting was so hilarious. There was nothing false about it, and when you know you're dealing with people who are being strictly honest with you, that's good."

Jones, still entertaining thoughts of being the front man, detested Lydon and didn't want him in the band. Lydon thought Jones was thick. Cook, who at the time had a mysterious apprenticeship in a brewery, refused to commit to music. Lydon liked Matlock at first but quickly found him unbearable. Jones despised Matlock. But Jones was scorned for his inability to play guitar very well, and so further auditions took place.

"Mick Jones came down." Lydon laughs. "Hair down to here. Nice pair of flares. He looked such a Clampett."

Jones: "It was such a laugh, man, auditioning these guys. I remember one guy, his name was Fabian Quest."

Lydon: "Yes!"

Jones: "He had a hundred footpedals and couldn't play a fucking note."

Lydon: "He had all his mascara on, and lipstick. Big hair. He looked like a fake northern tart."

In those embryonic days of the Pistols, a fellow from Shepherd's Bush named Wally Nightingale was in the band as a guitarist. He was soon jettisoned, on the instructions of McLaren, for not looking the part. The mention of him causes Jones to grimace.

"Ooh God. I hope he don't show up," he says. "He's around, I think." He looks up at Lydon: "Isn't he trying to sue us or something?"

Lydon replies levelly: "People have short memories, Steve, that's the trouble."

MANY PEOPLE'S ASSUMPTION, upon hearing of a Sex Pistols re-formation, was that, semen sandwiches notwithstanding, the deepest enmity would be between Lydon and Matlock. Lydon can still be withering on the subject of his former bassist ("Lets hope he's off the booze, hee-hee-hee"), but Matlock seems keen to mend fences.

In the past, their written accounts of how Matlock came to be replaced in the Pistols have varied (Lydon: "I instigated Glen's leaving the band." Matlock: "Malcolm played this whole game of divide and conquer"). What's more, Lydon claims outrageously in his book that the Pistols re-hired the "sacked" Matlock during the recording of Never Mind The Bollocks, to play bass for a session fee. " Shame on him, he actually did it," Lydon relates. "Isn't that awful? That, more than anything, explains my contempt for him tenfold."

Matlock insists this did not happen. His bass-playing, he contends, can only be heard on the three singles they made before he left: Anarchy in The UK, God Save the Queen and Pretty Vacant (a song that he mostly wrote). Jones confirms that he himself played bass on a few songs, reducing the contribution of Vicious to one song only, Bodies. Cook is adamant that Vicious played on more.

Matlock suggests that posterity has maligned him. "I thought John was great," he says defensively. "He was just such fucking hard work that he got up my nose."

Had Matlock not said that Lydon's lyrics for God Save The Queen were offensive?

"That's *bollocks*. The only thing that made me wince every time I'd hear it – and I still do – is when he rhymes 'an Anti-Christ' with 'I am an Anarchist'. It's such a cheesy rhyme. It's dreadful."

Now into a second bottle of chilled Guinness, Lydon is recalling some of the more eventful Pistols gigs. There was a disco in Paris, "on a lake in some big park. I remember Siouxie Sioux got beaten up outside because she had a swastika on. You wouldn't see that on us. Unfortunately, you'd see that on Sid, because he got it *wrong*."

Then there was the TV show they played in Rotterdam with a circus theme. The Three Degrees were co-headlining. During the Pistols' set, Lydon "kicked a dwarf off the stage".

Lydon: "I was *so* drunk. We were their top pantomime act and it didn't work out that way. We're *cruel* to dwarves. And anyway, we've always been, like, 'It's our stage, get the fuck off it.'"

The Rotterdam TV show was immediately followed by Matlock's last gigs with the band – at the Paradiso in Amsterdam. The Pistols agree the best audiences were always in Europe, particularly in Scandinavia. Back in Britain, since the Bill Grundy interview in December 1976 on ITV ("you fucking rotter"), they had only played a handful of gigs; only seven were salvaged from the month-long Anarchy tour, as show after show was cancelled by local councils.

"We'd sit around the bar or in the van," Lydon recalls wearily. "'It's grim up north' really took on a frightening reality. When we'd stay overnight somewhere, it'd be all nylon sheets and ten to a room. Really not pleasant. Not with the state of our socks."

Jones: "Cum stains on nylon sheets is not attractive."

"Steve's speciality," notes Lydon. "You'd get out of bed in the morning and the sheets are sticking to you."

Jones: "Looked like you'd got stockings on."

The last-ever English gig by the Sex Pistols took place in late 1977 and there is a dispute about it. Lydon and Jones have a feeling it was at Brunel University: "a very bad gig", according to Lydon, with no monitors, a "zonked" Sid on bass, and Nancy Spungen by now in the frame. ("That fuckin' bird," sighs Jones). But Paul Cook is right in saying that the last gig was at Ivanhoe's in Huddersfield on Christmas Day 1977. It was a benefit gig for local firemen, and

The pre-Vicious Pistols with Rotten and the former object of his scorn, Glen Matlock.

(Inset) The Pistols ham it up for a photo shoot after the press launch, March 1996.

"When Sid joined the band, the music went out the window."
STEVE JONES

their children comprised a large part of the audience. The Pistols played all their crowd-pleasers and Lydon dived into a big cake positioned in front of the stage. ("All these young kids have their little flags out," Cook recalls, "and there's us playing Bodies and Anarchy in The UK. Crazy…") Steve Jones has not played in Britain since.

The press conference at the 100 Club ended over an hour or so ago and at the photographer's studio everybody is agreed that Lydon stole the show. If they know him, they come up and congratulate him. Lydon's wife, Nora, offers him tissues, bottle-openers, whatever he needs. A loitering MTV film crew offers congratulations. An American named Mitch, who is co-ordinating the band's US press (not that they've done any yet), starts to read choice quotes from the conference back to Lydon.

"Don't do that," says Lydon, appalled. "I don't want to hear it all *again*."

As Cook tucks into mushroom soup, Steve Jones swaggers around exchanging wisecracks and Matlock sits by himself, with a hangdog look and a fag in a half-closed fist. Three days ago, the four Sex Pistols met for the first time at the Landmark Hotel in Marylebone. According to Jones, it went without a hitch. Lydon's even announcing loudly to anyone who'll listen that he's finding Matlock quite tolerable.

But remember who we're dealing with. As the MTV film crew swoop in for an interview, there is tension in the air. The Pistols demand that the crew vacate the studio and reassemble outside, within view of a local council estate. This seems to be a clumsy attempt by the Pistols to get back to their working-class roots.

All the cameras are set up outdoors. Once in place, the Pistols allow their young interrogator only two questions before dispersing in a flurry of profanities. They've blown the story, but it's clear what's happened: still feeling their way with one another, a bit hot and a lot bothered, the Pistols have had enough of being patronised, cosseted and second-guessed for one day.

JOHN LYDON IS an occasional epileptic, a brutal exposer of cliche and cant, and very hard to get to know. This is a pity, since he holds the key to this Sex Pistols tour. Infinitely cleverer than his bandmates, he is canny enough to realise that he stands to receive the biggest mauling should this all go badly wrong – as it very well might.

In room 368 at the Peninsula, with Jones gone, Lydon had proposed an intriguing analogy to part-explain his involvement in a Sex Pistols reunion. It was, he said, a bit like that Nick Hornby book, Fever Pitch (Lydon's an Arsenal supporter). Watching Arsenal struggle every week, Hornby knew the futility of the situation; could envisage an alternative way of life; and had successfully isolated the flaw in his psyche that drew him to Arsenal. Having done so, he still went anyway.

Lydon speaks matter-of-factly about his reputation in Britain, which has had good and bad points. He admits that this tour is the biggest risk he has taken since joining the Sex Pistols in the first place. (And he also lets slip that, contrary to belief, he could do with the money.) In the end, it all comes down to an irrational hunch. It could – just about, conceivably – be fantastic and there's an infinitesimally small reason why: asked which song he'd like to start the Pistols gigs with, Lydon replies instantly – Bodies.

Why. The. Hell. Not.

Even 18-and-a-half years later, Bodies is one of the most blood-curdling songs extant, and much depends on whether Lydon can get near its guttural roars and panic-ridden stuttering. It has nothing to do with his weight, or which city he calls home; it's about whether he can still sing songs like Bodies in the indescribably livid voice that moved US critic Greil Marcus to call him the first truly terrifying singer in rock'n'roll history. If there is any real point to this peculiarly quadrangular burying of hatchets, Johnny Rotten is the man who will decide.

GREEN DAY

A RIOT OF OUR OWN

It was a brawl broadcast on TV that finally broke Green Day in the US. But America's greatest modern punk band were no strangers to violence, police aggression and the wrath of their singer's mum.

FOR GREEN DAY guitarist Billie Joe Armstrong, the 25th anniversary re-staging of Woodstock ceased to be a festival of peace, love and understanding when he spotted bassist Mike Dirnt spitting three teeth and a mouthful of blood on to the stage. Security had him pinioned on the floor, his mud, blood and sweat-stained face slammed hard against a sound monitor.

Dropping his guitar, Armstrong dived in to rescue his friend. Punches rained down upon the pair of them. As a punk rock band, the idea of playing Woodstock II, a faux-nostalgic celebration of the original hippy festival, had always been a joke. Right now that joke didn't seem so funny any more.

In truth, Woodstock II – held over the weekend of 12-14 August 1994 and billed as "Three More Days Of Peace And Music" – had been descending into anarchy long before Green Day (literally) hit the stage. Days of torrential rain had transformed the 843-acre Winston Farm in Saugerties, New York into a mudbath. Camp-site facilities for the 250,000 people who'd paid $135 to attend were woefully inadequate, food and drink prices verged on the illegal and around 100 people an hour were turning up to the site's two field hospitals suffering from sprained ankles, hypothermia or both. Peering through the tinted windows of the stretch limousine that had been sent to ferry his band to the festival – an unexpected consequence of his band's third album, Dookie, having passed the 500,000 sales mark in the US – 22-year-old Billie Joe Armstrong observed the mud-people rolling around in filth with a mixture of incredulity, amusement and horror.

"It was the closest thing to total chaos I've ever seen in my life," Armstrong would later reveal. "I saw police and guards throwing down their badges, quitting on the spot, saying, 'I can't do this any more.' Technically, it was a human disaster."

Green Day had been handed a 3pm slot on Woodstock II's South Stage on the festival's final day. The decision to preface their much-anticipated performance with three hours of WOMAD acts was, at best, naive. Despite Peter Gabriel's repeated pleas for the crowd to show the African musicians onstage some respect, chants of "Green Day! Green Day!" rang out throughout sets

by Hassan Hakmoun and Geoffrey Oryema. Under the circumstances, Green Day's decision to open their 50-minute set with a song called Welcome To Paradise was wonderfully inappropriate, Armstrong taking huge delight in teasing the sodden, pissed-off, mainly collegiate crowd with the opening line, "Dear mother, can you hear me whining…"

ALL HELL BROKE loose. The crowd began pelting the stage with mud. Armstrong dropped his trousers and pulled ridiculous shapes at the lip of the stage. "Hey, come on, you assholes! Throw some more!" he implored. "Look at me, I'm a fucking asshole!" As mud rained from the skies, the security team took cover at the sides of the stage. Seeing the coast was clear, a stream of kids hurdled the barriers to invade the stage. Security guards began dragging teenage girls off the stage by their hair. Which is when Dirnt stepped in, and was sent crashing headfirst into an onstage wedge monitor. Which is when Green Day's set, arguably the most chaotic, charismatic performance in Woodstock's history, came to an abrupt, violent end.

The band were bundled offstage and ordered to leave the area to ensure their own safety. But their performance was the talk of the site. Even with Porno For Pyros, Bob Dylan and headliners Red Hot Chili Peppers (reportedly paid $1 million for their appearance) still to play, the day belonged to Green Day. And, all across the US, a TV audience of millions watching live on pay per view made a mental note to check out these weird-looking kids with the green and blue hair next time they hit a record shop.

Not everyone watching was impressed, though. When Billie Joe Armstrong returned to his apartment in Berkeley, California there was a letter from his mother waiting for him. Mrs Armstrong had indeed heard her son "whining"

Green Day enjoying the peace and mud of Woodstock II, 14 August 1994.

(Previous page) Billie Joe Armstrong pushes the band's latest album at the KROQ Almost Acoustic show, Los Angeles, 12 December 2004.

"Woodstock II was the closest thing to total chaos I've seen." BILLIE JOE ARMSTRONG

on TV and was disgusted by what she saw. His performance, she noted, was "disrespectful" and "indecent". Were his father still alive, she wrote, he would have been ashamed of what had gone down. Parents never did understand punk rock.

O N 16 FEBRUARY 1989, one day before his 18th birthday and one week before his band Green Day were due to release their debut album, 1,039/Smoothed Out Slappy Hours (aka 39/Smooth), Armstrong decided to drop out of Pinole Valley High School. All he needed was the assent of his teachers and Armstrong would be free. He made the rounds that morning with a glad heart: most signed his official drop-out slip without a word. One teacher,

however, looked confused when presented with the sheet of paper. "Who are you?" he asked.

Armstrong couldn't care less. He had his own seat of learning, a place where everyone knew his name. A former garage building located in North Berkeley just over a mile from the local train station, 924 Gilman Street was Armstrong's home from home. Opened in 1986 by Tim Yohannon, the founder of militant punk fanzine Maximum Rock'N'Roll, Gilman Street, as the club was known, was (and is) an all-ages, non-profit venue for underground music. Run by volunteers, with a policy of booking only non-sexist, non-racist, non-misogynist, non-major-label bands, Gilman Street gave the East Bay's strays and misfits a sense of community and belonging.

Together with his classmate Mike Pritchard (soon to be Mike Dirnt), Armstrong would travel down to the club from his home in the oil refinery town of Rodeo every weekend, begging for loose change for the price of admission to see local heroes such as Isocrisy, Stikky, Crimpshine and Sweet Baby. Dirnt and Armstrong

were already familiar with the sound of punk rock: at Gilman Street they saw the idea of punk rock become reality. Aged just 15, they were inspired to start their own band, Sweet Children.

"It was just, 'Well, here's some kids with just as crappy equipment as we've got, and they're making great music and playing gigs,'" Dirnt recalled. "It really was the classic realisation of, 'Hey we could do this.'"

"We played anywhere and everywhere," Armstrong recalls with a smile, "whether it was a bar mitzvah or someone's backyard or someone's bathroom. Part of the fun and beauty of punk was the same three bands borrowing one guy's amp or the seven bands sharing one drumkit held together by tape. We played every gig, wherever it was, and never cancelled anything. It just made us a better band."

A possibly apocryphal story from the time has one Sweet Children show interrupted by a telephone call from Armstrong's mother, insisting that Mr Punk Rocker come home to finish his household chores. But sometime in 1988, following the release of their Sweet Children EP, Sweet Children became Green Day, after a Bay Area slang term for a hazy day spent with an abundance of weed. "We figured we weren't gonna be children for too long," says Armstrong, quite reasonably.

Two years and dozens of Gilman Street weekend matinee shows later, the trio (then completed by drummer Al Sobrante, aka John Kiffmeyer) came to the attention of Lookout! records boss and Maximum Rock'N'Roll columnist Larry Livermore, who stumped up $600 for two days in a studio to record what became 1,039/Smoothed Out Slappy Hours. The album sounded raw and cheap, but the quality of Armstrong's punchy, poppy songwriting was evident through the tinny production. Green Day were happy with the results.

"We weren't able to have any expectations because there really were no bands, commercially, to aspire too," notes Armstrong.

Fast-forward two years, several hundred shows in squats, frat houses and community halls, and the arrival of a new drummer (the band poached Frank Edwin Wright III – aka Tré Cool – from Larry Livermore's band The Lookouts prior to the recording of their second album, 1992's Kerplunk), and it was increasingly obvious to Green Day that they were outgrowing their status as local heroes. 1,039/Smoothed Out Slappy Hours and Kerplunk had each sold over 30,000 copies. In some cities the band were pulling crowds of 2,000 people. In the wake of Nirvana's success, America's major labels had acted quickly to cream off the biggest bands from the nation's most credible independent labels – Butthole Surfers, The Jesus Lizard and Girls

"In our eyes, going to a major label wasn't selling out." BILLIE JOE ARMSTRONG

Against Boys from Touch & Go, Jawbox and Shudder To Think from Dischord, Helmet from Amphetamine Reptile, Babes In Toyland from Twin/Tone – and 'punk' was no longer a dirty word. The time was right for Green Day to take the next step in their career.

AFTER FIVE YEARS of looking out for themselves, the band finally signed with their first management company – Elliot Cahn and Jeff Saltzman, who already represented Mudhoney, Primus and the Melvins – and handed them a new demo to shop around. Warners, Geffen, Sony and leading Californian punk label Epitaph were among those who liked what they heard. While the band made fun of

PHOTO: JOHN POPPLEWELL/RETNA

Basket cases: (from left) Billie Joe Armstrong, Tré Cool and Mike Dirnt, January 1993.

The son of music industry veteran Bob Cavallo (manager of Prince and Paula Abdul), he flew out to Berkeley to meet the band in the summer of '93.

"I'll never forget when Green Day said to me – it was so cool – they said, 'We're going to be a great band. We're going to be a great band no matter what Reprise does for us,'" Cavallo said in 2005. "They knew what it took to be successful in the music business. They were like, 'We think we need the help of Reprise to realise our potential; however, we are fully confident that we are going to do it on our own anyway. So you're going to take the record that we make and you're going to send it to radio stations for us. So when they hear it, they're going to like it and they're going to want to play it.'"

Cavallo got his men. Green Day weren't the first American punk band to sign to a major, but in the early '90s taking the corporate dollar was still a contentious issue. That same year Chicago arts magazine The Baffler had published an article from former fanzine writer/ Big Black frontman/Nirvana producer Steve Albini entitled The Problem With Music, an acerbic dissection of the financial and philosophical ramifications of underground bands signing to major labels. In June 1994, Maximum Rock'N'Roll would borrow the final line of Albini's essay for a cover story attacking bands – Green Day among them – who'd "sold out" the scene. The cover line – "Some of your friends are already this fucked" – ran on top of a photo featuring a man with a gun in his mouth. Coming just two months after Kurt Cobain's suicide, the issue was the subject of heated debate throughout the rock world.

"In our eyes, going to a major wasn't selling out," shrugs Armstrong. "Instead, going to a bigger indie would have been selling out. If we'd gone to Epitaph – which is a label that wanted us, and a label I respect – I would have considered that more of a betrayal of Lookout! than us going to a major."

Work on Green Day's Reprise debut began at Fantasy Studio in Berkeley at the tail end of summer 1993. The band may have had a proper budget for the first time, but they weren't about to slack off: with Armstrong using a 100-watt Marshall amp borrowed from Cavallo, the band laid down 17 tracks in just 19 days, working 12-hour days to commit the songs to tape. The singer's vocals were completed in just two days, with several tracks recorded in just one take.

the attention coming their way – Mark Hoppus of Blink-182 recalls a gig in San Diego's Soma club where Armstrong mockingly encouraged the crowd to cheer as loudly as possible so all the A&R men in attendance would think the band was worth investing in – they certainly weren't naive when it came to business matters.

"We held off for a long time," Tré Cool told author Jon Ewing. "We wanted to hold out until we got complete artistic control. We wanted to be the bosses and not let somebody else tell us what to do. Of course, the first offer is bullshit, the second slightly less, the third still kind of sucks… We thought, 'Fuck this, it's our lives.'"

Reprise Records A&R man Rob Cavallo was finishing up production work on the debut album by The Muffs when Green Day's demo was passed on to him.

Green Day tour
American Idiot,
their politically
charged punk-
concept album,
Gillette Stadium,
Foxboro,
Massachusetts,
3 September 2005.

Dookie was released in America on 1 February 1994. It entered the Billboard album chart at Number 141, a position that seemed to make a mockery of glowing pre-release reviews. Filled with melodies, hooks, knowing ennui and rushes of hormonal teenage angst, Dookie was a punk album with a pop heart, an album about growing up without giving in to societal pressures. Though many of Armstrong's songs were written from the perspective of a teenage no-mark ("I write a lot about being a loser because I was conditioned to think that way"), a fierce intelligence simmered beneath the surface slacker attitude. Welcome To Paradise – a song originally recorded for Kerplunk – celebrated the dubious delights of a former hotel/brothel on West 7th Street in Oakland that the 17-year-old Armstrong had called home after fleeing the parental nest. Longview was a slacker anthem about masturbation, bong hits and daytime television. Pulling Teeth and She were bittersweet love songs, filled with images of violence and desperation.

"We knew that when we went in to make Dookie it was going to be a harder-edged album," says Armstrong.

"But we felt we were going with a label that would allow us to make records even if we weren't – quote, unquote – commercially successful."

The first single to be lifted from Dookie was Longview. The song's video – filmed in the basement of the Berkeley apartment on Ashby and Telegraph Avenue that Armstrong shared with Cool, their respective girlfriends and three others – saw the singer trashing the very room in which he'd written the song. It had the energy and attitude of Nirvana's Smells Like Teen Spirit video, a fact not lost on MTV programmers. By May, thanks largely to heavy MTV rotation, the song was creeping towards the US Top 30.

IN AUGUST, THE band jumped aboard the second month of Perry Farrell's Lollapolooza travelling festival, on a main stage bill that featured L7, Nick Cave And The Bad Seeds, A Tribe Called Quest, The Breeders, The Beastie Boys and Smashing Pumpkins. "When we were booked on that tour we were really nobody," says Armstrong. "But it was then that I could really feel something was happening. On

PHOTO: ROBERTE KLEIN/RETNA

that tour we were the first band playing, on at noon in these big sheds, and people were bum-rushing the show, bum-rushing the gates and turnstiles to come see us play. By the time we were finished on that tour we were outselling the bands who were headlining."

Green Day hysteria brought with it new problems. Two days before the band were due to play Woodstock II, at a show at the Lakewood Amphitheatre in Atlanta, Georgia, Armstrong asked the audience – as always, specks on the horizon on the grassy hill behind the expensive (ie corporate) seating – to get down the front to dance to Welcome To Paradise. In the frenzied rush to the stage, a woman security guard had her arm broken. With a threatened lawsuit hanging over their heads, management feared that things were in danger of getting out of control for the trio. So the band jetted off to Woodstock promising Cahn and Saltzman that they'd be on their best behaviour…

In the immediate aftermath of Woodstock II, sales of Dookie skyrocketed, passing the million sales mark within weeks. A second single from the album, Basket Case, hit the top of the Billboard Modern Rock Chart in August and stayed there for five weeks. The trio were fast becoming a phenomenon. Green Day were booked by Boston alternative radio station WFNX and the Boston Phoenix newspaper to play a free concert on 9 September at the Hatch Shell, an outdoor theatre on

ck'n'roll can be gerous and fun at same time." BILLIE JOE ARMSTRONG

the city's Charles River that traditionally hosted the Boston Pops Orchestra. Organisers expected 5,000 kids to turn up: unofficial estimates on the day put the number present at 10 times that.

By 7.30pm, the scheduled time of the show, the crowds in front of the stage were so tightly packed that movement became impossible. Three times the crowd were asked to move back by concerned road crew members looking to erect more safety barriers, but no one was prepared to risk missing out on seeing America's hottest new band. The trio kicked off, as always, with Welcome To Paradise, causing mosh pits to ripple throughout the crowd. To those unfamiliar with punk-

rock etiquette, the ritualised hyper-physical dancing looked suspiciously like actual bodily assault, and tension mounted as sporadic fighting broke out. The band got through a few more songs before Boston police decided to pull the plug for safety reasons. It wasn't a popular decision. Initially, aping what they'd just seen at Woodstock, the crowd threw mud: within minutes sections of the crowd were throwing bottles, cans, rubbish bins or whatever lay close at hand. As a full-scale riot threatened to erupt, the band were helicoptered away from the site. Police batons were drawn and scores of fans were led away in handcuffs.

Sitting in a Boston hotel room later that evening, Armstrong and his wife of two months, Adrienne, watched the riot unfold on a local news programme. Boston authorities were keen to point the finger of blame at the band. "Who is this Green Day?" the news announcer solemnly intoned. "This punk band from the wrong side of the tracks?"

The newlyweds could only look at one another and snigger. "It was just so funny to watch," Armstrong laughs. "Like, 'Holy shit!'"

A YEAR THAT had begun with Green Day playing a gig in the kitchen of a friend's house in California ended with them playing a December headline date at the 16,000 Nassau Coliseum and an Aids benefit show at the 18,200-capacity Madison Square Garden on 5 December. Dookie would go on to sell 12 million copies worldwide.

Many music business insiders saw the album's success as an aberration, a freakish post-Cobain sympathy vote for punk rock. As late as 2001 – after the trio had repeated Dookie's multi-platinum success with the darker, edgier Insomniac (1995), the superb Nimrod (1997) and the more acoustic-based Warning (2000) – critics were still making the argument that Green Day owed their entire career to Nirvana.

Finally, 2004's American Idiot album did much to silence those arguments. A wildly ambitious concept album, it chronicles "the alienation and disillusionment of the American citizen under Bush's post-War On Terror administration", complete with two nine-minute-long, five-part rock operas.

Picking up his group's Best Rock Album Grammy Award for American Idiot from Quentin Tarantino on  13 February (16 years to the week after he dropped out of high school), Armstrong commented, "Rock'n'roll can be dangerous and fun at the same time."

Anyone with memories of the band's Woodstock, Lollapalooza and Boston Hatch Shell shows knew exactly what he meant.

New York City Blues

The son of classical musicians, Godlis trained as a photographer in Boston before moving to New York in 1975 to find work. He quickly stumbled across CBGB, where he began shooting the performers and clientele – often without flash and using long exposures. To many who were there, the results summed up the atmosphere of that era better than any other pictures.

The naked city

Richard Hell, 1977

This shot was taken at 4am, following one of The Voidoids' sets at CBGB. Godlis describes the illuminated, rain-soaked streets as "looking like a film noir set". Understandably keen to escape the downpour, Hell made a dash for a cab.

Bad news

Dee Dee and Joey Ramone, 1977

Another atmospheric, street-lit image, this time capturing the Ramones' bassist and singer abusing their reading matter in the Bowery. Godlis was heavily influenced by Hungarian photographer Brassaï's night-time shots of Paris in the '30s.

The message

Ramones, CBGB, 1976

Joey holds aloft the famous Pinhead placard celebrating that song's "Gabba Gabba Hey!" chant on one side and its "D.U.M.B." refrain on the other. The track features on the group's second album, Leave Home.

Bum steer

Handsome Dick Manitoba and Jody, 1976

Dictators frontman Manitoba and girlfriend, pictured outside CBGB's entrance. The Dictators released their first album in 1975, when Dick was still essentially their roadie, though he guested on several tracks and was photographed for the front cover wearing a wrestling outfit.

Catch a fire

Punk haircut, CBGB, 1976

This shot, taken outside the club, shows a fan getting a quick trim courtesy of a cigarette lighter. "The people [at CBGB] were friendly and the drinks were cheap," recalls Godlis. "There were probably only enough people to fill a subway car in there."

L'ingénu

Tom Verlaine, 1977

Television's singer and sometime
lover of Patti Smith, photographed
at St Mark's Place. The session
had been commissioned for the
sleeve of the group's second
album, Adventure, though the
shots were never used.

Preppie love

Talking Heads, CBGB, 1977

Fronted by David Byrne, the group
were the Bowery's reserved, arty
outsiders. They arrived on the
scene via a prestigious CBGB
support slot with the Ramones,
and, with the addition of former
Jonathan Richman And The
Modern Lovers keyboardist Jerry
Harrison, they signed to Sire.

On the corner

Television, 1977

From the same session, the group at a junction on First Avenue. Says Godlis: "I was told to ring a certain number at a certain time. I called up and got Fred [Smith] and he set up the session. The band weren't very talkative that day, so I just kept quiet… and kept shooting."

Alone again or…

Joey Ramone, July 1981

The Ramones' singer regularly posed for pictures in St Mark's Place in the yet-to-be-gentrified East Village. By the time this shot was taken the group had become something of an unhappy marriage, with Joey and Johnny barely speaking, and Dee Dee increasingly dependent on heroin. Their latest album, End Of The Century, had been recorded in LA by Joey and producer Phil Spector, with limited input from the rest of the group.

A hard rain

**Debbie Harry and
Chris Stein, 1978**

This shot was taken outside CBGB, after Blondie had broken through as an internationally successful group. Debbie and Chris had lived together in a sleazy Lower East Side apartment, wallpapered with newspaper and magazine cuttings and full of voodoo accessories.

Girl interrupted

Patti Smith, 1976

"Patti was hanging out on the streets between sets [at CBGB] and I couldn't help butting in on her conversation because she was in the perfect spot for the shot," says Godlis. "She called me up years later and said, 'Sorry, I never thanked you for that picture.'"

Straw poll

Stiv Bators, 1977

Godlis shot the Dead Boys singer inside CBGB, as part of an "ugly competition". "I wanted to see who I could make the most ugly, and this one won," he explains. The runner-up was a picture of Patti Smith Group guitarist and Nuggets legend Lenny Kaye.

COMRADE, GOODBYE

Joe Strummer died on 22 December 2002. Charles Shaar Murray remembers The Clash's frontman.

SOMETIME IN 1979, I was interviewing Joe Strummer for the NME in the World's End pub on the King's Road. As well as giving me an update on all things Clash-wise in the run-up to their third album, London Calling, Joe was getting, as was his wont, all geopolitical on my ass.

"There's only 10,000 days' worth of oil left," he declared in those distinctively gravelled tones. "What does that mean?" I asked. "Only 10,000 days to discover an alternative energy source?" "Nahhhhh," he grinned back. "Only 10,000 days to play rock'n'roll."

Do the maths: 10,000 days from 1979 breaks down into a little over 27 years. Joe ended up with a few years less than that to play the rest of his rock'n'roll. That particular remark was memorable because of what it revealed about Joe: geopolitically suss enough to be informed about the oil crisis, while simultaneously sufficiently committed to the Big Rock and the Big Roll to want to spend whatever time remains for our so-called civilisation on making music.

The contradiction at the heart of The Clash was, ultimately, the contradiction at the heart of Joe Strummer. He longed for his band to be the biggest, flashest, craziest, most powerful full-on rock'n'roll experience in the world; at the same time, he wanted The Clash to be the voice of the global underdog and a positive force for good in the world. The conflicting imperatives of flashy success and collective personal integrity have pulled apart many bands, but never a better one.

"When I think of The Clash, I think of Paul Simonon slamming the bass," Joe told me over armagnac with Guinness chasers and mondo weed one 1999 night in Dublin after a gig by his new band The Mescaleros. "I've seen 10,000 bass-players using the same moves, and when all's said and done about the songs and the lyrics, I always think of Paul Simonon smashing that thing around. And that says it all. I'd like to think The Clash were revolutionaries, but we loved a bit of posing too.

"We were revolutionaries on behalf of punk rock. It was pretty dark in '74, '75. It all seems grey when you look back: I think of it in black and white. There was no MTV, no radio – it was quite a hard job to break it in America, and we did it by playing every shit-hole

Joe Strummer: not simply the heart of The Clash, but the heart of punk itself.

between Kitchener, Ontario and the Everglades. Now it's all fucking business. We may as well be in the business of making cheap plastic clips that they hang curtains off of. That's what rock'n'roll really is."

Except that once upon a time it wasn't. One of the greatest rock'n'roll experiences I've ever had in my life was attending a Clash show in New York in spring 1980. I was at the side of the stage, standing between Joey Ramone and David Bowie, when The Clash played White Man In Hammersmith Palais and London Calling back-to-back, and I was so giddily caught up in the transcendent emotional and sensual power of the moment that I didn't say hello to Bowie or Joey. The Clash – in their classic incarnation of Strummer, Jones, Simonon and Headon – could do that to a person.

(Right) Joe in 1980, trying out the first-ever typewriter to produce handwriting...

PHOTO: PENNIE SMITH

inside a five-year period, and that's a lot of yakking for one man to do in terms of lyric-writing, as opposed to gassing on generally. So I think it was pretty cool of me to shut up for a bit. I was exhausted: mentally, physically, every which way, you know?"

THE CLASH'S IDEALISM, their passion and the extraordinary response they elicited from audiences made them a tasty morsel for left-wing political groups to try to snap up. Fortunately, a maverick spirit kept The Clash and the left from getting too closely intertwined. "When they saw that we were making hay, the Socialist Workers Party tried to jump on the bandwagon. We didn't rebuff their overtures; we just didn't respond to them. We were just going, 'Fuck off, man! Smoke a bloody joint!' We were into getting the Rizlas out and playing Chuck Berry riffs! I'm much more of a Merry Prankster-type person than a committed anything."

And simultaneously, Joe's left-anarchist politics meant that The Clash would, eventually, have to step off the rock'n'rollercoaster. "The other thing was supporting The Who on the Combat Rock tour, and it was like seeing us in 20 years' time. I didn't want to be the new boss, same as the old boss, and I couldn't see any way around it "

What do I remember most strongly about Joe Strummer the person? His 'Joe Public' humanity. His warmth. His sense of humour. His speaking voice, slurred and phlegmy even when entirely sober. His infectious smile, particularly before he got his speed-rotted teeth fixed. His intensity and utter conviction, even (sometimes especially!) when totally wrong. His ability to be both eminently reasonable and completely unreasonable while remaining totally true to himself in either mode.

Tony Parsons referred, in one of the early Clash pieces he wrote for the NME, to the "savage warmth at the heart of the new wave", and there was no better exemplar of that "savage warmth" than Joe Strummer – not simply the heart of The Clash, but the heart of punk itself. The older, wiser, mellower Joe who returned with The Mescaleros in the summer of 1999 demonstrated that that heart was still beating. Until, one day, it stopped.

So farewell then, Comrade Strumski. Go straight to heaven, boy. Your name's on the door. Walk right in.

That night in Dublin, I asked Joe what was the worst mistake he'd ever made. He replied, "Could I have two for the price of one? Firstly, to fire Topper Headon, and secondly, to fire Mick Jones." What he'd realised, too late, was that The Clash was one of those Perfect Groups in which no one could be replaced without ineradicably altering the nature of the beast.

It was a massive loss to rock that the Perfect Clash ended up clashing: Mick had gone into diva mode and Joe, meanwhile, was turning, under the influence of manager Bernard Rhodes, into Joe Stalin.

"The five years, from '77 to '82," said Joe, "were very intense. Yak-yak-yak, non-stop yak. I didn't have any more to say. We'd done eight slabs of long-playing vinyl

what next?

Thirty years young, punk's legacy lives on as countless bands take their cue from the past...

IN THE DECADES that have passed since that first outburst of Filth and Fury, the sound, style and very meaning of 'punk' have changed immeasurably. In 1996, Johnny Rotten re-formed the Sex Pistols for filthy lucre and played the loveable curmudgeon on 2004's I'm A Celebrity Get Me Out Of Here; Joe Strummer left us far too soon in 2002; and the fashions that shocked a nation are now endlessly recycled in high street stores. The only fact that endures is: Punk's Not Dead.

In the early '80s, punk music went underground, but its influence remained. Its DIY ethic lived on in the indie scene, which maintained an 'us and them' relationship with the pop mainstream. Acid house's terrorising effect on Middle England recalled the furore punk had once stirred, and rave ringleaders The Prodigy underlined their punk lineage with dancer Keith Flint sporting a spiky makeover for their Firestarter video.

Punk was also invoked by Britpop, Oasis sharpening up their old-school rock tunes with a swagger that was equal parts Pistols and Faces. Manic Street Preachers assumed a punk stance in their lyrics, clothing and public statements. In this century, The Libertines' adoption of The Clash's Mick Jones as their producer/mentor connected a new generation of angry, idealistic youngsters to punk's original standard-bearers.

PUNK ALSO CONTINUED to thrive on the Continent: Germany gave us punk-metal fusionists Die Toten Hosen; Sweden offered ersatz garage-punks The Hives as well as the revered, deceased Refused, whose 1998 farewell album, The Shape Of Punk To Come, stands as an innovative punk landmark. Turbonegro, the pride of Norway, dress up as fake gay sailors with a denim-Nazi fetish and sing glam-punk paeans to gay sex and paedophilia.

But it is in America that punk has truly flourished. Its speed, brutality and brevity were vital influences on thrash metal and its offshoots. Guns N' Roses copped

285

Contributors

Nina Antonia is a freelancer writer and critic. Her books include The New York Dolls: Too Much Too Soon and Johnny Thunders: In Cold Blood.

Jay Babcock is the editor and publisher of Arthur, the US underground magazine. For more information go to www.jaybabcock.com

Johnny Black is a long-time MOJO contributor who has written frequently on punk rock. He has had several books published and maintains monthly music e-magazine Back On The Tracks.

Paul Brannigan is editor of Kerrang!, the world's loudest rock magazine. His writing on the giants of punk and metal has also appeared in Q and MOJO magazines.

Keith Cameron presented his own radio show on XFM until the station was bought by Capital Radio. He is currently a writer and sub-editor at MOJO magazine.

Peter Doggett is the author of Are You Ready For The Country and a former editor of Record Collector magazine. He is currently writing a book about revolutionary politics and music in the late '60s.

Ian Dickson has been photographing rock stars since 1972. His work has appeared in New Musical Express, Rolling Stone and MOJO. He shot many of the earliest UK punk gigs, capturing The Adverts, X-Ray Spex and the Sex Pistols. For more information go to www.late20thcenturyboy.com

Tom Doyle is a freelance writer, contributor to Q and MOJO, and the author of The Glamour Chase: The Maverick Life Of Billy McKenzie.

Ben Edmonds is former editor of Creem and a long-time contributor to Rolling Stone, among other publications. He is currently MOJO's US correspondent.

Pat Gilbert is a former editor of MOJO, an expert on punk and other youth cultures, and author of the acclaimed Clash biography Passion Is A Fashion.

Godlis is a New York-based photographer who captured many of America's greatest punk and new wave acts performing at the city's famous CBGB club. His subjects included Television, Blondie, Patti Smith, The Cramps and The Dictators. For more information visit www.godlis.com

Paul Gorman is a London-based writer whose books include The Look: Adventures In Rock & Pop Fashion and Straight with Boy George.

Bob Gruen began photographing rock stars in the early 1970s. After capturing the likes of John Lennon and Yoko Ono, he went on to shoot the Sex Pistols, Ramones, New York Dolls and Blondie. His books include The Clash and The Sex Pistols: Chaos. In 2004, he won the MOJO Image Award. For further information visit www.bobgruen.com

Ian Harrison is a rock critic, whose work has appeared in numerous music and lifestyle magazines, including MOJO, Select and Q.

John Ingham is a former staff writer at Sounds, and conducted the first interview with the Sex Pistols. He is currently a consultant on internet and mobile content strategies.

Nick Kent has written for New Musical Express, The Face, Arena, The Sunday Times, Details and many others. Now living in France, he works as a scriptwriter, TV director and contributor to various publications, including MOJO. A collection of his early work, The Dark Stuff, was published in 1994 to rave reviews.

Dennis Morris had his first photograph published at the age of 11. Based in London, he was well placed to capture the nascent British punk scene, taking iconic shots of the Sex Pistols, among others. His books include Bob Marley: A Rebel Life and Destroy: Sex Pistols 1977. For further information visit www.dennismorris.com

Charles Shaar Murray is the award-winning author of Crosstown Traffic and Boogie Man, a former associate editor of New Musical Express and a contributor to The Observer, The Independent and MOJO, among others.

Mark Paytress is long-time contributor to MOJO, among other publications. He has also written acclaimed biographies of Marc Bolan (Bolan: The Rise And Fall Of A 20th Century Superstar), David Bowie (Bowie Style), Siouxsie & The Banshees (The Authorised Biography) and Sid Vicious (Vicious! The Art Of Dying Young).

Andrew Perry has written MOJO features on, among others, The White Stripes, Nirvana and Nick Cave. He also writes for The Observer and The Daily Telegraph.

Ira Robbins is a veteran music journalist, based in New York. He currently operates www.trouserpress.com

Kate Simon became a star photographer at a young age. Her iconic images appeared in the music press, in major magazines and as album covers, including The Clash's debut LP. Her portrait of Bob Marley was named by the Capa Agency as one of the 100 Photographs Of The Century. Her book Rebel Music: Bob Marley And Roots Reggae was published in 2004. For more information go to www.genesis-publications.com

Ray Stevenson began taking pictures in the late '60s, shooting Jimi Hendrix and David Bowie, among others. His brother, Nils, worked with the Sex Pistols and Siouxsie & The Banshees, and through him Ray gained unprecedented access to the fledgling punk scene. His books include Vacant: A Diary Of The Punk Years 1976-1979 and Sex Pistols File. For more information visit www.photos.fsbusiness.co.uk

Gary Valentine is a founding member of Blondie and wrote some of the group's early hits. He's also worked with Iggy Pop, Lora Logic and his own groups The Know and Fire Escape. As Gary Lachman he's the author of, among other books, Turn Off Your Mind: The Mystic Sixties And The Dark Side Of The Age Of Aquarius; The Dedalus Book Of The Occult: A Dark Muse and In Search of P.D. Ouspensky. He reviews for The Independent On Sunday and The Guardian and is a regular contributor to Fortean Times.

THANKS TO Chris Catchpole, Patrick Fox, Eric Goode at www.themaritimehotel.com, William Howell, Debbie Keith, Music & Video Exchange, Reckless Records, Sister Ray, Shona Wong. ENDPAPERS PICTURE CREDIT: UrbanImage.tv/Adrian Boot.